An Interrupted Life

An Interrupted Life

A Holocaust Survivor's
Journey to Independence

Lisl Malkin

Full Court Press
Englewood Cliffs, New Jersey

First Edition

Published in the United States of America
by Full Court Press, 601 Palisade Avenue
Englewood Cliffs, NJ 07632
www.fullcourtpresnj.com

ISBN 978-1-938812-27-9
Library of Congress Control No. 2014930716

*Editing and Book Design by Barry Sheinkopf
for Bookshapers.com*

FCP Colophon by Liz Sedlack

FOR DEBBIE AND BRADLEY
AND FOR
MY GRANDCHILDREN

In memory of my mother, who saved us all, my father, who endured it all, and my relatives, who perished in inhumane conditions in Nazi concentration camps.

ACKNOWLEDGMENTS

I would like to start by thanking Barry Sheinkopf, of The Writing Center and Bookshapers.com in Englewood Cliffs, New Jersey, who taught me to write. Without his foresight there would not be a memoir. His knowledge, explanations, and editing are truly and deeply appreciated. His reassurance, guidance, and inspiration made the book a reality.

A big thank-you to my grandson Jack, who was instrumental in the idea of writing this memoir.

And to Ruth Seidenberg, Susan Teltser-Schwartz, and Thomas Kugler for cheering me on. Thomas's persuasiveness and promise of moral support convinced me to speak of my Nazi experience at his former high school in Germany.

I am grateful to Alex Herzberg, my long-time friend, who gave up many hours of spending time together while I was writing.

A very special thanks as well to Howard Rosenberg, Pulitzer Prize-winner in TV criticism, for his time, of which he gave generously. His comments, as well as his encouragement at critical moments, were invaluable. His insight, ideas, and suggestions, always delivered gracefully yet with candor, were enormously helpful. I'm grateful for the motivation he, a pillar of information, instilled in me, for his unwavering support, and for his ever-ready availability.

PREFACE

If I had not experienced the trauma—and many others that followed—of Austria's annexation to Germany in March 1938, and my eventual separation from my entire family, my friends, my home and culture, I would not have a story to tell about the Kindertransport (children's transport), the shockwaves inflicted by the Gestapo preceding it, and my life in England and the U.S. following it. But those traumas influenced and changed my whole life, and it's my story.

I lived in Vienna with my parents and older sister. My father, Richard Steiner, born and bred there, immigrated to the United States in 1940 at age fifty-one. My mother, Charlotte Deutsch, was Czech. After her marriage she moved to Vienna, and subsequently left for England in 1939, at age forty-two. My sister, Irenli, was sixteen when she left Vienna for Israel (then Palestine) in 1939. Each of those three people's stories is linked to mine although we lived on different continents.

When I left Vienna in August 1938, at age

twelve, for what was thought to be a visit to my grandmother and other relatives in Czechoslovakia, the trip turned into a nightmare of flights from and confrontations with the Gestapo.

My family was thus scattered to all corners of the Earth—not by choice. That was the only arrangement possible after *Kristallnacht* (night of broken glass), November 9-10, 1938, eight months after the annexation of Austria. The Nazis destroyed all Jewish-owned store windows, looted the shops, set most synagogues on fire, and arrested Jewish men in retaliation for a shooting of a minor official.

I had to return to Vienna in May 1939 (a feat unheard-of for Jews who had left) from a visit to the Czechoslovakia in order to join the Kindertransport, which left from Vienna for London. It was organized by Great Britain, which saved nearly ten thousand children from certain death just months before the outbreak of World War II. They were gathered, infants up to the age of sixteen, from Germany and Austria, some from Czechoslovakia and Danzig. No other country opened its doors in that manner.

I was born in Europe. You—my children and grandchildren—were all born in the U.S., and it is for you that I am writing the story of my early life, so different from yours. It describes how ordinary, normal life no longer existed after 1938; survival was the only thing that mattered. But it also affords me the privilege of being the narrator of circumstances that you, or your friends, may not have learned about otherwise.

I hope you will be able to visualize what I have gained from that experience, and, in the process, learn about Europe, the history at that time, the different values, and what it meant to be Jewish.

Ironically, the trauma of my early upheaval, although ever present and showing its ugly head unexpectedly, did have an unplanned, positive effect: I learned another language, experienced three different cultures, and discovered how to value people of diverse backgrounds. I earned advanced degrees, enjoyed a career, a great marriage, and was blessed with two wonderful children and five terrific grandchildren. In the process I achieved self-reliance and became more skillful in coping with hardships. It also taught me to appreciate the freedom we cherish in this country, which I treasure humbly and gratefully, holding my head high as a Jewish woman—secure and independent.

Last, but no doubt most importantly, this labor of love—culled from memories, a diary, letters, and photographs—encompasses my unbounded love for each of you. Although we live far apart geographically, your emotional closeness and caring provides the most important single aspect of my well-being.

1

MY FIRST HOME

THE YEAR WAS 1999. I'd flown to London for the sixtieth Anniversary Conference of the Kindertransport, the British rescue mission just prior to World War II that saved nearly ten thousand children, mostly Jewish, from certain death in Germany and Austria. I was from Austria.

"Hello, Lisl, welcome to London again," said Shirin Spencer, greeting me as I entered the building where the conference would be held. "It's so nice to see you. It's been a long time."

Shirin and her sister, Unity, had wanted to join me at the conference. We shared a history that had begun when we were girls. I'd touched base with them on previous visits to London, but this was a special occasion that marked our anniversary as friends, as well as that of the Kindertransport.

I had met Shirin when we were thirteen, three years older than Unity. Shirin's hair was light brown then. Now it was gray, but her eyes had retained their sparkle. And Unity was still attractive, still lively.

As soon as the first day's session ended, we huddled over drinks—all in our seventies—and before long we were recounting the lives we shared at 6 Downs Road, Epsom, Surrey, in the home of Mrs. Muriel Harter. The sisters were related to her through Gwen, her daughter, who had married the sisters' uncle.

Shirin had lived with her since she was five. Unity, the evacuee, had been relocated to Epsom for safety in 1940 to escape the London bombings when the Battle of Britain was raging, followed by the Blitz.

I'd been a refugee, and Mrs. Harter had become my foster mother.

Shirin, Unity, and I discussed the nights we'd spent in the cellar during air raids and also Mrs. Harter's Victorian values, the punishments we suffered—arriving late for afternoon tea meant being sent to bed early—and how differently she treated each of us. Shirin was definitely her favorite (the apple of her eye), Unity was tolerated (sometimes unkindly), and I had several confrontations with her.

As we sipped our wine, it became obvious that our memories hadn't changed, but our perceptions of those memories had. Both Unity, an accomplished artist, and Shirin, a gifted pianist, faulted Mrs. Harter for exercising too much control. They blamed her for having influenced their lives in a negative manner. She'd stopped Unity from pursuing a career in ballet, and prevented Shirin from contacting her family. She had diverted my plans, too. Instead of continuing my education, I'd had to go to work at age sixteen.

Despite that, I had truly appreciated Mrs. Harter. I felt grateful and valued her kindness and willingness to undertake the huge responsibility of bringing up a child she hadn't known. As an adult, I came to understand her values, the positions she took, and her behavior. I forgave her stern control. Shirin and Unity did not.

Before we bid each other good night, they asked if I had visited Vienna since leaving in 1939. "Oh, yes," I answered dreamily. And on the way to my hotel I was on memory lane, back in the reputed glittering capital of intellectual, social, and artistic fame.

I WAS BORN IN VIENNA OCTOBER 11, 1925, Lisbet Gertrud Steiner.

My parents, my sister, and I lived in Ober St. Veit, Rohrbacher Strasse 5, in Hietzing, the thirteenth district, always considered one of the most desirable ones. It had villas (single family houses), gardens, and small apartment houses. We lived in one of the latter, a well-kept building of just four apartments. We were not permitted use of the lovely garden behind the house. For as long as I could remember, my parents spoke of the landlord's openly anti-Semitic attitude—even *before* Hitler. His family and his mother occupied two of the apartments. The third one, consisting of six rooms, was ours. Irenli (as we called my sister Irene) had been born three and a half years before me. We shared a room, at times quite happily, but often disrupted by her bullying and putting me down. The fourth apartment, just below ours, belonged to Mr. and Mrs. Horeyshey and their son Kurt, a graduate student at the University of Vienna. They were Social

Democrats and our friends. My memory of Kurt as a lanky young man is based more on his actions than his looks. He used to come upstairs to tutor my sister, and often played catch with me, running up or down the stairs.

I especially liked his mother, a housewife, who was always jolly. She wore her wavy, light brown hair parted in the middle, combed close to her round face, which reminded me of pictures we used to draw of a smiling moon. She was unusually loving to me. When, as a little girl, I'd be angry with my mother, I'd threaten, "I'm going to leave home and I'm not coming back." I left our apartment and fled downstairs to Mrs. Horeyshey.

"So glad to see you, Lisl," she said, enfolding me into her open, welcoming arms.

"I've come to visit you, is that all right?" I asked.

"Of course. Would you like a cup of chocolate?"

"No thanks, I just had lunch."

That elicited a knowing smile from her as she turned to walk into another room, saying, "I'll be right back. I just have to make a phone call."

On one occasion in the winter, my mother appeared after a while with a sweater, jacket, mittens, and warm pants. I was taken aback. I wondered, *How long does Mama think I'll stay?* I was ready to go back up, but Mama had left. As soon as she did, Mrs. Horeyshey whispered, "I have a surprise for you after you put on your warm clothes." I got dressed quickly, eager to hear what she had in mind. It was revealed as we left the apartment and stopped in the storage room downstairs to pick up my skates. They were kept there with our oversize toboggan, tricycle, bicycles, and skiing equipment. That little room was next to the janitor's apartment, who, like the landlord, was suspected of anti-Semitism—only covertly in his case.

I loved accompanying Mrs. Horeyshey to the skating rink and seized every opportunity to do so. She was a good skater, graceful, despite being on the plump side, and she taught me the figures three and eight, as well as skating backwards, so that I learned to dance to the tune of Viennese waltzes that came blasting over the loudspeaker. She treated me to hot roasted chestnuts before we went home, too.

Sometimes our nanny chaperoned us to the skating rink. Anni was pretty, rosy-cheeked, twenty-two years old. She was easygoing and fun, and I liked being with her. She frequently mentioned to my mother, "I like Lisl so much. I would do anything for her." Often she called me "Liserl"—a form of endearment. At the time, my parents dismissed these remarks; it was easier to take care of me than Irenli, who had a habit of throwing temper tantrums.

None of us realized that, in years to come, those prophetic musings by Anni would become pivotal in my emigration.

IN MY EARLY CHILDHOOD, VIENNA was referred to as "a cultural jewel," a mecca for art, music, literature, psychology, as well as fashion, medicine and cuisine. Hungarian and Czech women arrived daily to buy the latest styles. Men and women visited doctors famous for their specializations. A goulash or schnitzel, with a glass of local wine, followed by a piece of apple strudel, was nothing to be sneezed at, even at small, obscure restaurants. The physical beauty of the city was enhanced by its buildings— ranging from Romanesque and Baroque to the famous landmark of the Gothic *Stephansdom* (St. Stephen's Cathedral), as well as the beautifully landscaped parks interspersed throughout. Relaxing in a coffeehouse, savoring a cup of coffee topped with schlag while reading the newspaper, added to the *Gemutlichkeit* (relaxation) of the city. Impressive museums were easily accessible. And, within a short distance, lakes for swimming and the Alps for skiing beckoned.

NEITHER OF MY PARENTS ENGAGED in sports, although Papa took us sledding, but they encouraged my sister's and my participation in skating, skiing, swimming, and hiking. Tennis would follow, as well as a trip to France for my sister, but neither was realized. Hitler's "Anschluss" of Austria in March 1938 put a stop to those plans. Prior to the annexation, our family vacations took us to beautiful parts of Austria, where lakes met mountains, and an annual trip to Misslitz, Czechoslovakia, my mother's birthplace.

In the summer we spent much of our time outdoors. Because we were denied use of the landlord's garden, Mama thought of an alternative. At lunch one spring day (Papa came home midday for the customary big meal), she said, "Why don't we try to lease the building lot next door and have our own garden?" The property belonged to the city.

"Great idea," Papa answered. "As soon as I get back to the office this afternoon I'll make some phone calls."

I, too, liked the idea because she was such a believer in *Sonne und frische Luft* (sunshine and fresh air) for us children, which often meant going for a boring walk. Thus, the garden, cultivated over the years into a grass lawn with flowers and bushes all around the perimeter, solved the problem for all of us. For me, it spelled happiness, or at the very least contentment—sunshine, freedom, running, playing, bending down to smell a flower only to learn that primroses look lovely but don't have a scent, and, in the fall, collecting the chestnuts that had dropped from the big tree in the far corner. The smell of the purple lilac bushes in the late spring caught my breath as as soon as I entered the garden. I'd stop, pushing my nose deep into the midst of the heavy blossoms hanging down. That aroma, instilled in me a lifelong love for purple lilacs.

The garden stretched like a funnel—broad in front, past the house, narrowing towards the back. That's where Mr. Horeyshey kept his bees. I don't know what the arrangement was. If he asked for permission, my parents probably just said, "By all means keep your bees there."

He looked the part of a high school principal behind horn-rimmed glasses, which betrayed a friendly, patient attitude towards us kids. One day he asked, "How would you like to hear—" he was careful not to say learn— "how bees live?"

"Oh, yes. Do tell us," Irenli and I, and a couple of our friends, including Herbert, insisted.

He explained the hierarchy of the queen bee and the workers. He allowed us to enter the bee house—provided we wouldn't touch anything—but not before outfitting us with special gloves, a helmet with an attached piece of cloth to cover our necks and shoulders, and a wire mesh headpiece to protect our faces. We were quite impressed, and, following his advice, we never got stung. Herbert stood close to me for added protection.

Fortunately for Mr. Horeyshey, our interest didn't carry us much beyond watching a couple of times, preferring to gather in the front part of the garden to play with our friends. It was large enough for ball playing, running, and chasing each other.

I spent many hours there with Herbert. He was my best friend, lived around the corner, and until we were ten years old we were inseparable. He was a good-looking boy with a straight, pointy nose, thin and tall for his age. Six months younger than I, he was strong, and my self-appointed protector at all times, mostly against Irenli, who was ready to bully me at a moment's notice. Whenever she called me names, or uttered a put-down, Herbert stood up for me. He often suffered having grass thrust in his mouth by his older brother, George, to prevent him from joining me in shouting insults at Irenli. He didn't mind, though, getting in trouble on my behalf. We stuck up for and supported each other.

One day, when we were little, Herbert and I were alone in the garden, playing behind a bush, when he beckoned to me: "I have a great idea for a game," he half whispered as soon as I got close enough. "I'll be the doctor, and you have a stomach ache, so you have to take off your dress and panties so I can examine you." I had always trusted Herbert, but troubled by this new game and feeling awkward, I asked, "Just how are we going to play this?"

"I'll show you, and we can take turns being the doctor."

Before I was able to reply, we were both startled by the click of the garden gate opening as Mr. Horeyshey entered on his way to his bee house.

By the time we reached our tenth year, I had become friends with Grete, a big girl with short blonde hair who lived on the next street, and sometimes the three of us spent time together. He and I enjoyed skiing on the *Roter Berg* (red mountain), within walking distance of our homes. It received its name from the tinge of red in the earth just below the grass-covered surface. The Berg was not high enough to warrant a ski-lift, but neither did it possess a rope-tow, which would have relieved the burden of a twenty minute walk to get there, carrying the skis slung over our shoulders. When, after several runs, I got too tired to continue, he gallantly carried my skis uphill. He didn't make the same offer to Grete, and she got mad, refusing to ski with us again.

Herbert loved me and I felt I had a brother and confidante, something I missed in my sister. That feeling has prevailed all through our lives. He lives near Philadelphia, and I telephoned him a few weeks ago to wish him a happy eighty-sixth birthday.

2

MY FATHER

IN THE SPRING MY PARENTS made a point of setting one Sunday aside for an excursion to the *Wienerwald* (Vienna Woods), at the base of the Alps on the outskirts of Vienna. I, dressed in a casual dirndl, and Herbert in his short lederhosen, were joined by his brother and parents, and sometimes friends from school were invited. Then all the songs we had learned about the joy of hiking, including Schubert's famous "Das Wandern," got belted out. My father, whose first love was music, was only too happy to encourage us and take on the role of guide in choosing the next song. We delighted in negotiating the well-marked walking and hiking paths, especially as the rays of the bright sunshine filtered through the trees, tracing patterns on the ground. Some trails were narrow, leading through heavily wooded terrain, others wide enough to accommodate a horse-drawn carriage. We also crossed meadows with alpine flowers and became familiar with their names and the wild mushrooms growing at the edge of the woods.

On one outing, when I was six or seven, I lost my rucksack. It got kicked down an embankment where we had stopped, near a break in the forest, too steep to climb down.

"My rucksack is gone!" I burst out, big crocodile tears flooding my cheeks.

"Never mind, Liserl, we'll get you another one," Mama said consolingly.

"But it had *Waldi* in it, a book, and all the other things I like!" I wailed. *Waldi* was my favorite stuffed dog, named after Tante Hajek's live Waldi.

"Don't worry, I'll fetch it," Papa declared calmly. No anger showed as he set out to retrieve it. We children continued to play, but after half an hour had gone by without a trace of him, we grew anxious. When he finally reappeared, more than an hour had passed. He looked bedraggled and sweaty, my rucksack—a little dirty, but otherwise intact—dangling from his scratched hand. I ran towards him crying, partly at the sight of him, partly due to guilt, and partly out of feelings of relief of seeing him at all, as well as my rucksack. I don't remember hiking in the Wienerwald after that.

Before that particularly fateful Sunday, at a previous outing, we stopped in Grinzing, a district in Vienna that has maintained its village character. It was, and still is, inundated with *Heurigen*, several on each street. These taverns serve new local wine, hence the term. Always a popular recreation area for local people, it is also on the tourist list. You are invited to while away carefree hours drinking, eating, and listening to Viennese music as each eatery vies for attention by displaying a colorful shingle, or a lighted board, announcing the specialties on its menu or the presence of musicians. We chose one of those.

The outdoor setting, with its red-and-white-checkered tablecloths, provided a casual atmosphere, enhanced by lanterns hanging from the chestnut trees all around. They were colorful, their bright light diffused by the leaves, and when they swayed in the mild evening breeze, they seemed to be dancing. The three musicians—all middle-aged men—moved slowly but purposefully among the tables as the customers relished their Schnitzel—always tasty. One of them played an accordion, and one held a harmonica to his mouth; the third, the tallest, was the violinist. They played popular Viennese songs, some old, some new, and encouraged requests from the patrons. When they approached our table, their spokesman, the violinist, caught my eye and asked, "What can we play for you, Fraulein?" I was in heaven.

"*Die drei Matrosen, bitte*," I answered sheepishly, barely above a whisper, glancing at Papa for encouragement and approval, and they began to play "The Three Sailors."

They sang with *schmaltz* and smiles, looking into my eyes, much to my embarrassment. After they finished they were still smiling—but facing my father—waiting to collect their tip.

It was all part of the *Gemutlichkeit*.

Papa fit into that. Rather than attend the five o'clock tea dance at Hübner's, he preferred going to his favorite *Kaffeehaus* close by with Mama, or even alone. He took me once because Mama needed peace and quiet at home to treat her migraine (Irenli was at a friend's house).

I was more than halfway through eating my cake when I announced, "Papa, I ate another cake once that I liked better."

He looked at me lovingly, smiled, and offered, "Well, then we'll just have to order another one. They are displayed on two shelves under the counter. Which of the ones you see there would you like?"

In the background the "Blue Danube Waltz" (immortalized by Johann Strauss, but hardly ever blue) could be heard playing softly on the radio, maybe followed by Beethoven, or a current, popular song. It was of no matter if you sat an hour or two with a cup of coffee and a glass of water that always came with it on a little tray, reading the newspaper, writing, or chatting with a friend.

Papa loved Vienna. He was born there, Richard Steiner, July 12, 1889.

He had one older brother—William, born in the Czechoslovakia; and two younger ones, Karl and Ernst, both born in Vienna. Another brother, Otto, had been killed in World War I, and a girl, Irene (after whom my sister was named), had died as a young child.

Papa was kind, loving, and he possessed a great sense of humor. In many ways he was more approachable than Mama. When I was very young, Irenli and I were allowed to come to our parents' bed on a Sunday morning, where he let us slide down his bent legs over and over for as long as we liked. This was accompanied by giggles and laughter from both of us girls.

Soon we were old enough for him to take us sledding on Anni's day off, and he helped with homework, too. I did not think him handsome, but his deep-set eyes expressed intelligence and kindness. He was compassionate, and so patient that we all took advantage. When he was bothered enough and his patience wore thin, he got angry.

Far from the reputation of European men eschewing "women's" work, when the time came that we no longer had maids, he helped with housework. I still recall how startled I was when I entered the kitchen one day and saw him washing dishes. He helped because he adored my mother.

My thoroughly Viennese Papa, with his love of music, especially opera—whether in person, or whistling along when he heard a familiar tune on the radio, or singing to accompany the voice on the gramophone, or humming in the coffeehouse—served as my and my sister's background to our daily lives.

One afternoon in the fall of 1937, Mama took Irenli to the opera, and I was promised a future visit when I was old enough to appreciate a performance. My father and I were sitting in the den, I on the sofa (a daybed), which had a throw on it that was really a Persian carpet, judging from its weight. As the sun caught the animals woven into it, I liked to think of them coming alive and sharing the warmth and coziness of the room, which was enhanced by the light coming in through the colorful curtains when they were not drawn aside.

We had just finished playing a game when Papa turned to me with a twinkle in his eye and said, "Just because Mama thinks you are too young to go to the opera with her and Irenli to hear *Aida*, don't worry—I will teach you the melodies, and we will sing them when they come home."

"But I won't remember them."

"Yes, you will. We'll surprise them as we sing them together."

"All right," I agreed. Not a bad way to help pass the time for an eleven-year-old.

"Wait a minute now," he continued. "I'm going to move the gramophone from the little cupboard in the corner onto the table, right here in the middle of the room, to get the best sound. Also, it will be easy to reach and replay whatever we need."

He then sang for me the eloquent, passionate aria "Celeste Aida" in the Viennese dialect. The melody remained the same, but the words changed into funny, somewhat crude language. He used the dialect typically to tell jokes or an anecdote.

He instilled in me a love of music, especially opera, so that even now I remember the German words of many operatic tunes.

PAPA EARNED HIS DEGREE IN electrical engineering, and after a dozen years working at AEG in Vienna (the equivalent of GE), he formed a partnership with Herr Hajek. The firm was called Hajek und Steiner, located at 36 Sechshauser Strasse. They employed ten or twelve men in the factory, which produced awnings and shutters. Their main customers were commercial establishments, stores, banks, and coffee houses. Business was good.

Visiting Papa at work was a rare treat. I remember Berta, the pretty, blonde bookkeeper, slender in a black dress with a white collar. Her office was small, with a window facing the busy street below. There was space for a desk and a table with a couple of chairs. "Would you like to type something, Lisl?" she asked each time, and I was thrilled to be allowed to pound on the typewriter for a few minutes.

The partners' friendship went so far as to make Herr Hajek's wife a periodic visitor to our home for a *Jause* (afternoon tea, which consisted of coffee and cake), usually accompanied by her mongrel dog, Waldi, the chief reason for her welcome as far as I was concerned, although I liked her well enough. I had always loved dogs, sometimes over people. Dogs were acceptable, whether mongrel, big, small, calm, frisky, or smelly. Waldi was a smelly one.

On one of her visits, when I was six years old, the doorbell rang, and I asked, "Who's there?"

"It's me, Tante Hajek. Open the door, Lisl."

"I don't see Waldi," I said after looking through the little peephole in the door.

"I didn't bring him today. It's raining, so he's better off at home."

"Then I can't let you in," I answered, and refused to open the door. I relayed my disappointment of not seeing Waldi to my mother, who rushed to the door to let Tante Hajek in.

Waldi was twice the size of a dachshund, which is what he was supposed to be, and his front legs turned out, producing a gait not unlike Tante Hajek's. He did not share her square face or droopy eyelids behind glasses; on the other hand, both were well rounded. I loved smelly Waldi, secretly feeding him forbidden tidbits of cake and cookies, so he could enjoy the desserts of our *Jause* as much as we did. In return, I thought he looked at me adoringly. I also took him for walks. On one of them, he spotted another dog and pulled the leash so hard that I fell. Anni was bent over me when I heard Irenli, who had also accompanied us, burst out, *"Blöder Hund!"*

"He's *not* stupid. You are!" I yelled back in his defense. He served as a substitute for the dog I longed for, which the landlord did not permit.

Because of the close friendship between the partners, Papa readily consented to Herr Hajek's request for his three sons to join the firm. Papa was too kind, and too lacking in business sense, to decline. It was not a wise decision. Anti-Semitism was prevalent in Austria long before Hitler's arrival, and the two older sons did not take long to openly show their Nazi sympathy, which they had been harboring all along. They set about, and succeeded, in elbowing my father out of his partnership a few months before Hitler annexed Austria in the spring of 1938.

Soon the maid was let go, and Anni was also gone by then. Both parents spent more time at home. When Papa was not on the phone, he and Mama sat in the den and talked in low tones, both looking very serious. He had laid out papers and pencils on the table, scribbled from time to time, then compiled some papers and stashed them on the daybed.

Adding to the gravity of the situation was that the gramophone had lost its importance. It was stowed away on a stool, unused, and covered up. The cupboard, its old home, was needed for my father's trade papers, letters, and other paraphernalia transferred from his office at the factory.

At age twelve, I did not grasp the seriousness of the situation, which was not discussed in front of me, but I realized it was not good; the carefree days of listening to records were no more.

THE NEW COKE-FED STOVE in the corner where the tall, old fashioned, green porcelain-tiled stove stood, had kept us warm as the wind howled through the coming cold winter days, and the gray clouds steadily turned darker in more than one sense. To keep the room warmer, the door leading to the dining room was kept closed. I sensed not to interfere and kept myself busy elsewhere. I moved close to the stove, and spread out my toys on the red flowers of the Persian carpet, and books on its blue designs.

In one way, life for Irenli and me continued unabated. We still had friends over for a *Jause*, we went to the movies, we gobbled up the cakes Papa brought home for us, Irenli still bullied me, and Herbert and I played endless games of Monopoly, but a new seriousness permeated the home.

Several weeks passed. Austria hadn't been annexed yet, but it had by then become difficult for a Jew to land a decent job. One narrow option involved opening a store.

On a cold, rainy December evening in 1937, as all of us were gathered in the den, Papa said, "Listen, I have something to tell you. I have a new job. I am opening a store."

"Oh, good. Will you sell chocolate bars?" I asked enthusiastically. For some reason I took it for granted that it would be a delicatessen store.

"No," he answered, throwing me an unaccustomed, earnest look. "The store will carry bicycles and sewing machines."

"That's really much better," Irenli added. "Will I get a new bike so I can get rid of the old one?"

Papa did not enjoy his new occupation. The fact that he received the sewing machines at a great discount from Arnold, his brother-in-law, who was in that business in Brno (Czechoslovakia), did not alleviate his distaste for his new career.

3

MY MOTHER

WE WERE GIVEN TO UNDERSTAND the store did reasonably well, but looking back I believe my parents barely eked out a living. In any case, several months after Hitler had annexed Austria in March 1938, the store was 'aryanized,' the term used for confiscating Jewish property and transferring it into Aryan hands. It meant the Nazis seized the store, and with it all salable items, furniture, as well as checkbooks and bookkeeping materials, so that my father's ownership was taken away without any compensation or trace that it had ever belonged to him.

During the store's lifespan, however, Mama had been of great help, able as always, to rise to the occasion, no matter how sudden or how difficult. Bright and enterprising, she kept up Papa's spirits, and became an excellent saleswoman as well, when helping in the store and out: She used her sales talents on friends, neighbors, and mere acquaintances. Her charming manner and good looks helped. Her high forehead and straight nose contradicted the proverbial "Jewish" look.

She was born Charlotte Deutsch on March 25, 1897, in Misslitz (Miroslav in Czech), in Czechoslovakia (now the Czech Republic).

As the oldest of nine siblings, followed by Olga, Mitzi, Poldi, Leo, Gretl, Yelli, Rosl and Lorly (Lore), she had learned to take responsibility early in life by occasionally taking charge of one or the other. That may have inadvertently earned her the role of 'rescuer.' She showed her proficiency at that again when she secured the freedom of my father, my sister, and me (in that order) from the clutches of the Nazis.

She had read a great deal on various subjects as a young woman and immersed herself in the joy of learning. Her lasting regret was the lack of formal higher education, which she would have enjoyed, something that was accorded to her brother Leo, the only male, and later to her youngest sister Lore, both of whom became lawyers. The others finished high school. Olga, the next youngest sister by one year, married Hugo of the prestigious Hauser family. That put pressure on Mama, since the older girl was supposed to get married first. At twenty-three she married Papa and moved to Vienna. I don't know (nor does my sister) how they knew each other. They might have met on one of her visits to relatives in Vienna, or, we suspect, theirs was an arranged marriage—not uncommon in those days.

Once Mama had entered the realm of Hausfrau and motherhood, even the presence of a maid, and later also a nanny, kept her from pursuing the reading she loved so much.

One of her tasks was to train new maids. It was not unusual

for young women to leave their homes in the country for the city. Young, bright-eyed Marie was one of them, newly arrived in our home.

It was a mild spring day—I was five—when Mama called me into the hallway where she was waiting for me with my favorite blue cardigan in one hand, using the other to push a lock of her thick, chestnut-colored hair off her high forehead, the way she often did.

"Get your *Dackel*, Liserl, and we'll take him for a walk."

I grabbed Waldi, my stuffed dachshund.

"Are we going to the park?"

"Not right now. I have to go to the police station."

"Why do we have to go to the police *again*?" I asked.

"To register Marie," Mama explained. "When we hire a new maid, I have to fill out a form to show she is living with us." Then she smiled and added, "Guess what else we'll do?"

It seemed to me we trekked to the police frequently, but I knew "what else we'll do" meant dropping in at the *Konditorei* around the corner from the police station where Mama and I would sit at a little table, each enjoying a piece of pastry.

I also remember *Waschtag*, the wash day—a busy time, requiring a lot of preparation. That was when the *Waschfrau* (laundress) came to wash the heavy bed linens and towels, which had to be carried into the attic, where she scrubbed each piece by hand in a big tub. Mama, instead of the maid, cooked a hearty lunch that day for everybody—all ingredients carefully chosen and bought the day before: potato soup (always a treat for me), a roll, a couple of thick slices of beef, creamed cabbage (another bonus for me), roasted potatoes, cucumber salad, and a piece of cake. Whichever Marie was the maid at the time carried the tray upstairs. Later in the afternoon, Mama would say to me, "Take this snack up to Frau Schmidt and ask her if there's anything else she needs," making me the proud messenger and carrier of the afternoon *Jause*.

The attic was hot, steamy, and stuffy, and smelled of soap. The steam was overpowering, which, in the winter, made the windows opaque. I didn't like it up there, but Frau Schmidt, big and strong, her face covered in sweat and her head tied in a dark blue kerchief that allowed a hank of hair to fall over her forehead and another to creep out near her neck, gave me a broad smile, and her kind remarks made me feel I had done an important deed by bringing her a snack.

Mama found relaxation a couple of times a week by playing bridge with her friends, either at home or in the nearby *Kaffeehaus* in the afternoon. Entertaining for dinner at home occurred rarely, except for occasional visits by relatives, and vice versa. Sometimes Mama suffered from migraines and had to lie down. When she felt well, she sewed a beautiful *dirndl* for me, a traditional costume I loved to wear. It consisted of a short white blouse with a drawstring inside the round, low-cut neckline, covered by a sleeveless dress patterned in pink and white squares. A white apron folded over the dress. Irenli had the same dirndl. There's another dress I remember. It was made especially for both of us by a Polish tailor who kept a makeshift shop in a basement nearby. Mama told us, "Mr. Namiz is not only an excellent tailor, but I like to go to him rather than to the dressmaker because he has had so much trouble finding a job."

"Well, if he's so good why can't he get a job?" Irenli asked.

"You may have noticed that he speaks Yiddish, not German," Mama made a point of explaining. "Some people look down on him," she continued, "because he's from Poland, and uneducated. That's not his fault. Jews in Poland were denied a proper education."

The dresses were exactly the same—soft brown velvet, a round off-white collar, and embroidered pastel flowers of pink, blue, green, and yellow flowing down on one side. The long sleeves ended in a cuff matching the collar. I hated that dress, although, or because, I received compliments that only caused me embarrassment. I was happy when I had outgrown it. Much to my dismay, I inherited Irenli's, which lasted for at least one more winter. Too shy to wear a big bow in my hair that went with the dress—too embarrassing—I refused to wear one.

Mama also made dolls' clothes for us, which we received as presents from the Chanukah Angel, invented by Mama to counter my Catholic friend Grete's bragging about presents she had received from Santa Claus.

At Chanukah, Mama decorated the round, green silk shade in silver and gold garlands. It covered the lighting fixture that hung over the dining room table and made up for not having a Christmas tree. We lit Chanukah candles for eight evenings on a lovely gilt menorah with standing lions engraved on either side of the panel. Our traditional dinner of soup, followed by a main dish of carp, potatoes, creamed spinach, and a homemade cake and cookies for dessert, was served every year. That, in turn, elicited my usual complaint: "It's carp again. I don't like how it tastes. Besides, I can still see it jumping around after the fishmonger cut off its head when we bought it this morning."

"Then why don't you just have the soup, and I know you like the creamed spinach, and potatoes," suggested Papa in his usual kind tone. "There's also a small piece of schnitzel you can eat."

The best part of the meal was Mama's specialty. She baked Chanukah cookies, which were available throughout the evening, ready to be gobbled up as we pleased.

We opened our presents, lit candles—an additional one every night—and sang "Maoz Tzur," in Hebrew, followed by a German song that recalled the revolt of the brave Maccabees and the rededication of the temple, where in the rubble of the destroyed temple, a small jug had been found that contained just enough oil to sustain the menorah for one day. Miraculously, it had lasted eight days.

Mama led us in the religious songs, with which she was more familiar than Papa, who preferred opera melodies. She taught us the tunes chanted at weekly services, which she knew from her days as a member of the choir at the temple in Misslitz before her marriage. I recognized them some fifty years later while at a synagogue in Portugal, and another time in Kenya. At first, I was rather surprised, but that was quickly followed by a sense of belonging, of being comfortable, thousands of miles from home.

It was also she who imbued us with the values of loyalty and cautioned, "Be honest, and remember to be considerate of other people, especially those who are not as fortunate as you are, and don't have as much as you have." I wasn't sure what to make of that. I didn't know any children who in any way had less than I, but it impressed me sufficiently to remember it and to practice it in later years.

The message to marry a nice man was also passed on.

Both our parents harped on learning. "Whatever you have learned, and whatever is in your head, nobody can take away from you." That last statement was repeated often after Hitler had occupied Austria, when we witnessed how easily friends and acquaintances lost jobs, houses, and even respect and dignity. My father was a prime example.

Even before the advent of the annexation, we were instructed not to show off or be loud in company, since that might attract anti-Semitic remarks and give the wrong impression of a Jewish personality. That was due partly to Mama's outer-orientation. Important to her was how other people looked, and the impression *our* looks and *our* behavior made on them. Those images increased my sense of inferiority, already fueled by Irenli's constant bullying. I grew up internalizing that attitude, conscious of the outside world. Irenli grew up saying, "I don't care. I do and say what I want."

There were times I didn't care either—when it meant going to museums or to certain relatives' homes. "Do we *have* to go to a museum?" I muttered. Like it or not, I schlepped along, though I expressed my dislike of visits to some people more forcefully.

"I don't *want* to visit Tante Ella. Onkel Eduard is nice" (he was my maternal grandfather's brother), "but she's too fussy. I'm always afraid of spilling hot chocolate on her precious carpet or light blue sofa," I remonstrated. "Besides, Irenli says the same thing about her."

"Oh, she's actually very nice, Liserl. You just have to be a little bit careful," Mama said, trying to be reassuring.

"She tells me not to drop crumbs from cookies," I remembered.

"If you look at her," Mama answered softly, still trying to impress me, "you'll see how beautiful she is. And she can sing." She had studied to be an opera singer, but Onkel Eduard, a well-known and highly respected ear, nose, and throat specialist, would not allow his wife to perform on a stage. I liked him. He smiled at me and he had a habit of winking at me when his wife gave instructions.

"She's really very pleasant, and—"

"No, she isn't. I told you how annoying she is. Irenli also doesn't like her. I don't want to go. I want to be with Anni and ride my tricycle and play in the garden with Herbert."

"Tomorrow. You can do that tomorrow," Mama answered in a tone no longer so forbearing.

She stored all kinds of little sayings in her mind. She used them, I now consider inappropriately, to exercise her control, although not consciously. Irenli had just thrown one of her temper tantrums, and after exchanging a few disagreeable words with Papa, Mama cried out, obviously overwhelmed, "If it weren't for Liserl, I would leave." I was horror-stricken, at age seven, to hear this from my mother. I came home from school fearful that I might find her gone, and henceforth decided I would have to be a good girl to keep her at home, too young to realize the burden put on me, and that it was an empty threat—merely her way of expressing a frustration of the moment.

Something else she declared, which, although I remember hearing it only once, made an indelible impression: "You can't burn a candle at both ends."

I interpreted that as a warning that she might collapse, or, worse—that I would find her dead on the floor one day. I asked myself, *Was I good enough today? Did I do what I was supposed to do?* I took it upon myself to act responsibly and to make life easier for her by being on my best behavior.

Occasionally, she nagged Papa until his good nature reached its limit, and when he reacted angrily, she mumbled, "Little pots boil over quickly."

Her threats occurred only a couple of times, but their imagery was strong enough to etch possible disaster on my mind. I didn't perceive our family's situation to be so drastic. On the contrary, both our parents expressed their love for us girls, and on the whole it was a harmonious home. Of course there was my sister's bullying and jealousy, but I didn't know any better at the time. I didn't understand why Mama felt that way, especially since she frequently prepared a special meal for Papa if he had had a hard day at work, making sure to tell Irenli and me, "Be nice to Papa. Let's all sing that song he likes from *Die Fledermaus* when he gets home."

Mostly, I remember Mama from my childhood days as kind, protective, and reliable, and I felt loved, although she was not physically demonstrative. I don't recall ever sitting on her lap as I did on Papa's. When she took us girls to the city, she bought for us, within reason, what we wanted. It used to be a fun day, sun shining, holding her hand, swinging the new parcel in the other, on the way to buying an ice-cream cone. We would savor it, sitting on a bench at one of the parks flanking the Ring. If it was too cold, we stopped at the well-known Demel's for a piece of cake with schlag.

Neither she nor Papa was strict. We were never spanked, or punished by being sent to bed early (we had no set bedtime), or had a privilege revoked. We were spoken to and given an explanation of why what we had done was wrong.

4

SISTERLY LOVE

THE RELATIONSHIP WITH MY SISTER the first twelve years of my life was strained and tenuous. Her unabated jealousy, interspersed by her bullying, and her delight in putting me down, was accepted by me as part of my life. I grew into a shy child, compounded by being small for my age. Even my thick, wavy, beautiful auburn hair, and lovely white skin, for which I received frequent compliments, did nothing, except cause embarrassment. I was dubbed cute, dear, well behaved, and 'chochem'(smart), when I unexpectedly answered a complicated question. Irenli referred to me as "*Das brave Liserl*" (good, little Lisl) "who, of course, didn't do anything wrong," when we were reprimanded. I didn't like any of those descriptions, but having received the labels I inevitably lived up to them. If Irenli told a story with much elaboration, I didn't bother to correct it. It was easier to keep quiet and let her babble on. I felt inadequate. Nobody asked my opinion. Maybe they did. I don't remember. Irenli didn't have to be asked. She volunteered. Of course, for me there was Misslitz (Miroslav) in Czechoslovakia (Czechoslovakia)—my second home and haven.

IRENLI HAD BEEN SENT THERE to Mama's relatives to ease the transition of my birth. When she returned, she realized the three-and-a-half years she had enjoyed as queen had become spoiled by an intruder. I have heard the incident told so many times that I have no trouble visualizing it.

Her feeling of having been dethroned made her decide to take action. Wrapped tightly in a blanket, she managed to pull me out of the crib and drag me to the kitchen. My mother found her at the trashcan, lid held high in one hand, the other clutching the blanket in a tight fist, lest I, then four weeks old, make an attempt to escape.

"You lied to me," she cried through tears covering her cheeks.

"She doesn't have red hair. It looks like carrots. We don't need her."

Irenli's antics continued over the years, and when she really wanted to scare me, she taunted, "Wait till you go to school. Mrs. Somerer is very strict. She is mean and nasty." Mrs. Somerer was the first-grade teacher, and Irenli succeeded. I was terrified of starting school. What a surprise to find the teacher was neither mean nor nasty.

There were times, of course, when we shared doing things together, and family outings passed peacefully. Sooner or later, however, the volcano erupted.

One such eruption occurred while we were vacationing at the *Wolfgangsee* in Austria. On a beautiful, cloudless summer day,

Irenli decided it was time again to do away with me. I was eight at the time; she was eleven. Walking along the lake where a springboard had been built at the deep end, I stopped near it and glanced around when, without warning, she pushed me into the water. It caused quite a commotion. Swimmers and sunbathers congregated to where I had been standing. I heard excited voices of a child drowning, and a woman jumped in to save me. It was a surprise to witness all the tumult, because I didn't feel I was drowning. I had managed to keep my head above water by flailing my arms, and was quite pleased with the accomplishment. Realizing that such a movement kept me afloat, I continued happily to doggy-paddle the rest of our holiday.

As for my part in our relationship, I was not totally innocent. I contributed my share to our difficulties by becoming sneaky, and I would plot my defense. The trick I liked to play on her usually worked. Our baby-grand piano stood on a red Persian carpet that had beige flowers woven into it. Quietly entering that room, I crawled under the piano, and using one of the flowers as a launching pad, I reached out and pinched her legs. She shot up, and the chase around the table began, ending in my flight to the toilet (a separate little room), where I locked myself in long enough to wait for one of our parents to settle the fight, or for Irenli to walk away calling me names.

On the other hand, I endured her threats. At one time she commanded me to say the word "Znaim" (Tsnime), the name of a town in the Czechoslovakia where my grandparents lived. We were staying at their house at the time.

"I can't say it," I answered.

"Yes, you can," she demanded harshly. "Say it."

"I can't say it," I insisted, my voice pretty steady, standing my ground.

"A child must be able to say Znaim." Her tone rising, she got up and stood over me.

"Well, I can't," I said loud and clear, determined not to give in.

"If you don't say it, I'll beat you up," she threatened.

"I *won't say* it," I maintained, facing her uplifted arm.

At that moment the door opened, and as I beheld my mother in the doorway, I yelled, "And I won't say 'Znaim.'"

Sure, there were times we got along, but she delighted in putting me down. Her oft-repeated remark was, "You have red hair. That's bad enough. Also, you have freckles, white skin, and you are short." She added what she thought were other defects as she thought of them, and I believed her. If I complained to Mama, she assured me, "Your hair is a beautiful color, the color Titian painted his women, and white skin is wonderful."

"You're only saying that because you love me, but Irenli is telling me the truth," I answered in disbelief.

It did not occur to me at the time that Kurt, the university student living in the apartment below ours, tutored her; I had no such need. Or that she, too, possessed defects, maybe different from mine, but she was not perfect.

Despite all that, I looked up to her. In my eyes she was talented, good looking, outgoing, and self-assured. She played the piano quite well; I had given up on it. She talked to people; I kept quiet in company. She spoke up; I was shy. She claimed what she said or what she did was fine; I was quick to doubt or accept blame.

My sister's bullying continued right into adulthood with few interruptions, one of which occurred after the annexation of Austria to Germany. I was at home alone one dreary April day looking out the window. As she approached the house, she looked up and waved to me. Not a show of great sisterly love; nonetheless, I thought, *Finally, she is nice to me.* I remember another time, a little over a year later, when I had written to her from England telling her how homesick I was. She answered from Palestine, where she had immigrated, "How can you be homesick for a country that threw you out, and people who kicked you in the behind? Be glad to be rid of them." That made an impression.

5

MY GRANDPARENTS IN VIENNA

BOTH MY FATHER'S PARENTS WERE born in a small town near Prague in the Czechoslovakia. After their eldest son, William, was born there, they moved to Vienna.

Several times a year we visited them. They lived in a part of Vienna that had once been the Jewish ghetto and still housed a large number of Jews. They seemed old-fashioned to me, as did their apartment, which always appeared dark, exuding an odor of un-aired rooms.

Grosssmutter welcomed my sister and me warmly. "Come in, come in. I'm so glad to see you." She ushered us through the large kitchen into the living room. Petite, and soft-spoken, there was an implied self-assurance about her, but somehow I felt remote from her. I perceived her as very old, perhaps because she moved so unobtrusively and slowly in her dark clothes and, because of her wrinkled face, I never noticed any other features.

On one of our visits, she announced, "I'll be right back with something I made just for you, dears." She disappeared into the kitchen and returned bearing two big plates of semolina, a big slab of butter swimming in the middle, melting as it dribbled to the outer limits of the plates. Both Irenli and I felt repelled as we slowly swallowed a few mouthfuls, wondering if Grossmutter was watching. We were used to eating semolina without the butter. Neither one of us could possibly say anything derogatory to that sweet, little old woman. It seemed helpful to look around the room while slowly stirring the food absent-mindedly. In doing so, my eye caught the big speaker of the gramophone sitting on a round table against the wall. It fascinated me, as it reminded me of labels on records, and ads of 'His Master's Voice', portraying a sitting white fox terrier, with one white ear and one black one, listening to music emanating from a large phonograph cylinder.

Grossvater, tall, big, and slow moving, now bald, and wearing glasses, also catered to us. His thick gray mustache, which had a few hairs sticking out of order, intensified the appearance of being strong and sturdy, but maybe he was not. Mama claimed he had never worked hard in his life, and that my grandmother had to take care of everything. I don't know what that meant, because I never heard what he did for a living.

On our visits he played dominoes with us, and he managed always to let us win. To prepare for the game, he said, "Let's get the table cleared off," addressing Grossmutter good-naturedly with a wave of his hand as he winked at her. "We need room here for the game." We usually played at the large table in the middle of the room after we managed to swallow the semolina. The adults moved to the brown velvet sofa that occupied the space between the two windows, or to some chairs in front of the heavy, dark red drapes, or the one big, red armchair by the gramophone. That's where Papa liked to sit, unable to resist playing a record of Viennese songs, or an opera, in muted tones that served as background music. When we finished the game, Grossvater got up, drew himself up to his full height, and announced in his deep, hoarse voice, "I have something for you." He mysteriously left the room and returned with either money—including old, foreign coins—or trinkets for both of us. I cherished those little nothings.

On another visit, Grossmutter asked me about my school, my friends, and what I was doing. I had graduated from elementary school at age ten, and was attending a lyceum (gymnasium) for girls for the second year, having formed new friendships. Herbert, also in a new school, and I were still good friends, but we saw less of each other. Grete had become my constant companion for the last two years. We walked to school, did our homework, and spent our free time together. As a Roman Catholic, she learned about the Jewish holidays my family kept, and I was invited to attend church services with her. A big, strong girl with short blonde hair and blue eyes, she had decided to let her hair grow longer.

I was shocked when Grossmutter, after listening attentively, asked: "She is your best friend? She wants you to go to church with her?"

The question reeked of rebuke. I tried to temper it. "Well, yes. Maybe she will come to temple with me."

"I am surprised. You know, dear, you are not supposed to do that. And remember, she is not Jewish."

Grandmother had never before voiced her opinion so directly. She usually deferred to Grandfather.

That conversation took place not long before Hitler annexed Austria, and maybe Grossmutter already suspected more than she let on.

Since they lived at the opposite end of Vienna, it was too difficult for them to visit us. We did, however, travel to the main synagogue in Vienna (Seitenstaetter Gasse) to keep them company every year for the High Holidays. Occasionally, we met Uncle Karl, and his wife Hansi and son Willy, at my grandparents' apartment. Sometimes they visited us in Hietzing. I don't remember going to their house. Uncle Karl was a fashionable, impeccably dressed gentleman, which my mother always commented on, and Tante Hansi's blonde, perfumed hair was always beautifully arranged under her various hats matching her outfits. Willy, who was my sister's age, seemed whiny and distant, and we were not very close. Having escaped the Nazis, poor Willy came to a terrible end several years later in New York City. As a young gay man, he invited another man to his hotel room, who, it turned out, was an FBI agent. Willy jumped out the window to his death. That was in 1941, when gay men were imprisoned in America.

My father's younger bachelor brother, Ernst, a jolly fellow, visited once in a while, too. He talked of getting married, but I never met his fiancée.

Grossvater and Grossmutter were alone in what must have been the darkest period of their lives. They had no children left. William, their eldest, had left Austria before World War I, and subsequently served in the Canadian army. Richard (my father) had left for the United States. The other two sons (Karl and Ernst), and their wives, had been arrested and later killed by the Nazis.

Then it was my grandparents' turn. In 1943, the Nazis appeared at the apartment to arrest Grossvater. Grossmutter insisted on accompanying her husband of sixty years—wherever the destination. In their eighties, they were deported to Terezin (in Czechoslovakia; the German name was (Theresienstadt). I am thankful that they were spared the horrors of Auschwitz, the death camp. Terezin was bad enough, but it didn't have gas chambers.

While I was very fond of my paternal grandparents, I did not love visiting them. Yet tears are running down my cheeks as I write, some seventy years later. I picture the SS (*Schutz Stoffel*), the elite fighting force, in their black uniforms, reputed to be even more cruel than the brown-shirted SA men, bursting into my grandparents' apartment to haul off Grossvater, handling him gruffly as they did so. I see little Grossmutter, frail, her wrinkled face, which must have been very pretty at one time, loyal and attentive to Grossvater, even in the face of death, by choosing to go with him—wherever that might be. They died in Terezin within four months of each other.

Without the chance to say proper good-byes to them prior to their arrest, or at a previous time when I unexpectedly and suddenly departed for Misslitz, I had no closure. I cry for having allowed the darkness of the apartment and the smell of un-aired rooms to overshadow my recognition of their kindness and, especially, my grandmother's sweetness. My tears are for times and opportunities lost forever.

6

MY GRANDPARENTS IN MISSLITZ

I N 2006 THE CITY OF VIENNA invited me (airfare and hotel paid) to return for a visit for one week. Hotel accommodation for one companion was also included. The offer was made as an apology for having thrown us out almost seventy years earlier. Because of my ambiguous feelings about going there, I asked my son, Bradley, and my grandson Ben, to accompany me. Thomas, who had been our exchange student from Germany in 1980, and remembered Bradley and me, flew from Berlin to meet us. We kept in touch over the years, mostly via e-mail. Wined and dined by the City of Vienna, it turned into a very pleasant visit. The highlight, though, took place somewhere else.

While there, we rented a car and drove to Misslitz, Czechoslovakia, my mother's birthplace and home of my maternal grandparents. We stopped on the outskirts to check if the cemetery we had just passed was the Jewish one. Thomas stretched over the wall and glimpsed a Mogen Dovid (Jewish Star), but we were unable to go inside—both doors were locked. Bradley, anxious to get a better look, stood on a small rock around the corner and started videotaping. From a row of houses across the street, a woman on a cane hobbled towards us and inquired what we were doing. Thomas, who knew some Czech, conveyed our mission. Miraculously, she was the person who kept the key to the cemetery, which she generously offered. We entered eagerly and looked in vain for some paths. Brown old leaves covered all of them. Careful not to trip, we pushed our way around tumbled tombstones, some with their tops chopped off, others leaning heavily, almost all damaged in some way. The cemetery looked uncared for and in utter disarray. I asked Ben, then nine years old, to look for a tombstone that said Isidor Deutsch—my grandfather. After several minutes of wandering through ruins, I heard, "We found it; here it is." I rushed towards Bradley and Ben, both facing a large, oblong, black granite stone—almost intact. Except for a scratch at the bottom of one corner, the stone was in perfect condition. My grandfather's name was engraved in large letters, followed by *4 Marz 1868–19 November 1933*, with three lines in Hebrew above the name. All four of us stood in speechless amazement. Thomas, who is Protestant (he had spent a year on a kibbutz in Israel where he learned Hebrew), broke the silence; he pulled a *yarmulke* (skull cap) from his backpack, translated the Hebrew, which lauded my grandfather—a respected, loved citizen—and suggested we recite the Kaddish (prayer for the dead). At the conclusion of the prayer, we again fell into silence, each one of us engrossed in thought. There was space on the stone for my grandmother, who, unfortunately, had to die in the

Terezin (Theresienstadt) concentration camp in 1944. I had
never been to the cemetery, and seventy-three years had passed
since my grandfather died. Bradley's comment, "Mom, with Ben,
we are five generations standing here. It's awesome," summed
up how we all felt. *(County of mother)*

Slowly, we wound our way to Mrs. Sindelarova's house to return the key. It was a mall house, very tidy. She, too, was small,
dressed neatly, her face wrinkled. We were both the same age—
eighty-one. She welcomed us warmly, and we managed to con-
verse. I hoped she had known my grandparents. She had not.
She was only a little girl during their lifetime. When I wanted to
leave after twenty minutes, she stopped me, stroked my cheeks
and looked terribly mournful. That was repeated at each attempted leave-taking. Finally, I backed out, but as I waved to
her, she stood in the doorway looking so forlorn and unhappy
that I turned back to give her a big hug. She had tears in her eyes.
Thomas, Bradley, and Ben followed, and also hugged her. She
then crossed herself, pointed towards the cemetery, and explained
that she says a prayer for all of them every day. Then I had tears
in my eyes.

From her house it only took a few minutes of driving to reach
the center of Misslitz. The visit to the cemetery, followed by the
meeting with Mrs. Sindelarova, was so extraordinary that I felt
exhilarated in the anticipation of seeing my grandmother's house.

We parked the car and walked briskly across the Marktplatz
(town center). The square cobblestones, the old, unused pump
just off center, were familiar, happily remembered sights. Excitedly, I approached my grandmother's house only to stop short as

a loud gasp escaped me. The house I had known was not there. Another one stood in its place. The buildings to the left—Grunbaum—and the one to the right—Kramer—where I often visited, were also gone, as were the next three houses. I was devastated. Either bombs, or combating the Russians in World War II, had destroyed them, and others had been built.

"Let's see if the big red iron gate at the far end of my grandparents' yard is still there," I suggested, hoping to salvage some part of their existence as I had known it. The four of us meandered around the block to the street running parallel to the Marktplatz, only to experience the second letdown. A fence surrounding a house replaced the gate.

Just a few steps away the Judengasse (Jewish Street) beckoned. In place of the sizeable temple, a plaque verifying its existence was all that was left. I looked for Tante Kati's house in the opposite direction—just a short distance from my grandparents' house—I couldn't find it. The visit I had looked forward to with such anticipation turned into a nightmare—one disappointment after another.

There was another street I recalled, but, fearful of yet another disillusion, I avoided it. It became too painful not to find again and again what I had remembered so well; also, the atmosphere of the little town had changed. No Jews returned to Misslitz after the war, and the Czechs threw out all the remaining Germans. Even the name was no longer Misslitz. Now Miroslav, the people neither understood nor spoke German or English. I wanted to get away. It was too upsetting to find the past erased everywhere I turned. It was *my* past, and although the structure of the Marktplatz and its cobblestones were unchanged, the atmosphere and the feeling of the place had changed into something totally different—like finding an old skeleton, flesh and blood and life gone.

As a last resort, however, I wondered if the swimming pool still existed.

On the short drive to reach it, I recounted to my three amiable companions how my aunt Gretl's boyfriend—the one with the dark, bushy eyebrows—used to hoist me onto his bicycle bar in 1937 as he rode along the dusty country road, passing geese and grazing cows on the way to the pool.

It was situated outside the village, at the entrance to a small forest, which harbored a creek. A pipe from creek to pool conveyed the necessary water, the dribbling of which was insufficiently fresh or plentiful to change its permanent color—dark green. Moss, also dark green, adorned the sides of the pool walls. No matter—none of that distracted from the fun of swimming and splashing in that luscious water for hours on end. My favorite snack—great tasting fresh country bread, buttered and salted, and homemade peach ice cream—were sold near the entrance and enjoyed on the wooden planks that flanked one side of the pool for sunbathing. The opposite side displayed an area of grass—sharp and prickly. Up a few steps, about twenty large wooden cabins that bathers could rent for the season stood attached in a row. They lent privacy for changing clothes, provided primitive furnishings—a wooden bench, a small mirror hanging on the wall, and a few clothes hangers. Bathing suits, hats, and other articles of clothing were left overnight, some items throughout the season. My grandmother had rented the same cabin every year—the second from the left.

WHEN WE REACHED THE POOL on an unusually warm day in October 2006, it was closed for the season. Standing on a rock on that clear day, I looked over the fence, and my eye traveled across the pool (still dark green) up to the cabins. All doors were closed except my grandmother's—the second from the left. Its door stood wide open.

Bradley asked, "Do you want to look for anything else, Mom? Or, would you like to walk in the little forest here that you said you liked?"

"No, I don't feel like exploring anything else. I remember Misslitz well, and except for the swimming pool, I can't stand what I am finding. I want to get away from here. Let's leave— the sooner the better," I answered, feeling rather downcast.

On the way back to Vienna, I tried to erase all I had just experienced, and to ease my pain and forget how Misslitz turned into Miroslav, I concentrated on my vision of it as I knew it in 1937 and before. The memory was too precious to allow it to be tarnished by the present.

To cement the memory, I talked to my three companions about Misslitz and started by telling them about how traveling there was always an adventure.

Papa, who did not accompany us, saw us off at the train station in Vienna. The rude customs official at the Grussbach border—inflated with his official importance—rummaged through the big leather trunk, totally turning the contents upside down as if he were looking for contraband. Closing it after he left the train meant going through the same ordeal every year, because Mama never heeded Papa's warning not to stuff the trunk to the brim. A piece of underwear, or the strap of one of her brassieres, invariably managed to dangle out after it was closed and locked. Passport control went faster and was more civil. At least that scenario helped pass the hour or so we had to wait for the connecting train. We had just finished a three-hour ride from Vienna. What also helped pass the time was the vendor marching back and forth, calling "*Horky parky/Heisse Würstel*" ("hot dogs" in Czech/German), which he carried in a black pail. Irenli and I watched through the open window as the aroma of the escaping steam filled our nostrils and teased our taste buds. If we pestered enough, Mama bought them for us. They came in pairs, wrapped in brown paper with mustard, if requested. They were not served in a roll as in America, and never with ketchup.

I adored visiting my grandparents in Misslitz. Both, Opapa and Babi, as we called them, were born in Moravia, Czechoslovakia, and had lived in Misslitz for many years. I loved them as well as my beautiful aunt Gretl, my favorite aunt Yelli, her son, little Stefan, and also Wolfie, Babi's dog. Of my mother's eight siblings, I felt closest to Gretl, not married yet and living at home, and to Yelli, married. She lived a few houses away.

My visits—a couple of weeks every summer and an extended stay in 1937—were very important to me. They represented a time to be free, to be just me, not to be criticized or judged, a chance to keep some distance from my bullying sister, and no need to be a good little girl to make up for her temper tantrums.

Last but not least, I enjoyed the freedom to roam by myself, to drop in on neighbors unannounced, or to run errands, always accompanied by Wolfie.

When I was very little, my grandfather was still alive. He was tall, always stood erect, and his intense brown eyes in his bald, egg-shaped head, smiled down at me when I tugged at his trousers to get his attention. When (I was told), at age two, I approached him with, "*Opapa, Krone, Gage, Stich*," he knew I'd asked for a Krone to buy chocolate at Stich's candy store, and he obliged every time.

Opapa suffered from headaches, but that didn't stop me, and any visiting cousins, from playing in the living room. I loved the interaction as there was always a lot going on. Invariably it became so noisy that Babi cautioned us to be very quiet, better yet to leave the room, so he could rest. I suspect now that her eagerness for such stillness was, perhaps, a ploy to also save a few minutes of peace for herself. She had a habit, for instance, of saying that the best part of the radio was that you could turn it off.

The day Opapa died in 1933, I was in Vienna. The phone rang on a miserable, rainy day in November. Disaster was written all over Papa's face after he had picked up the receiver to listen.

"What's wrong, Rikki?" my mother asked as he hung up the phone. Trying to compose himself as he reached for Mama's hand, he stammered something, and said, "It's bad news. It's your father, Lottie. He suffered a heart attack and he died this morning."

Hard as Papa tried to comfort her, Mama sobbed inconsolably. I began to feel sad, overcome by her reaction. I didn't quite know what to do. She was sitting in an armchair, so I moved next to her, kneeling on the floor, and put my hand on her lap. I was eight years old and had never heard of someone dying.

A large photograph of Opapa hung over the piano in my grandparents' living room, with his eyes following wherever you stood. That, and Mama's stories about him, kept his image alive.

She bore great admiration, respect, and a lot of love for him. He, in turn, had asked her opinion on important matters. He had danced with her at a ball. They had loved each other's company.

BABI, IN CONTRAST, WAS QUITE short, stocky, and tight-lipped, which belied her kindness. She wore her short white hair parted on one side, a dark barrette fastened on the other.

She was enterprising. Some time after Opapa had died, she had one of the rooms converted into an office. "I need it, now that I am taking care of much of the business, rather than just have ledgers lying on a desk," she declared proudly to my mother. She also had a veranda added to the kitchen, with flower boxes "where I can plant the purple petunias I like." I have always re-membered those flowers, and I usually buy purple petunias for my flowerbed in front of the house.

Curious to inspect the office, I made my way there the fol-lowing day through a corridor that connected another room to it. "Hello, Babi," I called, "I've come to visit." I wondered why she didn't turn around. She was hunched over her desk, sur-rounded by papers, and, pen in hand, she said quickly but kindly, "I can't talk to you now, Liserl, I'm busy. Come back later." She was busy with the stock market.

My grandparents were always in favor of having improvements made to their home. Theirs was the first one to have an indoor toilet, and, which I liked, Babi had had a kennel built for the dog, big enough for him to move around instead of being chained in the yard.

I don't remember ever being told off by her. She was gentle and loving, though not physically, and very approachable when not in the office. Yet there was another side to her. I don't think she liked any of her sons-in-law, or the boyfriends of her two unmarried daughters—Gretl, and Lorly, who was mostly in Prague studying at the university. I never heard her say anything derogatory about my father, but even as a little girl, I sensed there was no love lost. Others received nicknames, were criticized, judged, or looked down on. There were two exceptions. One, Arnold, was very wealthy, married to my aunt Rosl, who was very attractive and ten or fifteen years younger than he. They lived in Brno and he hardly ever visited. The other, Hugo, married to Aunt Olga, blonde and also attractive, had been a high-ranking officer. He must have looked good in uniform—tall, straight, stiff, and he never laughed. His family, who lived in Misslitz, may have rated a notch higher socially, although Opapa was highly respected. He was president of the temple, held other positions of honor in the Jewish community, and was equally well liked by the local village folk. My grandparents and two other families—the Fischers and the Hausers—constituted the ivy league of the Jewish community, and there was covert competition among them. Who the guests were, and the tablecloth and dinnerware that was used, were the subjects of importance. The other Jewish families fell into a category below. Son-in-law Hugo was a Hauser.

There was a divide. The Jewish population in Misslitz was sophisticated; many were educated, cultured, and able to speak Czech. Among themselves they tended to speak German—whereas the non-Jewish village population spoke Czech. My father, the old Viennese, liked to make fun, referring to Misslitz as "Big City Misslitz." In many ways, it was. Those who could afford it—money-wise and time-wise—traveled frequently to Vienna to shop, see specialist doctors, visit relatives, attend theaters, the opera, and museums.

Babi and Opapa were well off. They owned hundreds of acres of land on which vineyards and orchards of fruit trees were planted, which they rented out. Close to their house they owned a tavern, which was also rented out. The concrete yard at the house accommodated a small beer cellar on one side. The yard stretched considerably, starting at the home and ending at the next street, a block away. At that end, a big red iron gate, locked for privacy, was large enough for the beer truck to pass through. Farther down, on the right side, a fence surrounded a small plot of earth where Babi planted herbs and flowers in her private little garden. As a special favor, she allowed me to enter it and pick flowers for the dining room table. Wheelbarrows and bicycles stood around neatly piled.

My grandparents led a simple, but comfortable life. Surrounded by their servants and loyal staff, they ate well, had improvements made to the house to their liking, and enjoyed the respect and popularity afforded them as active members of the community. Misslitz provided their basic needs. For the purchase of clothes beyond the local dressmaker's ability, or for special items, they would hire a car and driver and spend a day in Brno, the second largest city in Czechoslovakia. Visits to Vienna were not uncommon, but involved an overnight stay.

Accompanied by her sister, Tante Hanni, Babi traveled to an elegant spa in Karlsbad every year. They spent a couple of weeks there for the cure. Hats, gloves, new dresses, stuffed foxes around their shoulders (the bushy tail of the fox swinging as they walked), they went off to see and be seen, sitting at their fancy hotel enjoying the five o'clock tea dance. The cure was for stomach ailments, which, apparently, by means of drinking warm or even hot water from one of the many surrounding mineral springs that were pumped into the city, alleviated the discomfort. Strolling past large hotels, under equally large columns supporting them, and nodding to acquaintances, offered a popular pastime.

I LIKED BEING IN MISSLITZ so much that, when it was time to return to Vienna at the end of the summer in 1937, I simply said, "I'm not going." I was eleven years old.

"What do you mean, you're not going?" Mama asked, surprised and trying to sound stern. "Of course you are."

I remained adamant in my refusal, and tension grew. Mama got angry, then anxious, because the bus was ready to leave for the station to catch the train to Vienna. After much fuss, and talk among the grown-ups, Mama said, "All right, you can stay for a few days. After that, I'm sure somebody we know will go to Vienna and bring you."

I was delighted to have time to spend with Babi, my aunts Gretl and Yelli, as well as Ernst, her husband. He allowed me to be 'useful' in his grocery store. He did not sell fruit and vegetables, but I do remember fresh, salty pickles. He also carried 'gourmet' items like imported chocolate. Wolfie, the fierce mongrel dog, my frequent companion in and out of the house, meant the world to me. The freedom I so cherished there, away from my sister, combined with the laissez-faire attitude, all of which made me feel like a big-shot, was perhaps, the most important for me, except—unrecognized in my child's mind at the time— for Yelli's presence. Sure, she was my favorite aunt, but it was her nurturing and hugs, embraces and kisses, that mattered—that physical show of love my mother seldom supplied. And she knew how to make me feel important. She would ask my opinion or advice and act on it.

The few days Mama had agreed to turned into weeks, which passed quickly. Almost every day that August brought bright sunshine in a deep blue sky, with little white clouds scattered here and there. There was usually somebody willing to take me to the swimming pool, or, if not, I found other ways to amuse myself.

A visit to my grandfather's sister, Tante Kati, who lived up the hill, a five-minute walk, was not unusual. She made me feel welcome whenever I turned up. Her divorced daughter, Ida, lived with her, as did *her* daughter, Mariandl, in her early twenties. She was friends with my aunts. Tante Kati would ask, "Lisl, would you go and pick some apricots for us?" I would hurry to the tree in her garden, careful not to step on any of her masses of flowers, whose colors and scents were gorgeous.

Other activities kept me occupied: errands to the dressmaker, delivering messages to relatives (rather than using the telephone), or shopping for a forgotten grocery item—always accompanied by Wolfie.

THOSE WERE THE MEMORIES THAT occupied me on the way back to Vienna from our one day visit to Misslitz in 2006.

7

MISSLITZ (MY SECOND HOME)

THURSDAY WAS A SPECIAL DAY. The market was held on the *Marktplatz*, the village square, where farmers from surrounding villages displayed their wares for sale. Misslitz was the biggest and most cosmopolitan little town in the area. There was a selection of clothing, knick-knacks, kitchen utensils, garden tools, small furniture, ceramics, toys, and food. Sometimes I bought some trinkets, but mostly I loved browsing, never growing tired of repeating the meanderings week after week.

One Thursday, Katcho happened to see me leave the house. She had been Babi's wet nurse for her nine children. Although no longer needed in that capacity, she had become a fixture in the house, she came every day for years to oversee other servants, me, and my grandmother, and generally to keep order. She was an impressive, good-looking peasant woman. Her forceful personality matched her tall, strong physique, as well as her tanned face, which had become wrinkled. She kept her head covered with a black kerchief, and it seemed that she wore several skirts or petticoats that swished as she strode in her high, black-laced shoes. She was Czech, but she had learned some German from Babi. I liked her, and we were able to communicate with each other quite well—a few German words on her part, a few Czech words on my part, mixed with sign language.

As soon as I returned from my morning's foray, she stopped me.

"What you eating?" she demanded in a friendly enough tone.

"A hot dog, of course," I answered.

"Where you buy it?"

After much pointing and explaining the direction where I had purchased that delicacy, she figured out I was eating a hot dog made of horse-meat, sold by a vendor she knew.

My grandmother kept kosher, and Katcho knew the rules.

"No eating that in the house," she cautioned. I was at her mercy and did not reply. She must have noticed how much I enjoyed eating that forbidden tidbit, because she continued: "I won't take it away from you. You not supposed to eat that, but you finish it, if you stay outside."

I liked her even more then—and at the same time felt adventurous and pleased with myself, because it tasted so good, and I had ventured into a forbidden field.

Katcho, sometimes we called her Katchova, sure knew the rules. When my grandmother arrived home late one Friday night, she calmed her, saying, "Not worry, ma'am, I already lit the candles and covered my eyes." She then spread her arms, and demonstrated how she brought them towards herself, adding, "I said welcome to Sabbath."

Another special day I loved was to be allowed to accompany Marianka, the maid (rather than the other way around) and her boyfriend to the Kirtag, if it fell on a Sunday during my visit. That festival took place on the Marktplatz, with loud drums beating out polka music. Taking me by the hand to dance with them on the large wooden platform, especially erected for the occasion, was pure joy. Sodas and beer flowed, and colorful balloons and streamers hanging on the lampposts floated all around. An abundance of candy and knick-knack sellers circulated through the crowd. Everybody was in a jolly mood as they jostled each other in their best Sunday clothes; some sported original national costumes, their beautiful colors swirling as they danced. Stuffed with sweets and drinks, I returned home tired from "dancing" (jumping around) to tell Babi all about it.

My grandmother employed another loyal member of her staff, held over from my grandfather's days. His name was Pavlov. A big, strong man, he was the driver of the old blue truck parked outside the entrance to the beer cellar. I used to watch, fascinated, as he loaded the heavy barrels. He often smiled at me or winked his merry eyes, especially when he told me to get out of the way, aided by a little wave of his arm, but always careful and patient when he spoke to me in his broken German.

"I would like to go on the truck with Pavlov," I surprised Babi one day by saying.

"You don't know where he is going or how long he'll be gone," she answered, taken aback by my unexpected request.

"Babi, you know how much I like driving in a car, so that's why I want to go with Pavlov. It doesn't matter where he's going."

"Well, I'll think about it, and check his schedule," she promised.

She did not take long before she returned to tell me, "He has a short trip tomorrow, and I will ask him to take you along."

I was overjoyed that she had given her permission and not made me wait in suspense. I gave her a big hug.

The next morning I woke up early, excited about the adventure that awaited me. I dressed quickly to make sure Pavlov would not leave without me.

Squeezed between him and his assistant, Janos, an amiable young man, I was delighted, no matter that the front seat suffered from lacerations, and that I had to move my legs and tilt my body sideways every time he shifted gears. Sometimes he and Janos, thin and hollow-cheeked, conversed in Czech; at other times they included me. His assistant told little anecdotes, his dark eyebrows arched, or hummed as we passed orchards, vineyards, and cornfield after cornfield.

That day's destination: a farmer, one of my grandmother's customers, in a small village not many miles away. Pavlov explained my presence to the surprised-looking man standing by the door of his beige house, eliciting a smile from his deep-wrinkled, sun-worn face. It must have been his day off. Both he and his buxom wife, in short-sleeved white shirts, hers followed by a blue skirt and white apron, welcomed us to sit at a round table in their large kitchen. The woman shook my hand as I entered and gestured me to the chair, from where I could see the flower boxes outside the window. The delicious smell of freshly baked

Buchteln (buns), filled with the customary prune or apricot jam, permeated the whole kitchen. One of these buns, served with a cup of hot chocolate, immediately endeared her to me. The men drank beer.

Before we took our leave, she handed Pavlov a lot of money—strange custom, I thought. As soon as we arrived home, I babbled to Babi what a pleasurable day I'd had.

During that extended stay in Misslitz, it was also fun to show off my expertise in riding Gretl's bicycle—no hands on the handlebars. Gretl (I never called her 'aunt'), one of my mother's younger sisters, looked stunning. Her smile revealed gloriously white teeth, her clear blue eyes never missed a trick, and the crowning glory was her naturally wavy blonde hair, which she wore pressed closely to her head. The fashionable clothes she liked to wear looked good on her tall frame. She was not a model, she was a little *saftig*, but she appeared in ads for toothpaste.

On rainy, non-swimming days, there were other options. One was to find my way to the bathroom, up several steps from the otherwise sprawling, one-level house. It was the equivalent of an attic in atmosphere, but much larger in size. Besides the bathtub, sink, and the necessary usual bathroom furniture and fixtures (no toilet, which was in a separate room), it included two big closets for off season clothing, fancy shoes stacked on a shoe rack, and the most interesting of all, as far as I was concerned, two trunks containing jewelry, hats, scarves, trinkets, and some old photographs. I considered it a treat if one of my aunts allowed me to watch her groping through, especially, as was often the case, if I ended up the recipient of one of those trinkets.

At age eleven, I was an ardent admirer of Gretl. One day I was allowed up in the bathroom and watched her put the finishing touches to her face and find the appropriate jewelry that matched her outfit as she took a last look in the long mirror that hung on the back wall, in preparation for an outing in the car with her boyfriend. I thought, *What a way to live! He drives a big car, and if he owns a chocolate factory, that would be perfect.*

She dealt generously with me—lent me her bicycle, passed on small pieces of jewelry (a pin of a small white dog comes to mind), and sometimes included me when she dated Rudi, the guy who put me on his bicycle on the way to the swim club. She had many admirers, and turned down several "good" marriage proposals. Finally, in 1939, after Hitler's occupation of Czechoslovakia, she married Hans Wilheim in Brno. I don't know what he did for a living, but I overheard Babi telling Tante Hanni, her sister, that he was kind, and good looking, but relatively poor. Her response was, "And for such a bargain, she had to wait so long?"

That was a typical remark for Tanta Hanni, known for her frankness that sometimes bordered on insult. She was a big woman, well rounded, capable, and very outspoken, not beyond using mild curse words, but she was bright and funny, and the fact that she was unique and different from anybody I knew fascinated me. She carried on her late husband's business of selling tools and farm machinery, and was very successful. Because of her *tête-à-tête* chats with Babi, I crouched under the table after dinner to listen to their business talk (for the most part not understanding it), past or present family scandals, rumors, and local gossip. When I was confronted with why I did not go to bed, I answered, "Because their talk is so interesting."

Much as I liked Gretl, my greatest love belonged to her younger sister, my aunt Yella (usually we called her Yelli), who had always been my favorite, and I hers. She was thin, with straight, short black hair, the ends of which pointed forward on her cheeks. That drew attention to her small, upturned nose. She was pretty and, like Gretl, wore fashionable clothes. I liked her, because when I was little, she had carried me, and even as I grew older, she often caressed me in a way Mama never did. She looked out for my interests, which of course Mama did also, but Yelli did it in a way that made me feel my needs and desires were important. I wasn't compared to anybody. What I said carried weight. My words counted as good, smart, and wonderful. I was not only out of reach of my sister's bullying, but I received hugs and kisses, and was embraced. She acted as my surrogate mother later, when I found myself once more in Czechoslovakia under Hitler.

She was married to a local man, Ernst, nicknamed Cokl (Tshokl), which afforded me the opportunity, especially on rainy days, to spend time in their beautifully decorated apartment, a flight up from his specialty grocery store. It was just a few houses away from my grandmother's. One of the rooms was furnished totally in Baroque style, and I was not allowed to sit on any of the chairs or the sofa, all covered in authentic silk fabric of blue-and-white stripes, with small pink and red roses woven through them. I found the bedroom very impressive, too. One side consisted of mirrors making up the whole wall. In the middle, barely visible, was a door leading into their spacious bathroom. The stylishly furnished living room, where I was welcomed, showed off a curved sofa, covered in a blue/gray wool fabric. That, and tables, chairs, and credenzas, were in modern 1930s design. They had a considerably large collection of records, which I spread out on the sofa—operas, operettas, *Lieder*, folk, and popular songs— and chose which ones to put on the gramophone, which I was allowed to put on the cocktail table by the sofa.

Stefan, their three-year-old boy, was taking a nap in the nursery while I played the gramophone waiting for him to wake up. Yelli dressed him in beautiful outfits. He was a handsome, bright, happy-go-lucky little boy who spoke Czech with his nanny and German with me. What he could not do, when I asked him, was to translate a word from one language into the other. That annoyed him. He and I played together, went for walks together, and as the days passed, and we spent more time relying on each other's company, we developed a closeness that grew into deep love for each other. He would routinely ask for me on awakening from his naps, ready for our daily walks. He was quick to learn the songs I taught him as we strolled or used the gramophone on rainy days.

THERE WERE NO STORES IN Misslitz that sold the kind of dresses Gretl and Yelli wore. They found a dressmaker who was able to copy fashions from magazines if they brought her the appropriate material. Often they sent me to pick up a finished blouse, or to bring accessories she had asked for. On those occasions, I would take Wolfie. He ran along happily, keeping an eye on me, never on a leash, which he did not permit. He also did not allow anyone to pet him except Babi and me. Irenli was terrified of him, because he snarled at her as soon as she approached him.

On one such occasion, after he had waited for me outside the dressmaker's house, I was on my way home when I encountered a bunch of village boys. All of them were between ten and twelve years old, still young enough to wear short pants. Some, I noticed, kicked stones out of boredom as they rambled aimlessly in the street. When they spotted me, they turned slowly in my direction. One of them yelled, "Hey, Tomato Girl," and I noticed how he gestured with his right arm as he swung it back and then forward, pointing toward me to signal to the other boys to move nearer to me. Although I recognized him—he was the butcher's son—I started feeling uneasy, because they had gotten too close for comfort, especially since by then they had all started to shout. They were beginning to surround me. I stood still and Wolfie took over. Their yelling was instantly drowned out by his loud bark as he circled around me to keep them at bay. They quickly scattered. As it happened, "Tomato Girl" had become my friendly nickname the previous winter when I skated with some of the boys on the frozen pond. I was surprised, therefore, to recognize the butcher's son as the ringleader of the group. He and I had been elected to be the last ones on the long line they formed, because that afforded the strongest pull at each turn. When I got home after that little skirmish, Wolfie, my loyal protector, in spite of his independence, came into the house. When Katchova threw him out (he was not allowed indoors), I sat with him in his kennel to console him.

The few extra days I was to stay in Misslitz, to which Mama had consented reluctantly, turned into three weeks, because I refused steadfastly on several occasions to travel with whoever volunteered to take me back to Vienna. Mama appeared in Misslitz one day to take me home.

With my mother's arrival, Babi, who had noticed my sadness at the inevitable task of returning to Vienna, turned to me, her hand on my shoulder, and said reassuringly, "You know, Wolfie should really be your dog. I am giving him to you, so now he belongs to you, but I will take care of him while you are in Vienna." Since I had always dreamed of owning a dog, it eased my departure somewhat as I took my leave of her, also Gretl, and especially from Yelli and Stefan, and from a life surrounded by undisturbed love.

Sadly, this—for me—idyllic existence was extinguished after the summer of 1937. Misslitz, my second home, holds only happy memories, in contrast to those of Vienna, which are stained not only by a deep hurt of suddenly not being accepted, and becoming an outcast overnight in the city of my birth, but by the terrible happenings that followed the March 1938 annexation.

8

ANNEXATION

MAMA AND I RETURNED TO Vienna, and it felt good to see Papa again, waiting for us at the railway station. He quickly stepped forward, and his welcoming arms embraced me in a big hug, followed by kisses on both cheeks. "Oh, it's so good to see you again, Liserl. I've missed you," he said, smiling from ear to ear.

School started shortly, and we all resumed our familiar routines.

By the time winter set in, and Papa had had his encounter with the landlord's teenage son (Papa had told him off for not greeting him or even acknowledging one from Papa), our daily life was still the same—but the atmosphere had completely changed. It was not long before I heard friends and relatives, who had come to our apartment one evening, make remarks like, "If Hitler comes, it will be bad for the Jews."

"Don't I know it," my father declared, as he sat down on his favorite blue chair, pushing the small light-blue pillow aside.

With a sigh, he added, "I already had a taste of it here in the house, and from my business partner and his two Nazi sons."

My uncle Karl didn't agree. "I'm not so sure. My position in my firm seems secure." He looked the part, too—always poised, and carefully and meticulously dressed.

On another occasion in our apartment, one rather large guy with a big stomach, cigarette in hand, sprawled out on the sofa next to my father's chair and blurted out, "My family has good friends who are Gentiles. We'll do all right. After all, we aren't like the Polish Jews. We have always lived here. We are educated and cultured. What can happen?" Having said that, he took a long puff on his cigarette, which stretched out from an ivory holder, and blew smoke circles as he looked smugly around the room. *My goodness*, I thought, *this 'Herr Doktor' must be someone very important.*

My political savvy at that time, age twelve, was based primarily on such overheard conversations, which were alternately conveyed in remarkably assured tones, or cautiously whispered by the various grown-ups.

A couple of months passed, and again I heard the pros and cons of the situation. My father's youngest brother, Ernst, solemnly declared, "I think this is going to be very bad. The best and safest thing to do is to leave here as soon as possible." He was a bachelor of medium height, slim, not as assuming as Uncle Karl, and closest to me in age. He was usually happy, laughed easily, and had a habit of blowing a stray piece of hair off his cheek. I liked him and was deeply affected by his words. In time, his views expressed my own feelings.

Soon it was March, and Dr. Schuschnigg, Chancellor of Austria, proclaimed over the radio, *"Bis in den Tod—Rot, Weiss, Rot"* ("Unto death—Red, White, Red"—the colors of the Austrian flag). It was too late. Death already stood at the door, ready to march in.

Hitler annexed Austria on March 12, 1938.

Suddenly and abruptly, my life was changed forever.

On that cold, gray day in March, several columns of German tanks and trucks wound their way into the city, one of them through our street. It was on a Saturday, and Papa was home, standing next to me at the dining room window as we watched the dark snake roll by. Every once in a while, that slow-moving monster stopped to feed into the main thoroughfare at the end of our street. The scene below—soldiers perched on top of tanks, others in their grayish uniforms, sitting close together in full gear on the trucks, rifles held upright—was very scary. Their helmets deep down on their foreheads also covered their ears and hid their faces unless they turned to face you. They were shouting excitedly—I couldn't understand what they were saying—and I was afraid those rifles held high with bayonets protruding even higher, might start firing at us.

I was petrified. I was witnessing something I had never heard of before, had never seen or read about before, and I became so frightened that my teeth started to chatter. Papa bent down to reassure me. "No need to be scared, Liserl. We are safe here in the apartment. They are just passing through," he added softly, putting his arm around my shoulder and drawing me closer. He then turned, suggesting, "Let's go and have a cup of chocolate."

"No, not now," I answered, tugging at his sleeve and facing the window again. As if drawn by a magnet, I had to see what was going on down below.

The shouting in the street was actually friendly, but I had been unable to discern that until I realized what was happening. I could hardly believe what I saw: Our landlord, his wife, and son came running out to the soldiers to lavish them with flowers and baskets of fruit. Other people came rushing, too, some waving little swastika flags. Suddenly, people appeared out of nowhere, and whoever was in the street ran towards the soldiers with raised right arms in the Hitler salute. Screams of "*Heil Hitler*" rose to our apartment. There was chaotic jubilation as people ran towards the soldiers, happily shrieking and laughing while waving the swastika flags. Just as quickly, and all of a sudden, swastika flags were flying everywhere—from windows, from doors, from rooftops.

At that point, facing my father, I pleaded, "Papa, let's leave. Ernst said to do that, too, when he was here the other day. It's not safe."

"We'll try, but we can't just pack up and go on the spur of the moment. We have to take care of a few things here first."

The very next day, the friendship that had existed between my best friend, Grete, and me was extinguished. She came to school in a blue skirt and white blouse, her blonde hair grown long enough to wear in braids. She looked very much like a member of the Hitler Youth. Other girls in our class commented, "Grete is not talking to you. Did you have a fight?" Everybody knew how close we were, and that we walked to and from school together every day.

She avoided me in school and out. She crossed the street the next day as her mother was walking with us because an SA man came towards us, and she, in her uniform, did not want to be seen with me. Her mother was quite embarrassed. (SA men were the brown-shirted storm troopers. They dealt roughly with Jews, overriding police authority. We soon learned that, if one of them passed by without stopping you, you breathed a sigh of relief.)

The situation at school changed quickly. The five or six Jewish girls banded together in the back of the classroom (where we had been assigned to sit), although the Gentile students still conversed with us—except Grete. When, the following month, a play was to be performed, not only had the Jewish students been stripped of their parts, they were also forbidden to attend just to watch.

The Jewish teachers, many of them professors, were dismissed immediately. I was thrown out in the middle of the school year, before the end of term. It was simple and unceremonious. One day the new teacher, who had taken the place of the dismissed Jewish one, informed me that my last day at school had come, and handing me my report card, said, "Good-bye."

The report card, besides my grades, bore a rubber stamp as follows: *"The student has declared that she is leaving the school. She did this freely and in an orderly manner, and she is free to enroll in another school."* I had done no such thing.

Jewish students in all schools were thrown out. The only educational choice left was to attend the all-Jewish school in the city. It was situated a distance from our house, and not an inviting prospect. I felt fortunate, as an unexpected alternative was presented to me later in the summer.

In the meantime, in July 1938 Herbert accompanied me to the swimming pool. We stopped short at the entrance, stunned to read a notice: *No Dogs, And No Jews, Allowed.* Even dogs were mentioned ahead of Jews.

Herbert, half Jewish, declared, "If you can't go in, I won't either." I knew how much he enjoyed swimming and encouraged him to do so, suggesting that I would wait for him, but after a short discussion we both returned home. It did not take long to see such notices posted at park entrances, movie houses, theaters—in fact, Jews were denied entry to all public places of entertainment or recreation.

FOR YEARS AFTER THE WAR, Austria maintained it had been Hitler's first victim, ignoring the jubilant welcome they gave the troops, their happy reception of Hitler, or their behavior immediately after the annexation.

In Austria, the Nazis unleashed their brutality on the Jews much faster than they had in Germany. What took the Germans several years, Austria contrived to achieve in weeks. Incidents of men being beaten, losing their jobs, memberships in clubs being denied and Jews openly sneered at, became a common occurrence—all of it happening abruptly, without notice, so that a knock on the door sent shivers down your spine. General discomfort, anxiety, and fear of what might happen next penetrated your very existence.

Any day during that summer, a piece of bad news would surface. Sightings of men being beaten, even being made to clean the streets with a toothbrush while onlookers laughed, sneered, and shouted anti-Semitic slogans, were reported. Jews were openly humiliated.

During this growing chaos (it was then August), Mama's youngest sister, Lore, arrived in Vienna from Misslitz. She was a twenty-four-year-old law student at the University of Prague, home for the summer. She was attractive—as all my mother's siblings were—and vivacious. Though not as tall as her siblings, her bright eyes and mischievous smile complemented her quick movements.

On the second day of her visit, she asked, "Lisl, how would you like to go back to Misslitz with me?"

"Oh, yes. I would love that. Sure, I'll go," I beamed without a moment's hesitation. There was silence in the room, and I glanced from Mama to Papa, both of whom looked serious. Smiling at me, Papa slowly turned to Lorly as he stabbed his cigarette into the ashtray, and said, "That sounds like a good idea. I think she will be happier there. She can go to school, and maybe things will calm down here a bit."

"All right," Mama joined in, "I agree, but I have to tell you that you'll be traveling without a passport. I can't give you mine, on which you are registered, because it is too risky to mail it back. If it gets lost, I can't get a new one issued, and that would be fatal. So, *halt den Mund* (keep your mouth shut, keep quiet), stay alert, and don't do anything foolish."

"I know, I know. I'll be careful," I quickly replied. I was overjoyed. "When are we leaving?" I asked, facing Lore, whom we usually called "Lorly."

"Early tomorrow morning. Is that all right, Lottie?" She asked Mama, looking at Papa at the same time. When my parents agreed to the early morning departure, I threw in, "Before I start to pack, can I just run over to Herbert to say good-bye?"

"I'll take you, Liserl," Papa offered.

"It's just around the corner."

"I know where it is," he said calmly, "but I don't want you out alone in the dark."

Papa and I set out for Herbert's house. The apartment was large, but we did not go beyond the entry hall after my father explained our visit, and that we only had time for a few minutes.

Our farewells were short, sweet, and sad, ending in a couple of tears.

"Well, Herbert, aren't you going to kiss Lisl good-bye?" his mother prompted as he just stood there, looking awkward and motionless, with his parents and my father looking on. He planted a quick little peck on my cheek, mumbling, "Good luck. See you."

"Yes, thanks. You, too," I replied, feeling equally embarrassed, trying to hold back tears.

I kissed my parents and sister good-bye early the next morning. Papa could not resist remarking with a smile, "You don't seem half as sad parting from us as from Herbert."

"That's because I'll see you soon, but I may never see Herbert again."

Neither was true.

9

CHAOS IN CZECHOSLOVAKIA

As PLANNED, LORLY AND I TOOK off early the next morning. We did not take the train, our usual way of traveling to Misslitz/Miroslav with Mama. Instead, we took a bus that was to take us to a different border crossing—Nikolsburg (Mikulov), just inside Czechoslovakia.

My uncle Viktor, married to Mama's sister, Mitzi, lived in Nikolsburg. He was acquainted with the Czech border guard scheduled to be on duty at the time of our arrival, and he had clinched a deal—either with money or wine—Viktor's business, to secure a safe entry for me.

The sun was blazing through the glass window of the bus, making a flash on Lorly's hand, which caught my eye. "How come you're wearing Mama's gold bracelet?" I asked in an ordinary tone, sitting next to her.

"Shush," and a sharp look, as she quickly slipped her hand under the jacket that was folded on her lap, was all the answer I needed. We continued the ride in silence.

Getting off the bus at the border presented no problems. The other passengers dispersed in various directions, not bothered by armed guards standing around, while we crossed a rather wide, open space—no-man's-land—on foot, in order to enter Czechoslovakia.

I turned and noticed we were the only people on the road. Trying not to show my uneasiness, I said, "Lorly, look at all the small houses surrounded by trees and bushes on the Austrian side, but I can't see any buildings or any people in what must be Czechoslovakia. There are just green fields everywhere." She didn't answer. No longer trying to deny my anxiety, I soon added, "How far do we have to go?" She pulled the beige jacket she was wearing tighter around herself, just as I pushed down my light blue dress that had been lifted by the breeze. A moment later, in what seemed like such peaceful, sunny surroundings, I heard shouts of "Halt! Stop!" coming from the Austrian side.

I took a quick look at Lorly and urged, "Let's run."

"No," she replied, "just keep walking, and don't turn around." I edged closer to her, reached for her hand, and as our steps quickened, my heart beat faster and faster, half expecting to be shot at.

We reached the gray booth at the Czech border, but when we entered, and Lorly mentioned his name in greeting, we found the man was not the one who was my uncle's friend.

The guard, his eyes set close in a square face, was in the process of buttoning up the jacket of his black uniform. He stood by the window, and barely acknowledged us as he pointed to a chair for my aunt. At the same time, he moved towards his upholstered armchair, and sank slowly into it. He pushed a news-paper and other papers aside to make room for ours. After a few minutes of looking at our documents, which seemed endless to me, he said, "The girl has no passport. She can't enter the coun-try." Those were his first words to us as he swiveled his chair to face Lorly.

I froze, afraid to meet his dark stare and, aware of his frown, I bent my head and looked down. Every time my aunt said some-thing to him, I heard him growl back. Attractive law student that she was, my twenty-four-year-old aunt Lorly started smilingly and charmingly to talk to him only in Czech, with no German words thrown in. Out of the corner of my eye, I observed a glim-mer of a smile on his ruddy face. Minutes—what seemed to me more like an hour—passed. They chatted; he shuffled through a pile of paraphernalia on the far end of his desk, pulled out a little scrap of paper, read it silently, and, turning to her, finally sighed, "Okay, go ahead."

So began my journey with the Nazis at my heels.

A few feet down the road, Uncle Viktor was waiting next to his old black vehicle. He was such a big, broad-shouldered man that it was comical to watch him squeeze into his small car. Re-lieved to see us, as were we, he eagerly listened to our tale of ad-venture, and we, in turn, were treated to a few choice curse words regarding the guard, his friend. Uncle Viktor enjoyed being a wheeler-dealer, even later during the war years in England, but I liked him for his charm, and willingness to be helpful.

He drove us straight to Misslitz. I was excited in the antici-pation of seeing my beloved Babi again, as well as Gretl, Yelli, little Stefan, who had turned four, and Wolfie, the dog, now mine. I was not disappointed. One and all gave me a warm welcome that paralleled my excitement.

Since Babi had no other visitors at that time, I was assigned the special guest room. Two beds with orange painted headboards, a night table between them, faced the windows. The white bedspreads, embroidered with multi-colored flowers, had matching curtains. A little lamp on the nightstand, a chair, and a chest of drawers completed the furnishings. To me, this room never seemed cozy, perhaps because it was cold summer and winter. Its location made up for its indifferent atmosphere. The bathroom was just a few steps up with its trove of treasures that always held a come-hither fascination for me.

EVEN MISSLITZ HAD CHANGED FROM the previous summer. The freedom I so cherished was now curtailed.

Babi enrolled me in the German-speaking school in time for the fall semester. It was my favorite aunt, Yelli, who helped me get ready to attend the first day.

I felt I looked good in my dark blue dress with a white collar and bow, wearing my favorite shiny black shoes. I set out on a balmy September morning, crossing the sunny Marktplatz, past Tante Hanni's house, to make my way up the hill to the school. With each step, I felt more excited and adventurous at the prospect of entering a new phase of my life. That euphoric feeling soon gave way to trepidations, with only a smidgen of optimism filtering through my increasing anxiety as I neared the school. I had been in a Lyceum in Vienna, and wondered how different the teaching would be in Misslitz, a village, although it had been elevated to a township. The two-storey school building had only one entrance, and it did not seem much larger than a big house. I entered the assigned classroom—it was either seventh or eighth grade. The teacher smiled on her way to the door to greet me. The high, Slavic cheekbones were the most prominent feature of her face that bore no makeup except lipstick. Her irregular teeth added to her plain looks, which receded once you were engulfed in her pleasant temperament. She showed me to my seat and introduced me. "This is our new student. Her name is Lisbet Steiner; you may call her Lisl, and she comes from Vienna." As if on cue, all eyes turned on me staring, followed by whispering. All I wanted to do at that moment was to disappear into thin air. They were all local kids, and I was the only new student. I wondered later that morning how, or if at all, I would be accepted.

I was more concerned with blending in socially than with academics. There was nobody with whom I became best friends in the short period of my attendance, but I was soon on friendly terms with all my classmates. I was even chosen as the treasurer for safekeeping the donations that had been collected for a forthcoming school performance.

BARELY THREE WEEKS HAD PASSED before my schooling ended. On October 1, 1938, Hitler occupied the Sudetenland—a border area around Czechoslovakia where mostly German was spoken. Misslitz was situated there. After the war, the Czechs threw out any Germans living in the area, so that today Misslitz is one hundred percent Czech in population and language. Hitler had occupied Vienna in March 1938. I'd left for Misslitz at the end of August 1938 and entered school there in early September.

There had been talk of the invasion, so that, on the last day of September 1938, or maybe October 1, my aunt Yelli told me, "You can't go to school today. Quickly pack your little suitcase. We're going to Brno."

"But why? What do you mean? What shall I pack?" I asked, totally perplexed.

"Lisl, take your underwear, socks, a nightgown, skirt and blouses, two dresses, and, if you like, a book and one toy. We're in a hurry. It's important, and I'll tell you all about it later."

She had engaged a taxi to drive to Brno (the second largest city, situated more inland than Misslitz, and not expected to be occupied). She, little Stefan, Babi, Gretl, and I piled in. Lorly was not home; she had returned to the university in Prague. I heard Gretl say to the maid as we left, "We're going shopping in Brno for the day. See you tonight."

From the conversation in the car, I quickly surmised that this was no shopping expedition. What I did not realize, as I looked out the back window, was that it would also be my last look at Misslitz for almost seventy years. Besides watching familiar houses rush by, a small white cloud in the otherwise all-blue sky caught my eye. In later years, when I thought of that cloud, it served as my special, loving treasure, holding all of Misslitz in its expanse—the Marktplatz, the people, their relationships with each other, and with me, Wolfie, the dog, and the other animals I knew, the weekly fairs, the gossip I wasn't supposed to hear, and the lively swimming pool filled with dark green, unfiltered water, and how it all fit into my freedom-loving life there.

As we approached the open road, my Jewish conscience began to bother me: *I have left with money entrusted to me. It does not belong to me. What will they think, what will they say about me at school? I have no way of returning it to them.* The fact that very little money was at stake did not console me. (This was Mama's influence.)

We passed through various villages and little towns, all of them crowded with trucks, soldiers, women, and children milling around. General mobilization was in progress to stop Hitler from occupying the Sudetenland. The taxi picked up speed. The next town was bigger and more crowded, more so since it was a warm, clear day, the sun shining unwittingly on the pandemonium below. Wives, relatives, children, and girlfriends were saying good-bye to army reserves and to young men freshly mobilized.

There was chaos as women and children jostled for positions at each side of the street. Some stood and waved; others crisscrossed the street, shook hands, hugged, kissed, and strained to reach the soldiers already on the trucks, to hand over hastily-put-together packages.

The next moment I felt a little bump, followed instantly by a second one, as the front and then the back wheels of the taxi drove over something before it came to an abrupt stop. Yelli grabbed Stefan, opened the door, and yelled to me, "Lisl, get out, quickly! Follow me." The other passengers also departed quickly. The driver was left to deal with the situation. The taxi had run over a child. The utter chaos and high tension in the crowd made Yelli afraid we might be lynched.

I did not know at that moment what had happened. I could only feel the emergency, the fear, and the need to act fast. We fled across the street into a store. The middle-aged man there took us to a back room to give us a chance to calm down. It turned out he was a friend of the family and a lawyer. We did not require his services, though his presence and advice helped reassure my aunts, and Babi. The stricken little boy had both legs broken, but he was otherwise unharmed. After a couple of hours of sipping tea, talking, discussing pros and cons of the situation, and looking for the driver, it was decided to continue our journey.

Our destination: the apartment in Brno—large enough to accommodate all of us—belonging to my aunt Rosl. It, like she, was chic, beautifully furnished in excellent taste. She and her two children, Dorrit (who, at sixteen, tried to, and succeeded in, looking like a movie star), and Frank (fourteen years old), were already in England. Her husband, Arnold, the wealthy son-in-law who never visited Misslitz, had stayed behind in the apartment. He was unable to separate himself from his business or his social obligations, preventing his departure, which, as a Czech citizen, was still possible at that time.

Arnold was suave; his black hair, parted on one side, always shiny and never out of place, was combed close to his head. He had a small straight nose and looked wealthy in his custom-tailored suits and shiny shoes, with a ring on his manicured finger. The cook/housekeeper, "Big Anna", was still installed in the apartment in my aunt Rosl's absence. She was nice enough to all of us for the time being, although I remembered Aunt Rosl saying how mean she could be. Even I knew she was a fixture in the family, having played a significant role once in informing my uncle of Rosl's love affair. How did I know all that? Those were the tidbits I relished gathering while sitting under the table in Misslitz late in the evening, listening to Babi and her sister, Tante Hanni, as they recalled the day's events, business deals, and gossip.

We continued taking our meals in Uncle Arnold's apartment even after we had moved out. Big Anna—tall, muscular, and often frowning in disapproval of someone—did the cooking. She was fresh, in charge, and nobody quite trusted her, but since we depended on her, none of the adults told her off. Different sleeping arrangements were in progress. Gretl had been in Brno before. She held a job as manager of a dental firm and had moved to a small apartment nearby. She must have been hired for her wonderful smile.

Babi and I moved to Gretl's former apartment, and Yelli found accommodations with Stefan elsewhere. Ernst, Yelli's husband, had been drafted into the army.

10

FLEEING TO PRAGUE

HE WEEKS ROLLED BY INTO November. We no longer took our meals at Uncle Arnold's apartment, but he had invited us for lunch. A little later, he handed me a letter my mother had sent to his address. It read: *Papa went on a trip. He was not sure how long it would take, and so I don't know when he will be home again.* I had just started to bite into an apple I had taken from the large bowl on the table. It stuck in my throat, making me choke. I understood that Mama was telling me Papa had been arrested and deported.

Mass arrests took place after Kristallnacht—the night of November 9–10, 1938. Thousands of windows of Jewish stores were broken—hence the name "Crystal Night" or "Night of Broken Glass"—burglarized and ravaged. In the days following, 267 synagogues in Austria and Germany were ambushed, set on fire, and left to burn to the ground. More than twenty thousand Jewish men were picked up randomly in streets or at home, arrested, and deported to concentration camps, my father among them.

That was the Nazis' retaliation for the shooting of a minor German official by a young Jewish man in Paris. It constituted the first official pogrom against the Jews in peacetime in Germany and Austria.

My father owed his arrest to our landlord's son who, a fervent Nazi by then, had reported him. We felt that was his revenge for having been reprimanded by Papa a couple of years earlier for neither greeting nor acknowledging him when they met on the stairs or at the door of the house in Hietzing.

From then on Mama's time was occupied with getting Papa released from Dachau, the concentration camp where he was incarcerated.

She told me later, "Papa ended up in Dachau only because of that brute, Wolfgang. Otherwise, he would have been detained at the police station and released, just like Herbert's father."

Papa was not politically active; privately, he was a Social Democrat. He did not subscribe to any political newspapers, nor was he a member of any clubs. There was really nothing of which the Nazis could accuse him, other than being a Jew.

Fears of being arrested or having your apartment searched, were uppermost in every Jewish mind. It put people on edge. Some reacted by not venturing outdoors, others talked only about that. Everybody was in a state of high anxiety.

The dreaded moment arrived: There was a knock on the door, and two young Nazis entered our apartment in Hietzing to make a search. They turned drawers inside out, plundered as they pleased, threw clothes and other articles on the floor. At one point, standing by the closet, my mother said, "I'll make this easier for you," took out a bunch of tablecloths, and placed them on a shelf that had already been raked through. She had some of the silver and money hidden in those tablecloths.

Papa was in Dachau; I was in Brno, Czechoslovakia; and Mama and Irenli were forced to leave the apartment in Hietzing after Kristallnacht. They sought refuge with one of Mama's sisters, my aunt Poldi, who also lived in Vienna, centrally located in the city. Two weeks later, she, her husband, and their daughter, Henny, left one night without a word, and escaped to Norway. Mama and Irenli were left as the sole occupants of the apartment, which was large, but old-fashioned and on the dark side. Mama sat in the living room in what had become her favorite little upholstered chair near one of the windows. She called Irenli over and said, "You know, our money is running out, and we have no income. We'll have to go to the soup kitchen from now on."

"No way will I go there," Irenli answered defiantly. "I wouldn't want to be seen dead over there."

Swallowing her pride, a daily occurrence by then for Mama, she made her way several times a week to the soup kitchen, returning with food for both of them.

Kurt Horeyshey (not Jewish), the son of our friends and neighbors in our old apartment in Hietzing, risked his life traveling across Vienna at night to bring food to Mama and Irenli a couple of times a week. Soon after Christmas that year, some Nazi youths broke into his laboratory at the university where he was working, demanding access to some instruments. When he refused, they shot and killed him.

While all that was happening in Vienna, I was in Brno instead of Misslitz, where I had been sent for 'safety,' but the terrible happenings were relayed to me in letters and, later, in person.

Registering me at a school in Brno was not an option—my illegal status prevented that. With time on my hands, Stefan (my little four-year-old cousin) and I took long walks, I ran errands for my grandmother, one of which was to fetch the meals Big Anna cooked for us, and, once a week, I meandered over to Uncle Arnold's store (he was the distributor of the second largest brand of sewing machines after Singer) to collect the generous allowance he had decided to bestow on me. I had also met a girl my age, Hannah, with whom I became friends. Her brown hair had a wave to it, like mine, and, like most of us, she wore it short. Quite tall and carefree, she was fun to be with. We used to go to the movies together, and laughed afterwards over jokes we told each other, based on what we had just seen.

Czechoslovakia was still unoccupied, but further mobilization was in progress. On one of my walks with Stefan, I decided on a shortcut through the park. It was winter by then, a cold, cloudy day, which shortened the daylight considerably. By the time we arrived home, which was hardly later than usual, Yelli stood at the door, frantically asking, "Are you all right? It's so late. It's almost dark."

"Yes, we are fine, Yelli," I answered, and eagerly told her, "Guess what? I taught Stefan another song, and showed him the shortcut through the park."

"I can't believe what I'm hearing." Yelli said as she put her hand on her chest, gave a deep sigh, half closed her eyes, and tried to suppress her anger but was unable to hide her anxiety.

"Didn't you see the soldiers milling around in Luzanky Park? They're mobilizing, and everybody is excited. It's dangerous."

"Why is it dangerous, Yelli? Two of the soldiers were very friendly and spoke to us," I answered naively.

THE NEXT FEW MONTHS WERE relatively safe for me, but all around me I sensed hopelessness. When Uncle Leo visited one afternoon, he told Babi, "My friend Paul just told me that the American Consul said he would have to wait about a year for his visa."

"What about you and Gerti?" Babi asked. Gerti was his wife.

"I wish I could give you good news," Leo answered gloomily as he stood by the door, running a hand through his dark brown hair. "It's all negative—from Brazil, England, America. One disappointment after another."

His big brown eyes looked as sad as the loose jacket hanging on his slender frame, cutting a very different figure from the boyish, confident lawyer I was used to seeing.

Gretl and Yelli had fared no better. Pessimism filled the air, and was beginning to affect me. I wanted out, but how?

Political news for Jews grew worse every day until the beginning of March 1939, when it became critical. Rumors abounded that Hitler might occupy the rest of Czechoslovakia.

One evening, Babi and I, Gretl and Yelli, with Ernst and Stefan, had an appointment with Uncle Arnold. We all gathered in his large living room. Besides the two black and beige striped sofas, one of which Stefan and I requisitioned, the leather chairs surrounding a round cocktail table were occupied by the adults,

Arnold sitting in his big black armchair with red pillows supporting his back. Big Anna served coffee to the grown-ups, while Stefan and I savored the cookies and snacks.

Babi spoke up: "If Hitler is going to occupy the whole country, I'm staying here in Brno, in Gretl's apartment."

"No, you shouldn't, Mama," Yelli, ever nurturing and looking out for others, answered. "You should come to Prague with us, so we can all stay together."

"If Mama stays, I will, too," Gretl put in.

"This is what I propose to do," Uncle Arnold then declared. "We'll wait for the eleven o'clock news and then decide whether to leave for Prague."

Soon after the news, he said, "Let's go." Once more I found myself leaving what I called home at short notice. I was told to pack a small suitcase.

"Don't take any toys," I heard someone say.

"O.K., but I want to take my favorite blue dress, the fancy one," I told Uncle Arnold, feeling sure he would allow it. After all, he looked like one of those 1930s Hollywood movie stars. Instead, I heard him say, "Better not—you won't need it."

It was March 1939 and snowing some. Uncle Arnold got behind the wheel, and after driving a little over an hour, we encountered a hill, not very steep, on which the car kept slipping and sliding. Unable to conquer that knoll, he pulled over to the side and stopped to look for chains in the trunk. Ernst said he would help put them on. Yelli, Stefan, and I waited in the car.

"That no-good, rotten, drunken bastard didn't put the chains in the car!" Arnold yelled angrily. Henry, his chauffeur, was showered with curses in Czech, German, and Yiddish. "We have no choice, we have to turn back," he told us, leaning his head inside the car. Back in Brno he found the chains somewhere in the car after all.

We started anew, hours having passed by then, so that it was early morning by the time we reached Prague. A policeman asked about our destination. "You may go ahead, if you wish," he said, "but the Germans are marching in from the North." We were entering from the East.

As we headed towards our hotel, Yelli explained to me, "I will only register one child and if they question me, I'll juggle your name and Stefan's to get around your registration." My status in Czechoslovakia was illegal.

The next morning I noticed German military boots that had been cleaned standing outside several doors. That gave me an eerie, nauseated feeling. Would they check up on me and catch me? The sight of what those boots stood for made me very fearful.

I breathed a sigh of relief when two days later it was decided we would move to another, smaller hotel. No German boots there—but after a couple of days the question of my registration once again surfaced. Yelli took me aside. "We have decided, Lisl, it will be best if we take you somewhere where you'll be safe, no questions asked, and it will be easier for you."

"Where are you taking me?" I asked anxiously.

"Not far from here, just outside Prague to a farm. I think you will like it and, of course, we will visit you and be in touch. Let's try it out and see how it works," she concluded, trying to be reassuring.

11

RETURNING TO BRNO

I WAS NOT HAPPY MAKING that move—and rightly so. The farm was not as I had imagined it to be: a farmer, his wife, children, animals, and the pleasant, easygoing atmosphere I had experienced when we stopped off at the farmers' homes, making beer deliveries with Pavlov during my stay in Misslitz.

The farm had a woman at its helm. There were no children or farm animals, except for one cow and some emaciated-looking chickens. Her sole interest lay in using me for work, although she was paid for harboring me. She was unpleasant and did not talk much except for giving me orders and telling me off. Language was a problem; I could not speak Czech, and she was either reluctant, as a Czech, or unable, to speak German. I have no recollection of details, but I do remember that I was told off frequently, as well as made to work hard carrying wood, buckets of water, sweeping, and cleaning. I was thirteen at the time.

Treated harshly and living under conditions I was not used to, I felt lonely and unhappy, and even more worried about my

---

future in that dead-end situation. Though I complained to whichever relative visited me, I spent several weeks there before I was taken back to Prague. No resolution of my illegal status was forthcoming.

The day after I was back in Prague, I attended what had become the customary twice-weekly meeting in Uncle Arnold's hotel room. His was the largest. Besides the bed, nightstand, and dresser, there was an alcove where we sat on upholstered chairs around a bridge table. The meetings usually took place in the late afternoons, and the discussions became the subject of intense debates of immigration possibilities. Whoever heard of a country willing to take Jews, even if only a rumor, presented it for its pros and cons. It didn't take long, however, before that theme had to be dropped, because the available countries quickly grew scarcer, and the only thing left that mattered was which country would allow immigration—no more pros and cons or other choices.

At one of those meetings, Uncle Arnold mentioned that he was preparing to visit (not immigrate) his wife, Aunt Rosl, and their children—Dorrit and Frank—in England. He addressed Yelli.

"Look, Ernst has been drafted into the army. Why don't I take Stefan with me to England? Rosl will look after him, and it will also make it easier for you."

"I'll ask Stefan and I will think about it," she answered.

"Don't take too long," Arnold cautioned. "I am about to make travel reservations."

Uncle Arnold still looked the same—the suave businessman—but Yelli, I thought, looked harassed and worried.

I was listening on tenterhooks, secretly hoping he would make the same offer to me, but not saying a word because I loved Stefan so much that I would have been happy for him to have the opportunity to get away.

Yelli asked Stefan, "How would you like to go with Uncle Arnold to visit Aunt Rosl?"

"No, no, I don't want to go. I want to stay with you, Mama!" he cried.

I chimed in, urging him to go, but after a couple more encouragements, he remained adamant in his refusal, which Yelli accepted.

I waited for what I thought was the appropriate interval. Then I faced my uncle, and pleaded, "If Stefan really doesn't want to go, would you take me?"

"Unfortunately, I can't. You are too old to go without proper documents. He can be smuggled in, but I can't do it with you. I would get in trouble and we would both be sent back."

I felt devastated. I was a fugitive, a hunted criminal on the run, all because of a stupid passport or, rather, the lack of one. Remaining in Prague had become untenable.

Other people, who had thought as we did that we could escape the Nazis by moving to Prague, were beginning to make their way back to Brno. My grandmother and Gretl had stayed there. The consensus was it would be best for me to return to Brno, where I could stay in the apartment with Babi and not worry about my status and registration procedures necessary in Prague hotels. My aunt Gerti, married to my mother's only brother, Leo, had also fled to Prague (Leo was to follow) and she announced her intention of returning to Brno to be with him and with her parents. I always thought she was beautiful. Her narrow nose topped by a high forehead, her black hair parted in the middle and pulled back, made for a striking, classic profile. I didn't know her as well as my other aunts, but I liked her, and her reputation for being capable and decisive. She was a lawyer, like Leo.

"Oh, good, Gerti, then I can go with you," I said, jumping up from my chair.

"Except it's not that simple. I would be glad to take you, Lisl, but I've heard that the Nazis in Brno take people off the train, and Jews are held for questioning upon arrival. If you are with me, your fate would be the same, and they would like nothing better than to detain me." Her uncle, a Social Democrat, was a cabinet minister in the Czech government, which made her a prime target.

"Then, with whom can I go?" I asked, feeling pushed aside once more, almost abandoned.

"We've had a long discussion on this," Yelli told me as she put her arm around me, "and we've decided the best for you would be to return by yourself."

"But what'll I do if someone asks me for papers? And, what if the Gestapo takes me off the train in Brno? Isn't there anybody I can go with?" I asked anxiously, feeling scared. The idea of traveling alone loomed like a nightmare.

"Liserl, you'll be safer going alone than with a grown-up. You'll see. You'll be all right." While Yelli's words sounded sincere and reassuring, they failed to make me feel it would be really safe for me to be on the train by myself.

The next morning Gerti handed me a sandwich she had made for me, and I received a present from Yelli—a traveling blanket – of brown and green stripes, which I loved. I kept it until a few years ago when, moth-eaten, I finally, but reluctantly, got rid of it.

Between hugs and kisses I was told, "Don't talk to anybody on the train. No Czech person will like to hear you conversing in German, and they may react negatively." Whatever that meant, I knew it was something not good. I was shy, so not talking wasn't hard.

Ernst took me to the train. It was a cold, cloudy day in April. That's how I felt, too. Even the not-very-big station, dark and gloomy, reflected my mood. We didn't talk much. He read some signs, and we found the platform easily for the train bound for Brno. A lot of people were scurrying around, looking serious on the smoke-filled platform. A woman accompanying a very young man in uniform gave Ernst a faint smile in passing, apparently approving his Czech uniform. As he put me on the train, he whispered, "The less the other passengers know about you, the better."

That last remark made me crouch in the corner of the compartment. Curled up in my new blanket, I looked out the window or pretended to be asleep. I probably did doze off. The journey proceeded without any incidents.

After several hours, the train pulled into Brno. My anxiety over being taken off for questioning returned, and I sat in full alert, preparing myself ready for the worst. Fortunately, it did not happen.

That day in Prague was the last I saw of Uncle Arnold. He returned from England, went back to his home in Brno where, many months later, he had himself smuggled out on a freight train, ending up in Palestine.

I RECEIVED A WARM HUG from Babi with the welcoming words, "It's wonderful to see you again, Lisl. I missed you a lot. Would you like to have something to eat?" They were comforting and reassuring words. She looked great in her dark blue dress. She was seventy years old then.

Gretl was also glad to see me. Just before we left for Prague, she had married Hans Wilheim, a handsome man. It was a simple wedding in Brno, performed by a judge, I believe, followed by a luncheon in a local restaurant. Babi, her sister, Tante Hanni, Leo, Gerti, Yelli, and I, as well as Hans's parents, made up the wedding party. Babi felt pleased about her daughter's marriage for the sake of security. Never would she have approved in earlier times. He was considered poor; he supported his parents, and did not have a prestigious job. In his favor was his pleasing, kind personality, and good looks. Many prospective bachelors had been introduced to and rejected by Gretl in years gone by, which made Babi's approval somewhat heroic.

My friend Hannah greeted me with, "I have great news. My parents and I will go to Argentina in ten days." I was pleased for her. At the same time, it made me wonder how and when I would be able to say that. Other people, too, were leaving, which increased my own strong urge to get away. Yelli, in her supportive way, tried to assuage my fear of being left by saying, "Ernst and I have applied to go to Australia through a friend of his. If it materializes, you can, of course, come with us." Those fruitless hopes were never realized.

I explained my unhappiness in a letter to my mother, who had been busy in Vienna, trying to have my father released from the Dachau concentration camp. He was in possession of an affidavit from the United States. That was a document, from an American resident, pledging financial support of the person therein mentioned, thereby eliminating the possibility of becoming a liability to the government. Papa's affidavit had been issued by a family member of the Bulova Watch Company. That, plus a promise to leave the country in two (maybe, three) months, served as an incentive to release a Jew from a concentration camp. It was, however, effective only in the first few months after the annexation. Later, releases from concentration camps were out of the question. Mama made several trips to the office of the Gestapo (*GEheime STaat POlizei*)—the secret police, which was in charge of emigration, to plead Papa's case. The man on duty on one of those visits urged her, "You should get a divorce from that Jewish man," obviously not believing her to be Jewish. In addition, Mama made a down payment for a ticket on a ship to Shanghai. "Come back in two days to pay in full, and we'll issue the ticket." On her return, she found an empty store where the travel agency had been. That was repeated a second time at another location. Those "travel agencies" were ploys put up by the Nazis—another mask under which they collected thousands of Reichsmarks from the Jewish population.

In the meantime, Mama was also worried about Irene, then sixteen years old. She had heard that the Nazis were seducing and raping young girls. Through her volunteer work at the Kultusgemeinde (Jewish Community Center), she heard of the Youth Aliya. Teenagers could go to Israel (then Palestine) to live and work on a kibbutz. Mama enrolled her.

"I'm really not too keen on going," Irenli told her.

"And I'm not happy sending you so far away either," Mama answered, "but it's better to be safe there than to stay here."

For us, Palestine in those days seemed every bit as remote as traveling to the moon.

Actually, Irene had been scheduled to go to England. Her piano teacher had found an English family willing to take her. The Quakers, who had been instrumental in that arrangement, however, had no control over what happened next. The office in London that handled these affairs moved to another location, and, in the process, her papers were lost. Several weeks, then months, passed with no word from London. Letters and telegrams from my mother remained unanswered.

In those days, Mama was the rock of the family. She succeeded in having Papa released from the concentration camp, made Irenli's departure to Palestine a reality, and then turned her attention to my emigration.

12

GESTAPO INTERROGATION

TWO DAYS AFTER IRENLI LEFT Vienna in March 1939, Mama sent her a telegram that Papa had been released from Dachau. She did not tell her that her papers to enter England had finally arrived. It was too late. She had already embarked on a ship in Italy bound for Palestine.

Mama had thus managed to have her husband home again, and to send her older daughter to safety, which made her optimistic about her decision to visit the English consulate on my behalf. She wasted no time. "I am in possession of papers for Irene Steiner to immigrate to England," she said to the consul. "I would like you to change the name from Irene to Lisbet Steiner, her younger sister, after I explain the circumstances to you."

"That cannot be done, Mrs. Steiner," the consul said politely but firmly.

That was Mama's first visit. She was not put off that easily. She returned several times, persisting and insisting, and finally he did what she wanted—change Irene's name to mine.

Mama was delighted. She wrote to me: *I have been able to secure a place for you on a Kindertransport leaving for England in a few days. It leaves from Vienna. That means you have to come back from Brno.* (The Kindertransport was the rescue mission that took place in 1939, nine months before the outbreak of World War II. The United Kingdom took in nearly ten thousand unaccompanied children, infants to age sixteen, from Nazi Germany, Austria, and a few from Czechoslovakia, as well as some from Danzig.)

There was a slight problem. I was stuck in Brno, and, a few days later, the Kindertransport left without me.

In the meantime, I heard of several people who had managed to leave the country, which drove me to write to my mother: *Everybody I know is leaving. I am going to be left here to die.*

That everybody was leaving was, unfortunately, not true.

Mama answered by return mail. *I promise I will not leave without you. If we cannot leave at the same time, I will make sure that you get out before I do, and I am convinced I will be able to do that for you.*

A promise from my mother calmed me down, but in order to return to Vienna, it became my responsibility to go to the Gestapo to obtain permission from them.

It was April by then. On a Thursday, I made my way to their headquarters, carefully carrying my birth certificate—the only document in my possession—terrified of coming face to face with the brown-shirted SA or, worse, the SS in their black uniforms (whose reputation of cruelty surpassed the SA), and becoming engaged in the unknown. Butterflies in my stomach tumbled over each other, alternating with tight knots.

They always requisitioned the largest houses or old mansions for their headquarters. This one, too, looked like a palace. Scared to death, I held myself tightly together so as not to tremble, and slowly climbed the wide, red-carpeted staircase. It seemed to me my heart was beating loud enough to be heard by anybody passing me. The stairs led to a long hallway, which was lit by a beautiful chandelier. There were several doors—the one I had been told to enter by an SA man downstairs stood ajar. I peeked in hesitantly. Two SA men sat behind a large, wide desk, which stood almost in the middle of the enormous room. I entered but stood still, waiting to be acknowledged or told to come closer. They took their time. Afraid to look at them, I cast my eyes down onto the blue carpet. Barely turning my head, I noticed a long table with some upright chairs surrounding it, and on the paneled wall behind it, stacked folding chairs.

Finally, I lifted my head, still waiting, feeling more afraid with each minute that passed.

One of them was fair-haired, his narrow eyes half squinting, his big hands resting on the desk. He stared straight at me. The other one, dark-skinned, looked no friendlier. Both appeared to be tall and strong, and the four eyes glaring at me instantly intimidated me even more. I was afraid my knees would give way. The blond one spoke first, his solitary gold tooth visible as soon as he opened his mouth.

"What do you want?" he snapped at me. He frowned angrily as he flung these words across in his harsh, loud voice.

"I n-need a permit to travel to Vienna," I stammered, barely above a whisper.

"No time for that today—and speak up. Come back next Tuesday," I heard, in the bristling tone from the blond one as he turned his back to me.

I left feeling even weaker and shakier than I had when I entered.

The following Tuesday, making sure I looked neat, my blouse tucked into my skirt, and my hair brushed, I kissed Babi goodbye without telling her how very afraid I was, to spare her an additional worry. She surmised my feelings, gave me a hug, and with a smile said, "We'll go out for a nice *Jause* this afternoon and talk."

I felt nauseous as I approached the Gestapo headquarters. Once more, I stood waiting in the room. I went through the same procedure—standing in the room waiting. I felt even more afraid than the first time, having had a taste of their gross manner. Fear gripped my whole body. I could not think straight. I was petrified.

This time, the dark-haired SA man looked up. I think he was Czech. His face and his whole demeanor seemed somewhat less stern, less tense that day. At least I thought so, since I was desperately hoping for a less scary aura. The shape of his moustache reminded me of my Uncle Viktor, but the intimidating atmosphere still prevailed.

"Oh, it's you again," he growled as he motioned with his arm to come closer. Neither of them acknowledged a greeting.

Haltingly, I repeated my request from where I was standing. I couldn't move. My legs were glued to the floor. I tried to speak a little louder, but my voice gave out.

"You'll have to come back with a photograph." He wasn't really any friendlier than the blond one, except the tone of his voice was less harsh. I left with a sigh of relief, anxious to get away from those demons as fast as possible, only to become acutely aware as soon as I hit the street that it was only a temporary feeling.

The day for the third visit approached. Terror-stricken by then as thoughts of their snarls rushed through my head, I was unable to eat breakfast. Babi thought I should have some food before setting out. I couldn't. I was ready to throw up.

At the Gestapo headquarters that day, the words, "We are busy. No time for you today. Be here tomorrow," were almost welcome. Getting away from those goons was a gift, even if short-lived. That day, on my way out, I noticed the crystal chandelier and decorative lamps on the paneled walls. They do not deserve such beautiful surroundings, I thought.

By then, my knotted stomach had become constant. It wasn't a question of getting used to the frequent trips to their office. On the contrary, my fear of those two monsters had built up. The accumulated terror grew worse before each appointment. I never knew what command would be thrown at me. I was in a panic just thinking about my next confrontation. I had trouble falling asleep, and when I did, I dreamed the dark one was standing over me, ready to crush me.

In addition, Tante Hanni, Babi's big fat sister, suggested, "I think you should stop going, because I've heard of bad things they do to kids. We'll manage all right here staying together."

She had a reputation for being outspoken, sincere, and witty, and I basically liked her. I half believed her. At the same time, I suspected that her suggestion might be grounded in a little selfishness. I fetched the lunch/dinner that Big Anna cooked for her, my grandmother, and me every day from Uncle Arnold's apartment. I ran errands for them. It was useful to have me around. I did not mind. The necessity of my presence made me feel important.

I tried to act as grown up as I possibly could. I told myself to think before answering, not to let on how terrified I was, and to be polite to these demons.

When I returned for my next appointment, those resolutions flew out the window. Instead, panic set in as, once more, I stood in the middle of the room, feeling sick and weak, unable to think as I heard the blond one snarl, "Hey, you, step up. Do you think we have all day for you?" As I winced, he turned to the other one with a wink and a smile, tossing his head in my direction. I tried not to tremble, breathlessly approaching the desk to put the photograph on it. "You only brought one? We need two."

With a malicious grin, the gold-toothed one added, "You should have known that," and turning to the Czech one, he snorted loudly, "She's wasting our time."

I had to prepare for the fourth round with the Gestapo, and the fifth, sixth, and many more. My visits to their headquarters lasted for three and a half weeks, during which some of the same questions were hurled at me. I felt worn out, belittled, humiliated, and fearful even on days when I did not have to appear there. I became depressed and pessimistic about my future. My physical being in general was in disarray. I suffered from stomach aches and diarrhea, and frequent nightmares, and was haunted by similar visions during the day. On days between visits, I was plagued by worries of whether I had answered their repeated questions satisfactorily and always in like manner, to avoid being caught saying something differently. I could not understand their visible joy at my fear; it showed, despite my determination to keep it from them. The gold-toothed one took special pleasure in my terror, flashing his wicked grin whenever I winced. Unaware that the next visit would be my last, my thoughts went back to Tante Hanni's warning, which only served to increase the pain in my already-knotted stomach. I felt weak in body and spirit, and was seriously contemplating giving up the hopeless struggle when a voice in me urged, "You have to face them if you want to get out, so just grit your teeth and go."

And so, once more, terrorized, feeling weak, dehumanized and shaky, with my stomach in knots and trying hard to hide my fear, I made my way to the Gestapo headquarters.

The last interrogation, fired at me in quick succession, started with:

"Name of your father."

"What does he do?"

"Name of your mother—what does she do?"

"Are they leaving Austria?"

"Where are they going?"

"Where is your father?"

"He is in Dachau."

"Why is he in Dachau?"

"He was deported there after Kristallnacht."

"He must have done something."

"I don't think so."

"What do you mean? Don't you know?"

"No."

"What newspapers did he read?"

"I don't know."

"Did he belong to some organization?"

"I don't know."

"Was he a member of a club?"

"I don't know."

"You don't know very much, do you?" the blond-haired one growled at me—sarcastic, suspicious, angry.

"She is only a child. What do you want?" the one I thought was Czech interrupted.

Their questioning continued, becoming ever more sarcastic and threatening, and I kept up my denial of having knowledge of anything that I thought might possibly harm my father.

We had by then reached the point where I was told, "We can't issue a permit for you to go to Vienna."

"Then give me a permit, please, to travel to Nuremberg, to join the Kindertransport there."

"No, no. What do you think we are—a travel agency?"

"In that case, I have to go back to Vienna, just for one night, to be on the Kindertransport, which leaves from there."

"Don't you know a Jewess who has left the country can't return?"

My frustration and anger had reached such a pitch, it overcame my terror, and I burst out, "Yes, I know, and I don't want to go back for good ever again."

"What? You're going to answer us back?" bellowed the one with the gold tooth as he banged his fist on the desk, leaning over as he half rose out of his chair. "You are going to be fresh with us? We know what to do with kids like you. We have a big cellar here where—"

At that moment the lights went out. I grabbed my birth certificate from the desk and ran out of the room and down the flight of stairs, stopping only for an instant to check the direction in which the soldier, rifle slung over his shoulder, was heading. He guarded the entrance as he marched in goose-step fashion back and forth, so that, when he turned to the left, I ran out to the right and continued running across town until I reached my grandmother's apartment. I was too terrified to stand still and wait for a tram.

A couple of days later, there was a knock on the door. I was sure the uniformed young Nazi standing at the entrance had come for me. My poor Babi must have thought so, too. Her face totally lost its color. I thought she would have a heart attack. But he had come to check on something entirely different.

In my panic, harboring an even greater drive to leave the country, I wrote to my mother:

I tried and tried, but I can't get anywhere with the Gestapo here. They absolutely refuse to allow me to go back to Vienna for even one night. I can't join the Kindertransport. What is going to happen to me?

My mother then took drastic measures. Anni, our nanny

when I was a little girl, had always told my mother she would do anything for me, she liked me so much. She was married by then, and her husband had attained an important position in the Nazi party. Mama approached her, explained my situation, reminded her of her oft expressed willingness to do anything for me, and told her frankly, "Now's your chance, Anni, to do so. Promise me that you will ask your husband to get in touch with the Gestapo in Brno and have them issue the permit for Lisl." Anni followed through, and a few days later I received the permit. Besides doing this out of her love for me, she did ask for our silver, all of which, plus some money, Mama took to her late one evening.

I left Brno, grateful that my mother had once more restored happiness in my life, and that I had won out over the Gestapo.

The intimidation they instilled, their verbal and emotional abuse, and the fright and terror they caused had occasion to replay itself some forty-two years later (I describe it in Chapter 38). It left a life-long scar of mistrust of, and intimidation by, authority figures.

YEARS AFTER THE WAR, I conducted a lengthy search for Anni that snaked through various administrative offices in Vienna for several months, only to find out that she had died. I wanted to thank her. I learned that her husband had also died quite young, and that her only child, a daughter, had died as a child.

13

KINDERTRANSPORT

MY FATHER HAD BEEN RELEASED from Dachau only a short time before my return to Vienna. When he and my mother greeted me at the station, he looked different beyond belief—his head totally shaven, he was thinner, his suit hanging loosely, with a downtrodden look about him, but he was totally elated the moment he spotted me. He had been incarcerated from November 10, 1938 (Kristallnacht) until the end of March 1939.

My overnight stay in Vienna kept me busy, telling my parents about my life in Czechoslovakia for the past nine months. They kept me pretty much at home. I neither said 'hello' nor 'goodbye' to anybody, just unpacked and repacked, only to say goodbye to them once more the following night. There wasn't much to pack. There were restrictions on what we were allowed to take—one small suitcase and a backpack. I was too old, I felt, to take my favorite doll. I did pack my stuffed dachshund on wheels and a little stuffed, white poodle.

I was overjoyed to have the opportunity to join a Kindertransport--out and away from all that had become ugly and detestable to me. What an adventure lay ahead. England, I thought, here I come.

My spirits high, the three of us left for the Westbahnhof just twenty-four hours after my return from Czechoslovakia. It was an unusually dark night for May, cool enough to warrant a light coat. Somewhere in the crowded station, which was lit poorly, we met Uncle Karl, Tante Hansi, and Cousin Willy, seventeen years old, who had come to say good-bye to me. The grown-ups circled around slowly, all looking sad and worried, and all in dark clothing. Willy was clowning, doing tricks with his umbrella. I laughed; my parents did not. At one point during the long evening, a big cardboard with a number on it was hung around my neck. A girl my size stood next to me, smiled, and said, "Isn't it exciting?"

"Yes," I answered, "It's great".

We milled around behind a barrier, making that part of the platform over-crowded. Conversation was sparse, but much was expressed in body language. All of us young people were beaming, excited by the anticipation of freedom. All parents were deeply concerned, visibly upset, and troubled by the knowledge of uncertainty and fear of a dangerous future. When it was time to board the train, we had to cross a barrier beyond which parents were not allowed, but not before receiving last minute instructions: "Be polite, be a good girl, learn and study as much as possible, write to us, and ask if Papa can come to England." The train finally departed at eleven o'clock at night. I found out later that all of us received similar instructions from our parents. As

I smilingly waved good-bye to them, I will forever remember them standing next to each other, grimacing, a forced smile superimposed on their tragic, teary-eyed faces. Fate had made us children mature beyond our years, but we did not understand— and our parents did—the uncertainties that lay ahead. Yes, we had matured, but we could not fathom what it must have meant to those parents, parting from their children and sending them into the unknown.

THAT TRAIN TO FREEDOM FOR which I had so ached, and for which I was so willing to submit to any hardship to make it a reality, spelled victory over having been thrown out of school prematurely, facing signs that read *No Dogs and No Jews Allowed* at the swimming pool, as well as at all other public places— movies, parks, playgrounds, being snubbed by my best friend, spat at, made fun of, dealing with my father's arrest and deportation to Dachau, and living in constant fear caused by the Gestapo's terrorizing threats and abuses while in Brno. A bright future was waiting.

Sitting tightly packed in the compartment with people I didn't know did not matter. We must have been six girls of various ages, facing the same number on the opposite bench. It didn't take long before chatter started, and I was so impressed by an older girl telling us how fluent her English was. As one of her curls dropped over her forehead from her bushy hair, she gave an example: "I had a had on my had." I admired the extent of her knowledge, making me keenly aware of my lack of it. I knew only four or five words, and had no idea that she was mispronouncing two-thirds of what she said.

Nobody fell asleep for the longest time. Later, she threw up, barely missing my arm. I rushed to the open window in the corridor to prevent a similar fate. Each of the transports had a couple of adults chaperoning the children. The one assigned to us had instructed me not to eat anything, but I'd been hungry and downed the roll of ham and cheese my mother had packed as soon as she left our compartment. The accompanying adults had to return to Vienna, or their families were at risk.

The train made its final stop in Germany at the border of Holland. Uniformed SS and SA men boarded and took off one boy. The rest of us shivered as they conducted random searches of our luggage. Fortunately, they did not find any hidden jewelry, which by that time it had been forbidden to take out of the country—but some parents had sewed it into their children's clothing. The boy was returned to the train unharmed. The SS and SA men left. We felt relieved.

A few minutes later, we entered Holland. Dutch women passed hot chocolate and orange juice through the windows. We rejoiced. We were free and we were safe, at last. Some of us spat out the windows and cursed the Nazis out loud.

Thirty-six hours after leaving Vienna, we arrived at our final destination at Liverpool Street Station, London. It was May 16, 1939. We had traveled through Germany and Holland, embarked in Hook in Holland for an overnight boat-ride across the Channel, disembarked in Harwich, England, and taken the train to London.

I have no recollection of the journey on the boat, probably because it occurred at night and I slept, tired from the long train ride.

I found myself on the platform in London trying to close one of the locks on the suitcase, which had snapped open from being over-stuffed, when I heard, "Hello, Lisl, nice to see you. Can I help you?" It was Eric Sanders (formerly Schwarz) from outer space it seemed, suddenly standing beside me. He was nineteen, lanky, a volunteer for one of the refugee committees. I knew him from Vienna, where our families had been friends. He fixed my suitcase and vanished as suddenly as he had appeared.

The customs officials pushed us through fast, without much fuss. One of them asked me, "Do you have any liquor?" I didn't understand, so he threw back his head and held his fist to his mouth. Then, for the next question, he pretended to smoke; I shook my head, he smiled, and said, "Okay."

The eighty children on that particular transport were assembled in a large hall at the station, so dark and ugly that the sunshine could not penetrate its dirty, grimy windows. All of us had traveled alone. Parents were not allowed on any Kindertransport trips. I had been cheerful as I said good-bye to mine, because I was sure I would soon see them in England, but as I sat there waiting to be picked up, I was abruptly jolted into reality. I didn't know where I would be going except that it would be to somebody's home rather than a hostel. I had no idea what the person I was about to meet looked like. I had not seen a photograph, nor had received a letter, nor any communication. A woman entered the hall, and I thought: *I hope she isn't the one for me, she looks ugly.* More sponsors came and left with their assigned children, and the hours passed with only a few of us left sitting and waiting. That's when the last ounce of cheerfulness left me. I worried whether she would turn up at all, and the possibility of that not happening plagued me. What would I do then? What would happen to me? We had been forbidden by the Nazis to take money with us, and I had no way of acquiring any. I neither spoke nor understood English. Overnight, without notice, I was not only separated from my parents, but from my emotional support of friends and family, from my culture, from my familiar surroundings. I felt alone—all alone. I became more and more scared as harrowing memories of persecution, and the interrogation by the Gestapo in recent weeks, began to occupy me.

In the midst of this misery, I heard my name and the number that was on the tag around my neck being called, and I met Mrs. Harter, my new foster mother. Tall, elderly, still good-looking, she displayed an authoritative manner. She did not give me a hug as I noticed some others had to the children they picked up. She shook my hand, and after greeting me and introducing herself, she said, "We have to go to another railway station to catch a train to go home." My blank expression clearly showed that I didn't understand, so she repeated it in broken German—very broken. We took a taxi to Waterloo Station, where we walked at a leisurely pace alongside the waiting commuter train until she opened the door to a first-class compartment.

It looked scrumptious. The trains I was used to in Europe had an entrance/exit door at either end of the carriage. A long corridor stretched between them, from which you entered an individual subdivision. This one was different: The compartment had an exit door on either side. That made it totally disconnected from other parts of the train, and, at the same time very private. Instead of wooden benches or meagerly upholstered seats, I was greeted by soft cushions, beautifully covered in a beige fabric, with large red and green flowers, and some brown leaves woven into it.

Pretty tired from the long trip and from the anxious waiting period, I sank exhausted into this flowerbed, but I noticed as I faced the opposite side that the flowery pattern continued on the backside of the seat, which had a mirror above it. The luggage rack was wide and spacious, with a little guardrail running alongside the front. The white ceiling lamps, covered by lampshades, could be turned on and off. Windows, even the floor, were spotless.

We were the only two occupants. I was impressed and somewhat surprised to be sitting in first class for just a twenty-minute ride. I wondered if that luxury was a forerunner of what would follow. I did not really know what to expect. Mrs. Harter barely spoke because she knew so little German. I spoke little because I was shy. Not being engaged in conversation, my thoughts began to wander again—to my parents, my home, my friends—and I was worried about the future. I turned my head away from her, gently pulling aside the curtain on the window, and pretended to look at a passing countryside bathed in sunshine. I didn't want her to notice the tears rolling down my cheeks.

14

MY THIRD HOME

T LAST WE WERE "HOME" in Epsom, Surrey. The taxi we had taken from the local railroad station turned into a curved, sanded driveway and stopped at the front door of a sprawling house—6 Downs Road. Gwen greeted us. "Welcome, welcome to Ingleside," she said, smiling as she reached for my hand. She was Mrs. Harter's daughter—tall, blonde, beautiful, about thirty years old.

She ushered me into the hall, where a large, oval oak table was covered with newspapers, magazines, and a pile of unopened mail—including, I recognized later, letters in my mother's handwriting. She had sent several, none of which had been answered, asking for information of my sister's immigration status. (Irenli was initially supposed to have gone to Mrs. Harter). I bent down to pet the old dog, a small black Chinese pug, when a young girl appeared with *her* young black Chinese pug. She was Mrs. Harter's great-niece, about my age and height. "Hello, I am Shirin, and this is Peter, my dog. We want to welcome you," she said, all smiles, as she pushed some hair back behind her ear. She had lost one of the barrettes.

Mrs. Harter's sister, referred to as "Auntie Gwen," was also there—a sickly older woman who occupied a bedroom next to her own sitting room, carpeted and upholstered all in red, in that seventeen-room house. I didn't get to know her, or even see much of her, because she died shortly after my arrival. That still left the housekeeper, the daily maid, the gardener, the cat, and, a few weeks later, the refugee chambermaid, and Unity for me to meet.

We were still gathered in the hall when Mrs. Harter turned to Shirin and said, "Darling, why don't you take Lisl upstairs and show her her room, and then come on down for tea."

As we climbed up the back stairway, Shirin explained to me, "We and the maids are not allowed to use the front steps over there, carpeted in red, because we might leave fingerprints on the white walls." She pointed as she spoke. I got the general picture.

My room was in the attic, and I liked it as soon as I entered. It was light and airy, the curtains, with blue flowers printed on them, stirring in the breeze as the late afternoon sun filtered in. As far as attic rooms go, it was comparatively large, its two dormer windows overlooking the garden. A chest of drawers, a closet, a chair, and a small desk supplied plenty of space to house my meager belongings.

"I must show you something," Shirin said, pulling my sleeve to introduce me to a secret space under the roof; it necessitated stooping so I could slither in. In time, it turned into a very important territory—a stronghold for my 'important' possessions. Impatient to see what lay beyond the windows, I was greeted with a view of two lawns. The upper, surrounded by beautiful, multi-colored rose beds, was set up for croquet (a game I had yet to learn and enjoy); the lower, laid out as a grass tennis court, was soon to be tried out by me.

Shirin seemed eager to please. "I'll be glad to help you unpack later, but we'd better go down for tea, so we don't get into trouble being late," she told me, again smiling, this time because she had to use her hands, and other body language to make me understand.

Afternoon tea was a meal. Each of us had a designated place at the round table in the dining room. When guests were invited, the children (later three of us) sat at an upholstered bench at another table that stood in the bay window with a lovely view of the garden. "I would like you to sit over here, next to me," Mrs. Harter told me as she pulled the wooden armchair back. Usually, she poured tea for everybody from a bone china teapot into large, floral patterned china cups. Milk was added and I was expected to drink that and like it. That was bad enough, but that awful concoction was handed to me in a cup twice the size of an ordinary one, with offers of a refill as soon as I had suffered half way through. The only time I'd ever had to drink tea was when I was sick—chamomile tea. There were two kinds of bread on the table, of which we had to eat at least one slice of the brown before filling up with a piece of the white with butter or jam. After we had eaten the bread, we were allowed to tackle the cakes and cookies. Before the war, cheese and fruit had also been available.

Gwen circumvented the rules by clasping her stomach, announcing, "My system can't tolerate the bread," then proceeded to pick and choose as she pleased from the other foods. I would have liked to do that, too, but couldn't think of an excuse.

She knew exactly how to do what she wanted without getting her mother angry. She had studied dancing as well as acting, and she used both to her advantage. Beautifully coiffed at all times, two locks of her blonde hair covered her high forehead, and her makeup achieved a natural look. She went to great lengths to make sure not to overdress. I don't remember seeing her wear much jewelry, if any. She liked brown or gray tweed skirts from Harrods, which had a flare that showed off her good posture when she moved—gracefully like a dancer.

Gwen had only been married a couple of years when her husband, Sidney Carline, a painter, died of pneumonia. She'd moved back with her mother, and in many ways took care of her.

Shirin's mother, Hilda Spencer, was Sidney's sister, which made Gwen Shirin's aunt. Hilda was nervous and not a healthy person, and Stanley, Shirin's artist father, wasn't around much. That's how Shirin came to live with Mrs. Harter when she was four or five years old.

When tea was finished, Shirin and I had to help Mrs. Hopper, the housekeeper, clear the table and wash the silver. It was necessary to pass through her sitting room to reach the pantry, which had a double sink and many cabinets for the china. That room was light because the large window had no shades. By contrast, curtains covered the closed windows in her sitting room, making it dark so that the book and glasses she had left on the table were barely visible. This fitted her character. No smile ever crossed that woman's tight lips. Her black-rimmed glasses and perpetual frown stood in contrast to her starched blue overalls as she over-saw our housekeeping duties, which at that point meant separat-ing the heavy silver forks, spoons, and knives before washing them. Each category needed to be carefully submerged into a vase-like container of water, making sure not to scratch them in the process, before they were washed.

Mrs. Harter believed in routines and discipline. On certain days after tea, she reminded Shirin, "It is time for your piano les-son, dear." Both of us followed her into the living room.

Shirin played the piano rather well. Mrs. Harter sat on the blue linen upholstered sofa listening. She made her repeat sec-tions of the Brahms piece she was studying over and over. I curled up in the oversized matching armchair, then crouched on the floor in front of the fireplace, which, a few months later, in the winter, would become a sought-after place, warming your be-hind while the front of you froze.

"Well, that will do for today, darling. Practice tomorrow be-fore our next lesson." Mrs. Harter stood up and left the room. I wondered why there wasn't some praise, if not for Shirin's good playing, at least for her effort. Thin and small-boned, she looked quite little and forlorn sitting at the grand piano.

After the second night of my arrival, I wrote in my diary: *It seems my life in Vienna and Czechoslovakia is a million years ago, and is an equal million miles away. Everybody is very nice to me, but I'm so homesick I can hardly stand it.* I cried myself to sleep the first night—and many more that followed—consoling myself that I would write to my parents first thing in the morning and ask them to answer right away. That thought was rapidly interrupted by the realization that I had no stamps, or money to buy any. I was in awe of Mrs. Harter. I had no choice but to summon up enough courage to ask her to mail the letter.

Three days after my arrival, she called me into the living room to tell me, "Lisl, I want you to meet Jean. I have asked her to come three days a week to help you with English. She speaks German, so it should work out well."

Jean had a fresh, open country look—smiling eyes and rosy cheeks in a round face with a beautiful English complexion. She was about nineteen, always cheerful, and easy to be with on our walks. In addition, at Mrs. Harter's insistence, I had to sit, grudgingly, for an hour every day and translate the book *Heidi*.

"Jean, would you please look over what I translated?" I felt free to ask her. I knew Mrs. Harter would look at it also, and I didn't want it to appear too bad. It worked. The three and a half months available before school started were enough for me to understand and speak English, albeit on a primitive level. At least I hadn't failed Mrs. Harter in that. I felt she must have been very disappointed that I was not able to play an instrument (something she had stipulated), and when she took me into the garden a week after my arrival, and handed me a pencil and drawing paper, saying, "Why don't you sit down and just draw something—the flowers, or a bush?" it became apparent instantly that I had no talent in that area either. That added to my feelings of inadequacy, manifested in not speaking the language, wearing different clothes, being unfamiliar with the food (and not liking it), and the strong feeling of not belonging, perhaps not even being wanted—simply being an outsider, alone in luxurious surroundings, and, perhaps most of all, that there wasn't anything I could do about it.

Lottie, the chambermaid (not a professional maid), arrived at Ingleside a few weeks after I did. She was the refugee from Czechoslovakia, and she spoke German and Czech and some English. She was charming, good-looking, and moved like a cat. Her job was to vacuum and dust, and she served at table. I was delighted to have a friend, an ally, a confidante. I had someone to whom I could talk about my loneliness and about being told off. Mrs. Harter's inflexibility and strictness bothered me. Sometimes Lottie cautioned, "Don't take everything to heart." She had her own problems getting along with her new employer, who acted no differently with her.

Lottie used every opportunity to travel to London to visit her boyfriend. She was twenty-two then, and after a few, brief weeks she left, moved to London, and shortly thereafter married.

To leave Nazi-occupied territory had been my greatest wish, and I'd been willing to do anything to achieve that goal. Reaching safety in England had been an adventure, an ideal, dominated by happy thoughts of seeing my parents in a few short weeks. It had never occurred to me that it would be anything but that. It also hadn't occurred to me that it would be anything but enjoyable.

I was consumed, the first few months, with feelings of responsibility for procuring my father's entry into England. I summoned up enough courage to engage Mrs. Harter in my quest, pleading with her, "It is most important for my father to get out of Austria. He has an affidavit, and he's only waiting for his visa for America. He would not stay in England and be a burden to the country. Would you please ask Mr. W. if he has done anything yet, as he promised?"

"You must understand, it is very difficult," she answered without elaborating.

At the time, I felt she was turning a cold shoulder. For that, but even more for her strictness and inflexibility, I dubbed her "The Dragon" in my diary. In my loneliness, my fervent wish and greatest desire was to be united with my parents again—and my sister, whom I loved despite her bullying.

MRS. HARTER WAS SEPARATED (not divorced, because that was not done) from her army colonel husband, who lived in London. I never met him. She was a capable manager who set rules that had to be obeyed or punishment followed. She never wavered. She was controlling, much too strict in my opinion—after all, I had been brought up in a permissive, middle class Jewish home, and had to adjust to an upper-class, Church of England household, with a firmly established order. She obsessed over good manners and good speech, both of which were impeccable in her, and she expected no less from those living in her house. She corrected the way I brought the soup spoon to my mouth. "Don't turn the spoon, Lisl. Take small sips as you hold it straight, keeping it level." We happened to be sitting in the living room when "God Save the King" was played on the radio. We had to stand up immediately. Every Tuesday at lunch, we had to speak French.

She was so old-fashioned, I decided. After all, she was about sixty years old. Still, I had to admit that she was good looking with her Roman nose, her gray hair that had a lot of black left, and the blue sweaters and cardigans she favored enhanced her lovely, clear blue eyes. As for the long strand of pearls she wore every day, she explained, "You have to wear them—otherwise they turn yellow." Her tall, statuesque frame exuded strength and power. Her erect posture and decisive, firm step gave her an aristocratic air, even when walking the dogs. She was not always serious. She certainly laughed at a funny story, but never in a shrieking, loud voice. She sometimes expressed anger or pleasure just by movement of her eyes, the latter accompanied by a faint smile. Words were not always necessary.

Mrs. Harter's open-heartedness (which I did not recognize at the time) was overshadowed by her Victorian values, to which she steadfastly clung, and which were often the cause of rifts between us. She won in the end, of course, and although I endured the punishment, I was never convinced that she was right. Her reasoning was too strict, her rules too illogical.

She was concerned about my physical safety, but not about my emotional wellbeing. Auntie Gwen had died, the war had started, Shirin had moved into one of Auntie Gwen's rooms, and I was brought down from the attic into a large room opposite Shirin's; it had been the guest room formerly. It was safer there, and easier to reach the cellar during air raids.

In spite of all my complaints about Mrs. Harter, I was eager for her to accept me and like me, just as I tried to like her, so that after I had been assigned my new room, and I heard her go past it to kiss Shirin good night, and again pass my room on the way out without stopping in, I wondered what I had done wrong that day, how naughty I had been, and thought that I had better try to do things her way.

Since my parents had no strict rules for my sister and me, and we were certainly allowed to ask questions, I was dumbfounded one day when the daily maid appeared. Skinny as a toothpick, I looked at her and asked Mrs. Harter, "Is Margaret pregnant?"

"Please, darling, we don't discuss these things," she replied as she turned away from me. She *was* controlling. On the other hand, some of my questions, and my behavior, meant I was difficult from her point of view. I made my own rules. I refused to sew or ride my bicycle on a Saturday. We were not very observant in Vienna, but since there was no synagogue in Epsom, and I knew no Jewish people, I had to preserve my identity, so that when she confronted me one day with, "Lisl, it would be nice if you were to become Church of England," I answered,

"Never. I can't, and I won't do that."

She never brought that subject up again.

Ironically, I did internalize her rule for speaking correctly, and am aware of her standard for good manners, especially table manners, although much has sunk into deterioration by now. It bothers me when I hear "there is" instead of "there are," and I find myself making a silent correction.

Shirin called Mrs. Harter "Minniehaha," and I received permission to do the same. There was no Hiawatha, and I never found out where the name originated.

During my first summer there, in 1939, we drove to Littlehampton by the Sea, in Sussex. I had never been to the ocean, and the novelty of the crashing waves, the sand, the seashells, the taste of salt water, was a new-found delight. Minniehaha had rented a house for three weeks. She must have taken a maid along, because we made the trip in two cars. There were still rules, if not totally relaxed, somewhat easier to follow. We took the dogs for a walk in the morning, I still had to do the translating, and we spent the afternoons at the beach. The house was an all year, fully furnished home with enough bedrooms to accommodate Minniehaha, Gwen, Shirin, me, and she had invited Shirin's sister, Unity, and their mother, Hilda.

Much as I enjoyed the seashore, I again felt victimized when, on the way back, Minniehaha instructed me to ride in the car with Peter, because he was prone to suffer epileptic fits. Shirin rode in the other car. He was her dog, and I resented the idea that he might be sick on my lap, and that I would be responsible for him. Fortunately, the trip back was made without any incidents.

After we returned to Epsom towards the end of August, there was constant talk of war, and, indeed, Britain declared war on Germany on September 3, 1939. Any chance of Papa coming to England thus vanished. I said prayers every night for his health, safety, and general welfare.

By that date, England had admitted close to ten thousand children, albeit with the stipulation that they had to come alone—no parents allowed. Adults were allowed to enter if they had enough money to sustain themselves for five years without working. The other option, for a woman, was to accept a position as a maid, or, for a man, to work as a handyman. Under that ruling, my mother arrived in July as a maid. Her job was in

Sussex, quite a distance from me, and she was only able to see me when it was her day off, every other Sunday, but she told me later that in the six weeks she worked for the Aisher family before war was declared, they had made great efforts to bring her mother (Babi) and her husband (Papa) to England. They had offered their little guest house on their premises as a home for the three of them. Time had run out. It was too late. Their offer was truly magnanimous. Babi, at seventy-two, could not work, and Papa was capable in his profession and knowledgeable about music, but not much of a handyman.

15

LIFE IN ENGLAND

THANK GOODNESS FOR GWEN! At first, whenever Minniehaha told me off, Gwen threw me a sympathetic look. In time, I was able to express my hurt feelings to her, and she mediated. She didn't say she would talk to her mother, but she listened patiently and tried to reassure me: "You know, Lisl, you probably didn't mean to be fresh, but Minniehaha is used to doing things in a certain way, and she expects the children to comply without answering back."

"I wasn't fresh. I just asked a question," I said in a bewildered tone.

But Gwen put in a good word for me, because on days following our talks, Minniehaha often acted in a more understanding, kinder manner towards me.

Gwen kept to herself quite a bit; at other times she hovered around Minniehaha and, genuinely concerned, asked, "Mother, do you think you should go there?" or "Do you really think you should do that? Maybe you should take a rest." I used to wonder whether she visited a boyfriend on her mysterious trips to London, ostensibly to see her father, because she was beautiful, kind, and compassionate, but I never even came close to asking her. Shirin explained to me once rather philosophically, "Gwen is sad. You must know she is still in love with Sidney, and she thinks about him, which means she mourns him."

I admired Gwen for being calm, always pleasant, never angry, and looked forward to her return from her London day trips. It just felt better to have her around.

One of my bigger showdowns with Minniehaha occurred on an afternoon while Gwen was in London.

"May I tell you about it?" I asked Gwen the next day, trailing behind her as she made her way to her sitting room, and when she nodded, I stepped up next to her, dying to talk about it in her sanctuary, which possessed an unwritten aura of privacy. It was a large room with multiple windows facing the garden, a desk in one corner, a comfortable sofa covered in flower-patterned linen material, and several chairs around a table. "I was late for tea coming home from school yesterday," I started, even before we sat down. "Greg was outside the house as the sentry." (The house next door had been requisitioned by the Canadian army to accommodate twenty soldiers). "They all know us, and we even know some of them by name." I continued, "He stopped me, and asked, 'What did you learn at school today?' I told him about Mrs. Toy's history class, and I mentioned Mrs. Robertson, my favorite teacher, and then he smiled, took out a photo, and, pointing to a girl, said, 'That's my daughter, Betty, back home in Canada. She's a year younger than you, and she also has red hair.

I'm going to ask her if she likes history, too.' After a few more minutes of chatting, we said good-bye. He added, 'Run along now, and be a good girl."

I had apologized for being late for tea, but when Minniehaha heard why, she became very angry that I had stopped to speak to a strange man, a soldier yet, and didn't I know better.

"Was that so bad, Gwen?" I inquired quite innocently. "Shirin and I have seen him and exchanged words with him for weeks now when we're out in the garden."

There was a punishment, of course, for my poor judgment— an especially early bedtime and stern looks.

Gwen tried to calm me by explaining Minniehaha's concern for me. The punishment still didn't make sense to me.

I was naive enough that I saw nothing wrong with that encounter. I might have put it in the category of bad manners, since it made me late for tea. I simply added it to the list of what was expected of me. I thought I knew exactly what I could and could not do. I did not always abide by the rules, but this was a new one.

Good manners, so important to Minniehaha, had one exception. At teatime, the thirteen-year-old dog had a chair with a pillow on it placed at the table between her and me. Most of the time he sat quietly, drooling, having lost most of his teeth.

When the postman rang the bell with the afternoon mail, Johnny jumped on the table, his front paws crunching the tablecloth which, in turn, made the plates clink against each other and push the cups together as he barked loud and long, slobbering and hissing through his toothless mouth. After he calmed down and settled on his pillow again, Minniehaha, staring at my cup full of tea, said, "Darling, you didn't drink your tea."

"And I'm not going to. Johnny spat all over it."

Silence followed. That, and when I refused to convert to the Church of England religion, were the only times I strongly answered back.

LONELINESS AND SORROW ON A continuous rather than temporary basis were new feelings for me to deal with, and I had to do so on my own. While Gwen offered a glimmer of hope, I felt restrained talking to her, too. She was very nice to me, as was Minniehaha usually, in her own way, but the failure of communication contributed to the altercations. It wasn't a question of language. It was their way of not expressing feelings. I missed Lottie, because after she left I had no one to whom I could totally open up. I couldn't vent to my mother about any of the incidents on the phone, since there was a chance of being overheard, and I didn't want to add to my father's worries by writing to him.

I was free, but my life had changed. It was necessary to adjust to a new culture, to get used to a new language—and learn to speak it—to a different upbringing, different expectations of me, different rules of conduct, different food, a different school, and different friends. I was still miserable three months into my new life. I decided I had to work hard at all the differences to reach my goal of being accepted into the fold of what made up the family. The fact that I had learned to speak English quickly, that I was able to attend school, that I tried—and partially succeeded—

to obey new rules, and that I had acquired manners good enough to please Minniehaha, didn't bring the results I had hoped for. What mattered most and was the most urgent, I had no power over—combating my loneliness and longing to be accepted. I yearned for love, if not physical, at least verbal, and some nurturing and support, something Minniehaha was unable to provide. We were studying *Macbeth* at school, and because I didn't recite some lines out loud, although I knew them, her way of encouragement was, "If you don't say the lines, you'll never learn." Being naïve, still shy, and lacking self-confidence only added to my insecurity and not knowing what to do about it.

One of the bright spots—nothing important—occurred when Gwen invited Shirin and me one afternoon to her bedroom to try different lipsticks. Her room, directly over her sitting room, was just as large and airy, and it also overlooked the garden. A large portrait that Sidney, her deceased husband, had painted of her hung over her bed, which had a luxurious blue silk cover that fell loosely to the floor. We had fun sitting at her makeup table applying to our faces different colored lipsticks, eyebrow pencils, and painting our cheeks. When we finished piling on makeup, we stood in front of the long wall mirror, laughing and joking while making faces and clowning. Besides providing fun for young girls, I was fully included.

Shirin fared much better than I. She didn't get punished as much. She was definitely the favorite, with "darling" this and "darling" that. When I was addressed as "darling," it was usually followed by a reprimand. She was smart, thin, angular, and she was deceitful. When I needed new shoes, having outgrown the old pair, Shirin announced one afternoon, as we were finishing tea, "That's strange. I dreamt I was sitting in the garden and my little pet, Peter, carried this beautiful pair of shoes in a bag—the ones I had seen in the store and liked so much—and dropped them by my feet." I recognized her ploy but could not comment. In her deceitful way, she usually managed to get whatever I received too, whether she needed it or not. It was not so the other way around. Shirin took advantage of being the apple of her eye, and I wondered how it escaped Minniehaha.

On another occasion, Minniehaha took Shirin to the cinema without me, because, she explained, "You would not have liked that film." *How does she know what I like or don't like?* I noted in my diary. Certainly I could not have said that to her. It was to make up for my having been invited by friends from school the previous day: Shirin had not been included.

Minniehaha was very concerned with Shirin's feelings. I was left to cope with mine on my own, which was frequently not the best way. I had always been a good little girl, but I was no longer little, and I didn't want to be good. Besides, I was a teenager, nor did it help that I felt very uncomfortable physically. I suffered from frostbites, called "chilblains" in England, that reared their ugly heads, first on my toes, and later also on my fingers, on which they turned into large, painful blisters, caused partly by the weather, partly by malnutrition as the war progressed.

Slowly, and grudgingly, I learned to like Minniehaha, doubting, nonetheless, that she felt likewise, because she had trouble calling me "darling." I remained unsure, harboring feelings of being an outsider, longing for full acceptance. It finally came—

from a strange source.

I was riding my bicycle one morning when the air raid sirens started to blast. It was in the early fall of 1940 by then. I was approaching a public air raid shelter as people were hurrying inside, when the policeman guarding the entrance called out to me, "Come along, dearie, there's room for one more. Just lean your bike over here and come on in." Never mind the air raid: I felt so good, so warm inside, so happy, and oh, so accepted. I had been publicly included instead of excluded, the first public turn-around from the dreadful notice at the swim club in Vienna only thirteen months earlier.

While in the shelter, savoring what had just occurred, it dawned on me that other good things were happening. I liked it when Minniehaha took me along for a ride in "Bluie," as she liked to call her little blue Ford. I loved the bicycle she'd bought for me, and I saw an entry in my diary that soon after my arrival she'd bought me two dresses. She sent me to a private school for which she had to pay. She hired Jean, the young woman who helped me with English. She did not ask to be compensated for any of these expenses. On the contrary, she refused any offers.

16

SIR EDWARD AND LADY NORTHEY

INNIEHAHA SANG IN A CHOIR, as did Gwen, and I enjoyed being taken along in Bluie for the ride to Dorking, a town not far from Epsom. I liked the trip much better than the singing, which Vaughn Williams conducted. Neither his fame, nor his ability, nor his accomplishments much impressed me.

She also took Shirin and me to a philharmonic concert. I liked *that*. Beethoven's *Ninth Symphony* was somewhat familiar, but it also meant traveling to London by train, and climbing to the upper level of a double-decker bus, which gave me a chance to see some of the city on the way to Albert Hall.

Mrs. Harter never took me to London to go sightseeing, but one spring day she did say, "If it won't rain tomorrow, I will let Shirin accompany me to go shopping, and you may come, too, Lisl."

"Oh, yes, thank you. I would love to go," I quickly answered. She visited department stores on rare occasions. Her favorite one was Selfridge's, at the top of Oxford Street, where she shopped for Shirin and me. Her limit in a store was two hours, less if possible. She was very focused—she went straight to the section she needed, bought, and left. Afterwards, we walked down Oxford Street, then took a bus to Trafalgar Square. On the way we passed another store—C&A—which she dubbed "Common and Awful," and we did not go inside.

One rainy day—it was drizzling on and off—I happened to join her for grocery shopping on High Street in Epsom. We ran into Lady Northey, Minniehaha's sister-in-law. She was tall, of stately demeanor, stern looking under her gray hat; she looked unattractive to me. After exchanging greetings, this personage appraised me and, turning to Minniehaha as she glanced disdainfully at me, said, "Muriel, is that child really so fat, or does she have too many clothes on?" She spoke slowly, and pronounced each word clearly and meticulously.

"Well, she's not fat—a little on the heavy side, maybe, but the mackintosh she is wearing is slightly big for her."

As I looked down at the rather stiff orange oilcloth hanging on me, I heard, "I see. I hope she does not present too much of a problem for you."

I was livid, and I hated her from that moment. My shyness stopped me from speaking English, which obviously made her think I also did not understand, which I did quite well by that time. In contrast, Minniehaha's answer sent *her* up a notch in my liking of her.

The following weekend, sunny and pleasantly warm, we paid a customary visit to Lady Northey and her husband, Sir Edward.

We were invited for tea. On each occasion, we sat on the lawn in the beautifully kept garden, partly shaded by the old oak tree nearby, lush bushes, and creatively shaped flowerbeds all around. Lady Northey presided over the tea ceremony. Comfortable white wicker chairs, with green-and-white cushions, sat in a circle around a bridge-sized table, covered in a white embroidered tablecloth. Little finger sandwiches, pastries, and a cake were elegantly displayed on the table. The white vase in the middle, full of red and pink roses, and the silver cutlery at each place setting, dazzled by the sun, looked like a painting. Lady Northey started to pour the tea from a Royal Doulton teapot that matched the cups and saucers and little cake plates. She concentrated hard, which seemed to prevent her from smiling. After I had eaten some pastry, she asked, "Would you like another piece?"

"No, thank you," I remembered to answer politely, dying for another one but afraid to say so, instead waiting for her to ask, "Are you sure? Do have another piece," the cue for saying, "Oh, thank you. I would love it," and trying not to grab it too quickly. I thought I was acting exactly right. She didn't ask. I avoided looking at her as my dislike of her deepened.

Sir Edward was Minniehaha's brother, about seventy years old. His round, wrinkled face, and the twinkle in his eyes, gave him a jolly expression. He used to chuckle after his little anecdotes about Africa, amused by his own stories. Shirin called him Uncle Eddie. I addressed him, if at all, as Sir Edward. He had just finished telling a joke when he caught my eye and, smiling at me, said, "You may call me Uncle Eddie, if you wish, Lisl."

In my craving to be accepted by the family, my impulse was

to dash over and throw my arms around his neck for fulfilling my secret, inner hope. Instead, hands folded in my lap, I smiled, looked at him, and demurely replied, "Thank you very much." No word from Lady Northey, but I didn't care—I was pleased as punch.

I didn't know it at the time, only found out years later, that "Uncle Eddie" had been a major general in the British army, had been a highly decorated recipient of many medals, and had been knighted for his bravery in World War I. He had been appointed an early governor of Kenya.

On another visit, the butler, donned in tails, a white bow tie, and white gloves, and bearing a silver salver on which he had placed the afternoon mail, headed towards us as we sat in the garden. He lowered his arm to enable Lady Northey to reach for the solitary postcard. After reading it, she replaced it, looked up, and said, "Thank you, Charles, that will be all." He bowed, turned around, and marched back to the house. Then she turned to Minniehaha. "Muriel, the bakery is having a sale on Tuesday. Are you interested at all?"

I knew enough etiquette to keep quiet. However, on the way home in the car, I could no longer contain myself. "Because the bakery is having a sale next week, Charles had to get dressed up—tails, tie, white gloves—that's ridiculous," I burst out.

That spelled another early to bed, Minniehaha's comment ringing in my ear, "You do *not* make remarks like that. If you have nothing nice to say, don't say anything at all."

17

THE WAR YEARS IN ENGLAND

AMA AND I LIVED SAFELY in England, far away from the Nazis. She arrived in July 1939. Irenli was settled in Palestine. Our greatest worry was Papa, still lingering in Vienna. We had managed a sparse exchange of letters through Aunt Poldi, who had fled to Norway and later to Sweden, but that, too, soon stopped. It had been the sole feeling of any closeness to him. He was hiding from the Nazis—-I don't know where or how—-while he waited for his visa to come to America. I constantly prayed for his safety and well-being.

Great Britain declared war on Germany on September 3, 1939. I went to school carrying a box that contained my gasmask. Every once in a while we had a practice air raid in which we were told to assemble in the basement with the gas masks. It only took a few minutes of wearing them to feel the discomfort of the rubbery smell, the eye visor fogging up, and after taking them off, every student had red marks on her face where that heavy piece of equipment had scraped her skin.

Blackout was strictly enforced. Air raid wardens making the rounds after dark were quick to knock on any door, even if only the slightest glimmer of light was visible. Later, fines were imposed. Mail delivery was curtailed to once instead of twice daily. The annual Derby meet was canceled. Instead, we walked the dogs there on the overgrown grass track. Food became rationed—-meat, butter, sugar, and other items. During days of plenty, four ounces of butter were allotted; in lean times, we had to make do with two ounces for the whole week. Imported fruit and vegetables faded into memory. On the other hand, rhubarb must have produced a bumper crop. We ate it boiled, baked, grilled, hot and cold, to the extent that I couldn't touch it for years after the war.

Air raid shelters built above ground—-public and private—no longer looked strange. Ingleside, Mrs. Harter's house, had a large enough cellar to enable beds and cots to be installed, which we used nightly during the months of the Blitz. We simply went to bed in the cellar, knowing sooner or later the air raid sirens would blast. The Blitz (lightning) was the German onslaught on Britain through sustained bombing. They dropped incendiary bombs over the whole country, but mostly in London, from September 1940 until May 1941. The city suffered for fifty-seven consecutive nights of bombings. Hitler's goal to demoralize the British into surrender did not materialize.

Although Epsom was considered a "safe" area, it was close enough to London to set off the local sirens when the German bombers attacked the city. Minniehaha transmitted her strength to us children. We were not afraid of the air raids during the

Blitz, or, during the Battle of Britain (July–September 1940). We had been instructed what to do to feel safe. We knew to stay away from windows to avoid broken, flying glass, and we learned that if a shelter was not available, the safest place was under the stairs. Our war knowledge was supplemented by realizing that if we heard the whistle of a falling bomb, it had already passed us. When the German bombers were chased by the RAF (Royal Air Force) fighter planes, they sometimes dropped bombs indiscriminately to lighten their load. On one such occasion, we heard that special whistle. It hit the house bordering ours at the bottom of the garden, shattering glass in ours. There were a lot of different noises, all loud—the explosion, the droning of the planes, and the *tac-tac* of the anti-aircraft guns. It seemed they were vying with one another.

Mama had come to visit me one weekend and had to stay overnight. Traveling in the evening was too risky. The sirens had blared earlier, and soon we herd the noise of the German planes on their return flight. We crouched fairly near to each other. Should I move very close to her in case the next bomb is a direct hit? I wondered. A picture of my father losing both of us flashed through my mind, which made me create some distance, but within a second I snuggled up to her, because the thought of possibly staying alive while she didn't was more than I could cope with. Those thoughts, of course, took only a fraction of a second.

Everybody carried on as usual during the bombardments, but, several months before the onslaught started, Churchill had made no bones in one of his broadcasts about the possibility of

Hitler staging an invasion. In one of his famous speeches he declared, "We shall fight them on the beaches, we shall fight on the landing grounds, we shall fight in the fields and in the streets, we shall fight in the hills; we shall never surrender."

We all believed him, and we were all willing and ready to act exactly as he suggested. I did wonder how I would react if I found myself face to face with a Nazi, but I was so inspired by his speech that I was sure we would "never surrender."

On the other hand, his fear of spies entering the country, if there were an attempted invasion, was so great that he ordered mass internments of Austrians, Germans, and other "enemy aliens." Czech citizens were considered "friendly aliens," which meant Mama's two sisters, Mitzi and Rosl, were exempt. Mama thought she, too, would escape being interned after she was sent home from a court hearing. In her phone call, she told me, "I am so happy that, after all these weeks of uncertainty and apprehension on both our parts, my case has finally been settled." She was recalled a week later, because, although born in Czechoslovakia, she was now an Austrian subject, and on September 20, 1940, she was interned at Holloway Prison in London. That was to be merely a stopover before being transported the next day to the Isle of Man, where the internment camp was situated.

Almost as soon as she arrived at Holloway, she was struck with phlebitis, and she could not be moved. At first, she was in the prison hospital, later in a cell, locked up at night. That was more than she could stand. She demanded to see the governor of the prison.

"The governor doesn't see prisoners," the warden told her.

"I am not a prisoner, don't you understand?" Mama answered. "I must speak to him."

When the audience was granted, she said, "It is not right the way I'm being treated. I am not a criminal. Bad enough to be in a cell, but to have the door locked at night is inhumane and dangerous. If the prison were to be bombed at night, I would be trapped and helpless."

Nothing changed for several days, which made Mama request another meeting. At that one she said, "The woman in the next cell has had several privileges granted, among them a carpet, some furnishings, and food brought in." That woman was Lady Mosley, wife of the well-known fascist and Nazi sympathizer, Sir Oswald Mosley. "I think I deserve the same accommodation."

"Mrs. Steiner, you are a rebel," the governor told her, "But I know how you feel. I have issued orders for your cell to be open and unlocked at all times."

Three weeks later, Minniehaha took me to visit Mama. She had complained about the prison food in her letters and asked for certain items, all of which Minniehaha bought, and then some. She waited for me while a stern faced female guard made me follow her through the first locked door. She was wearing a blue uniform with a broad, brown leather band around her waist that had about a dozen old fashioned keys hanging from it. One in particular struck me as being at least a foot long. It reminded me of the witch in 'Hansel und Gretel' when she pulled it out, grimacing as she ordered, "Stand over here, please," pointing just behind her. She unlocked the door ceremoniously, motioned me to pass through, and ordered, "Wait here." Then she used that long key to lock the door again. We crossed a small courtyard, she unlocked and locked another heavy door, and even a third in the same way——the two last ones in silence, merely motioning to me with her arm and her stern, narrow-set eyes focused on me. The windows in the courtyard were undersized and narrow, covered by crossbars. I thought I was passing through a movie set, it was so unrealistic, very unsettling and a bit scary. In my diary I wrote, *It is all like a dream again, and I thought the 'dreamtime' had ended as soon as I left Austria. To think that my mother is in prison because the police made a mistake....*

Mama was sitting at a table in a very small room that had one window, narrow like the others, and also covered by heavy crossbars. The cloudy, sunless day added to the dismal, harsh atmosphere. She had trouble standing up but made the effort as soon as I entered and gave me a long embrace. Still holding her, I said, "Look, Mama, I brought you all the things you asked for, and also some chocolate and cookies that you like." She was thinner and did not look well, but I was glad to see that she wasn't wearing a prison uniform.

"You know, Liserl," she told me, "since I made a fuss, I have been treated quite well, but the food is just awful."

Trying to cheer her up, I told her, "Mrs. Barclay asked her brother to help get you out of here. He's a lawyer who deals with cases like yours, and she said it shouldn't take too long." Mrs. Barclay was my teacher and owner of the school.

"I should be out of here by now," Mama said sadly.

I didn't know what else to tell her about her situation, so I spoke about my school friends. Actually, I had also asked other people for help in getting her released. I again felt it was my responsibility (as I had a couple of years earlier regarding my father) to keep after whoever would be able to be of assistance.

"Fifteen minutes are up—time to leave," I heard an official voice loud and clear, unmistakably that of the unpleasant guard.

Mama and I hugged and kissed, and I said, "I'll ask Minniehaha to bring me again soon." I turned to leave, feeling frustrated. I knew I hadn't helped Mama very much in convincing her that she would be released soon, but there wasn't much I could do.

In December, Minniehaha made arrangements for me to visit Mama again. She was supposed to go to the Isle of Man internment camp the next day. She started to cry this time as she said good-bye to me, which made me cry, too. What was to have been an overnight stay at the prison turned into three months of pain and extreme unhappiness for my mother—-much more than I had been aware. Her long prison stay was an oversight of proper documents for her transfer to the internment camp.

After several months on the Isle of Man, she came to stay with me at Mrs. Harter's, looking well, except that her beautiful chestnut-colored hair had turned gray.

Minniehaha, who had frequently been nice to me (I noted in m diary), had invited Mama. She soon told Mama what to do, just as she did me. That led to utter disaster, and I couldn't understand why Mama had accepted the invitation, except that I believed she wanted to be near me. She was treated as half guest and half maid.

One afternoon, Minniehaha, Gwen, Mama, Shirin, Unity and

I were sitting around the big, round dining room table for afternoon tea, which passed pleasantly enough. The customary white and brown breads, butter and jam were laid out, as well as cookies and cake, and whatever meager fruit was available at the time. Minniehaha offered Mama some dessert. "Won't you have a piece of the pound cake, Mrs. Steiner? She asked good-naturedly. "I bought it at the bakery this morning; it is quite delicious."

Mama declined, but I popped up, asking, "Oh, may I have a piece? It smells so good."

"Just a minute, Lisl. Did you have your slice of bread yet?" Minniehaha asked in her usual authoritative tone. I hadn't but thought, since my mother was sitting there, she would let me skip that routine of having to eat bread before we were allowed to tackle the desserts. I caught Mama's sad expression as she bent her head slightly, without making a comment.

We finished tea and Minniehaha turned to Mama. "Mrs. Steiner, would you mind clearing the table and washing the dishes? Mrs. Hopper" (the housekeeper) "is off today."

Looking back as she was about to leave the room, Minniehaha noticed that I had started to help my mother. "Lisl, you can't do that now. You and Shirin are supposed to walk the dogs, remember?" Instinctively I would have answered, "Can't the dogs wait half an hour?" I was sure Mama felt the same way, but neither of us answered her. Mama looked at me and, in an artificially cheerful voice said, "Go ahead, dear, I'll see you later."

Mama tried to be helpful by taking over the early morning tea routine (bringing a cup of tea to everybody in their rooms before breakfast was served downstairs), which Shirin and I, and also Unity later, when she was old enough, had to take turns at. An hour later, with everyone present at breakfast downstairs, Minniehaha didn't hesitate to criticize Mama. "Mrs. Steiner, I know you wanted to be of help, but you should have been more careful about spilling the tea. Next time take a napkin along so you can wipe the saucer before serving the tea." Listening to her finding fault, criticizing Mama, and especially, issuing orders to her, tore me apart. I knew Minniehaha could be cordial, but why couldn't she refrain from treating my mother like a maid, and worse, humiliating her? I wondered if the fact that she was taller than Mama and exuded an imposing presence made her act that way.

The following week, happily welcoming a warm, sunny day, I had laid out the books I needed for homework. Sitting at the long table placed in the bay window of the dining room I looked out longingly at the lawn, set up for croquet. Mama and Minniehaha entered the room discussing where to store some dishes in the cupboard. "I think, Mrs. Harter," I heard Mama say, "the blue ones should go on the top shelf, because they are seldom used."

"Good idea, Mrs. Steiner," answered Minniehaha amiably, "I hadn't thought of that."

Without addressing her by name but catching Mama's eye, I asked, "May I postpone doing homework? I just want to go out and practice shooting the ball through the hoops for twenty minutes."

"Sure, Lisl," Mama answered, "Just don't stay out too long."

"Listen to me," I heard Minniehaha declare. "I am the one

you have to ask for permission. Besides, I think you know perfectly well that you have to finish your homework before you may go out to play." Mama kept quiet. I thought I saw her bite her lip as a frown crossed her forehead.

It had become my fault that the two important women in my life had disagreements. I had no idea how to reconcile their conflicting values or feelings. It was great when they got along, but when they clashed, usually ending wordlessly on Mama's part, I felt deeply wounded. Clearly, I was to listen to Minniehaha rather than to my mother if there was a difference of opinion, which reduced Mama to a nonentity. She tolerated Minniehaha's views, even if contrary to her own, without protest, to protect me.

After that confrontation, Mama and I were sitting in the living room, chatting. Minniehaha entered, looked at us, and with a "hm" threw her chin up and forward and left the room in a huff, obviously assuming we were discussing the recent incident. We were not. Mama was listening to my school activities, and eager to hear about my new English friend. Just the same, Minniehaha's attitude left me uncomfortable and with a sour taste.

I spoke to Mama the next day. "This is an impossible situation, Mama. I can't please Minniehaha, and I'm not able—-allowed—to stand up for you, or receive instructions from you."

"Yes, I agree," she said. "I realize how insurmountable these circumstances are."

I wanted Mama to move out. I saw that as the only solution. I don't know if I actually said that to her, but she did just that after about two weeks. In those days the choice of jobs for women refugees were still to work as a domestic. She could not find a job in Epsom, which would have been the ideal answer to the problem. That's when she heard of the housekeeper position in Purley, near Croydon, and set off.   She was also in charge of eleven-year-old Juliet after school. Both her parents worked. When she told me how much Juliet liked the birthday cake she had made for her and the little party she had arranged, I was jealous that Mama couldn't do that for me, and that that kid Juliet had my nice mother instead of me. I rode my bicycle there sometimes to visit her, if she did not have time off to come to Epsom. When Yom Kippur approached, however, Minniehaha did not allow me to go there to attend temple services with Mama. As usual, she gave no explanation of her refusal. At the time I thought she was mean.   Now I know she was concerned about my physical safety, but again, as usual, she did not deal with my feelings

Minniehaha's treatment of my mother troubled me. She had shown compassion by taking me—-a total stranger—into her household, and I had witnessed her kindness towards others—-like visiting the daily maid with food when she was sick, and bringing Unity, the evacuee from London, to live with us, but I hadn't figured out at that time that in her mind dealing with people was categorized according to her view of the degree of need. Once past that, you became subject to her whims, which did not necessarily fall under the umbrella of good manners, so very important to her, or thoughtfulness.

18

SCHOOL

INNIEHAHA PAID FOR THE PRIVATE school in which she registered Shirin and me. The all-girls Sherwood School, only a few minutes walk from our house, had been converted from a private residence on a large piece of property. The brick building, not much larger than Mrs. Harter's home, Ingleside, consisted of three stories and a basement. It easily accommodated between fifty and sixty students. We made use of the basement later in the year, during air raids.

The grounds were impressive. A patch of grass, surrounded by bushes and trees, gave the appearance of a small forest, through which a path led to a large lawn on a lower level.

Both of us were enrolled in a three-year program, adjusted for completion in two years.

Mrs. Barclay, owner of the school, was waiting at the door when Shirin and I arrived on the first day of school. She was a short woman, plain looking, pregnant with her second child. "Welcome to Sherwood School, Lisl," she said amiably, shaking my hand. "Let me introduce myself. I am Mrs. Barclay, and I am the headmistress. I am so glad you are joining us. I think you'll be happy here, and we are certainly glad to have you."

"Thank you," I answered meekly.

"I want to tell you one thing before you start," she continued. "I am placing you in a lower grade than Shirin, although you are the same age, but I think it will make it easier for you to catch up with English, and then you'll be able to join your age appropriate classmates."

We studied *Macbeth* in the first semester—four months after my arrival in England—and we had to learn by heart: "If it were done, when 'tis done, then 'twere well it were done quickly." The "if," and the "when," and the "were," which I translated into German to better get the meaning of the passage, became so indistinguishable and incomprehensible that the teacher released me, saying, "If you just learn to read it well, that will be all right."

Two years later, fluent in English by then, I fared much better with *Julius Caesar*. The role of Cassius was assigned to me, and I can still recite the eulogy Mark Antony delivered at Caesar's funeral.

In the beginning, the girls at school were not always friendly. I overheard one of them telling her friend, "Goodness, we have so many foreigners in the country, even here at Sherwood." At that time I was the only foreigner there. Within a year, though, an English girl, Ann Stanley, became my best friend. She was quite tall and a bit of a tomboy, wearing her straight, light-brown hair shoulder length, with a band to keep it out of her eyes. She had a lovely smile, which helped persuade me when she asked,

"Say, Lisl, how about the two of us signing up for the three-legged race at the end-of-term games?"

"You are joking, Ann, of course," I replied, aware of the enormous difference in our height.

"Oh, let's just give it a try. Come on. We're both fast. We'll have some fun."

The odd couple received more than the usual applause, accompanied by loud laughter when we emerged as the winners.

The teachers were first-rate; acceptance by the other students changed the atmosphere, both of which helped to make learning agreeable and pleasant. My favorite teacher was Mrs. Robertson, widowed, about sixty years old. She used to look over her oversized orange-framed glasses rather than take them off. She must have felt cold all the time. She was never without her sweater. Her good nature shone through her gray eyes, still clear, which smiled as she spoke in her Scottish accent. In the beginning, she stayed after school to assist me with schoolwork, but those efforts soon turned into helping me emotionally as well. Her kindness, understanding, diplomacy, and listening skills endeared her to me.

One day I confided, "Mrs. Robertson, I didn't understand what went on in the Math class today, and Mrs. Harter told me if I don't make more of an effort to speak, I'll never learn."

"Don't worry, Lisl, you will learn, you'll see, and you will be able to do it all. Now, show me what you can't understand in Math." Her soothing words caressed me like a lullaby, and I felt they were not idle words—they came from her heart. That made them encouraging. I looked upon her as my source of comfort and stability. Mama was stuck in prison, ill, on her way to the internment camp, and Minniehaha was unable to provide such support.

Mrs. Robertson was right. In due course I caught up, reached the same class as Shirin and other students my age, and did well.

A new girl, Ruth, arrived at the school from Germany. She seemed self-confident, I decided, because of the way she strutted around, her stringy, short black hair ending in line with her very pink, blown-out cheeks. We were friendly but not friends, perhaps because by the time she came I had befriended Ann.

There were other changes, too. It was 1940 by then, and one day at lunch, Minniehaha announced, "I have something to tell you. Unity, Shirin's younger sister, will come to stay with us at Ingleside."

"Is she going to live here, and go to school with us, and be with us all the time?" I asked eagerly.

"Certainly, at least while The Battle of Britain is raging daily over London, which makes it unsafe for her to continue living in Hampstead."

Her arrival equalized my position somewhat: She was the evacuee from London; I was the refugee from Vienna. She had more trouble getting along with Minniehaha than I did. Although she was almost four years my junior, I liked her right away. She was very pretty, sincere, much more outspoken than Shirin, and much less attuned to Minniehaha's rules and regulations. I had gained a partner in crime, so to speak.

The fact that Minniehaha was also providing a refuge for Unity helped me to reach some understanding of what she had done for me by taking me into her home, and I tried hard to make adjustments as I grew older—but it seemed there were always new ones.

Unity was broken-hearted one day. She was practicing her ballet steps in the hope of ultimately becoming a ballet dancer, when, Minniehaha, having watched her, said, "I think, Unity, you are going to be too tall to be a ballet dancer." She stopped paying for her classes.

When Minniehaha left the house soon after that, I tried to cheer Unity up. "Let's slide down the banister!" I suggested.

"I don't like it, I tried once. They're too short."

"I don't mean the back stairs. We'll go down the front ones, the forbidden ones. They're great for that," I urged. She was willing and didn't say, "But we are not supposed to," which made me like her more.

My maternal grandparents, Adele and Isidor Deutsch

My paternal grandparents, Therese and Benedikt Steiner

With Irene (right), 1928

My mother (second from left) with five of her siblings

With Wolfie, 1931

*Yelli Horner, my favorite aunt (left) with her
brother Leo and his wife Gerti*

My aunt Gretl, 1937

My passport photo, 1937

At Ingleside, Epsom, 1939. I am at left.

Mrs. Harter, 1939

With painter Stanley Spencer, 1952

Edgar Foltin, 1952

My father and mother, 1947

With Jack at the Schiffli Convention, 1957

Richard at age 2, August 1960

My mother, October 1964

Ginny, 1975

At Bradley's law school graduation, 1988

Bradley and his wife Sandy, 2002

Debbie and her husband Jon, 2005

19

VISITORS

HILDA, SHIRIN AND UNITY'S MOTHER, visited sometimes in Epsom. She had divorced Stanley, their father, because of his newest love-interest, Patricia, whom he had married. Her lesbian partner attended the wedding and, to his surprise, accompanied them on their honeymoon. I overheard him tell Gwen that he had been unaware of Patricia's lesbian relationship. He was already a well-known artist in Britain, and, the story went that, Patricia's only interest in marrying him was to further her own career as an artist. When I met him in Epsom, he hadn't been living with Patricia for some time, and he wanted to live with Hilda again, herself a talented artist, but she declined. It came to pass that both Stanley and Hilda were visiting Mrs. Harter at the same time. Although divorced, they got along quite well. He decided to make a pencil sketch of me, but since I didn't want to be bothered to sit still that long, Hilda agreed to read my homework to me while Stanley drew me. He later dedicated the drawing to my mother. Hilda was patient, accepting, and behaved in a rather saintly manner. She wore her gray hair, parted in the middle, pulled back into a bun. Her eyes, dulled from pain and no makeup, made her look older than her years—that, and also the fact that she was not a well person. She was a Christian Scientist, which caused her to bear considerable pain and discomfort years later when she died of cancer.

Stanley Spencer arrived unannounced at Ingleside one afternoon. When the doorbell rang, I went to see who it was, Minniehaha just ahead of me. "Why, Stanley, hello—come in, won't you?" she said, smiling, but surprised nonetheless. A little man in a loose overcoat stood in the doorway; he had no hat, gray hair mixed in with black shaggy ones dangled over his forehead, and his glasses were balanced on the tip of his nose. A small suitcase, partly hidden in shadow by the late afternoon sun, stood behind him. As he took a step to enter, Minniehaha asked, "Where is your luggage, Stanley?"

"Right here." He reached for the case.

"I don't mean your paints," she answered. "Your suitcase containing clothes."

"I don't need one. Here's my toothbrush." He grinned as he pulled it from his pocket, held it up, and, rolling up his trousers, added, "and here are my pajamas!" which he wore under his suit.

Minniehaha's face turned white. He had come because he had no home—Patricia had thrown him out—and no money.

Stanley was given the room next to mine in the attic. When it was my turn to take early morning tea to everyone, I noticed all kinds of books in his room, several on the floor near his bed. They ranged from *Alice in Wonderland* to political ones, to books on other painters, to yesterday's newspaper.

With Stanley around, teatime became long and drawn out. It was always interesting. He liked to talk politics, he often criticized the government, but when I once made a remark—nothing bad, just not complimentary—he turned on me, became very defensive and very patriotic. At other times, if Minniehaha had just told me off, he would wink at me, later instructing me, "Don't worry, don't take it to heart. You're O.K." He and I got along very well. I was unaware of it at the time, but we had formed a bond. Both of us were outsiders in that family.

He did not permit criticism. One day, I heard Minniehaha tell him, "I don't understand, Stanley, why you can't make any money. Look at your brother—he has a wife and child, and he does all right."

"So?" Stanley shot back. "I have *two* wives and *two* children." He neglected to add that he did not support any of them, including Patricia, who had never consented to a divorce.

Daphne was his new girlfriend. Tall and buxom, she towered over him, her long blonde hair flowing down over her shoulders. She frequently came to tea. What a motley crew Minniehaha had accumulated. When Daphne's presence and her trailing him became too difficult for Stanley, he asked me whether I knew of a bus he could catch to go to London to get away from her without being followed.

When he settled down to paint, it was in Gwen's sitting room. She arranged to have all her furniture pushed aside to make room for a canvas several feet long and two or three feet high. He had been commissioned by a government agency to paint *Shipbuild-*

ing on the Clyde (a river in Scotland). It was considered an important contribution (though paid) to the war effort. Some drawings were on large pieces of paper and drawing pads. He had also brought with him scraps of paper, including toilet paper, on which he had made sketches, all of which were strewn around the floor. Those scraps, the pads, plus his memory, forged the finished product. Sometimes he didn't mind being watched as he painted. He was immersed in putting finishing touches to *The Riveters* (another painting in the series) when he turned to me and said, "See, I remember this man's big nose. I have to get it right." He stayed at Ingleside several months, at the end of which the finished products were exhibited in the National Gallery in London, later at the Tate Gallery, and they were ultimately housed permanently in the Imperial War Museum.

In England, he has been considered one of the greatest British artists of the twentieth century. In the United States, he is barely known. He was Knighted by Queen Elizabeth II in 1959. He died later that year. He painted beautiful landscapes, which he sold to make money, but his preference was to paint religious subjects. He is not a painter easily understood on first viewing. The Tate Gallery archives the bulk of his work. It held a retrospective in 2001, at which time his daughters invited me to dinner at the gallery and a special private viewing before the show opened to the public. His paintings today sell for millions of dollars. In June 2011, one of his oils sold in London for £5.4 million (over $8 million).

20

LEAVING SCHOOL AND WORKING

Y TWO YEARS AT SCHOOL CAME to an end, and I took the School Certificate, the end exam, that also served as the entrance exam to Cambridge. Results were to be announced later in the summer.

In July 1941, I wrote in my diary: *I am very unhappy, and feel as sad as the dark sky. Today was the last day of school. My report card read in part: 'Lisl's diligence and her intelligent learn-ing deserve that she pass the School Certificate.'* Under the head-ing of *Exercise* it said: '*She has the makings of a good tennis player, but her game has been hampered by a rather unsatisfac-tory racquet.'* General Progress: '*Her perseverance and unselfish attitude are deserving of success. She would be happier dealing with people rather than in a business or office routine.'*

Instead of feeling proud and happy, I'm crying. I am fifteen, feeling like ten. If only I could go back to school for at least two or three subjects, but this is such a sudden, total break. I can't imagine going to a trade school or secretarial school. The whole process of saying good-bye to students and teachers was so, so sad.

I hadn't realized how vulnerable I had become to any parting or ending of relationships, and how earlier experiences had become embedded in me to surface each time as a wrenching, chronic happening.

Toward the end of August, I was busy preparing to donate some of my clothes to a sale being held for waifs and strays when Mrs. Barclay, my headmistress, appeared at the house. I had always liked her because she had been supportive and encouraging. I was glad to see her. She smiled, offered a big "Hello, Lisl," and continued, "Well, I suppose I better tell you the news at once. I have the results of the School Certificate. I am afraid you have not quite managed it. You didn't get through."

"Am I the only one?" I asked, dazed.

"No, Ruth didn't make it either," she answered.

Ruth was the best student in French in the whole school, and she had failed French. Ruth's theory was that our failing was due to the hostility in the country towards Germans and Austrians, because a Czech girl she knew had passed. The mistake was that we had taken five subjects, all of which needed to be passed. If you took six and failed one, you still passed.

Minniehaha put her arm around my shoulders, whispering, "Never mind," and Mrs. Barclay's eyes empathized. She looked at me kindly and said, "How about walking back with me and taking a look at the new kittens in my house?" I declined. Instead, I ran to my room and cried my eyes out. I liked Mrs. Barclay more than ever—she showed such understanding.

My mother wanted me to continue with my studies at another school. In a letter I found recently, she wrote to my father (in the U.S. by then), *I have told Mrs. Harter that I will scrape enough money together to let Lisl continue her academic studies. She did not like the idea. I tried a second time, but she would not hear of it. I am afraid if I insist, her anger might affect Lisl adversely.*

Minniehaha had made a decision: I was to attend a secretarial school. The main study in that six-month course consisted of learning to type fast and to write shorthand. The stenography was a very handy tool all through college in later years, and is even useful to this day.

She explained her decision—much to my surprise—by telling me, "You may wonder why Shirin is going off to boarding school. I am not paying her tuition—the Spencer family is taking care of that, and I can't afford to pay for you. It will be best if you go to a secretarial school and then get a job." That was one of the very rare occasions she offered an explanation.

My facial expression must have revealed my feelings, and she continued, "I know you would prefer to study. Maybe you will be able to take some night courses." She had had an income from Burma but lost it after the country was occupied by Japan. Before the year was up, we moved out of Ingleside with its beautiful, large garden, to a smaller house.

A NEW ROUTINE WAS UNFOLDING. After the six-month course at the secretarial school, I found myself on the commuter train to London every morning. In the beginning, I was unhappy and trying not to show it, as I was crammed in with what seemed to me mostly old men. Going to work at sixteen, instead of to school, was not what I wanted. I found a job as a secretary to the senior partner in a father-and-son law firm on St. Swithin's Lane in the East End, London's business district. The old man, Mr. Ed, bald and round-faced, with round glasses, was always dressed impeccably in a dark suit, stiff shirt collar, and bow tie. He was patient with me and pretty nice to work for.

Alan, his son, almost bald, had a long face and an insincere grin when something was not to his liking, and most of the time he was a pain. His secretary, two years older than I, who had been in the firm for some time, warned me about his moods. She also explained much of the office procedure.

Mr. Ed, my boss, was very hard of hearing, so whenever the air raid sirens sounded, sometimes more than once in a single day, I entered his room to advise him to go downstairs, as we had all been instructed. "No," he would say, "I'm going to stay here."

"But, Mr. Ed, you could be hit by broken glass from the window behind you. You are supposed to go downstairs," I insisted.

"No, no, you go ahead." I did. That became the pattern every day during the Blitz.

There was another woman on the staff, and Jim, the young office boy. He usually stood by the door, holding it for all of us to pass through quickly in an air raid, and was, gallantly, the last one to leave the office. Just eighteen, he was waiting to sign up for the RAF. He was quick to help me move a chair, show me something, or carry some of the heavy books I was about to take to Mr. Ed. He did all that with a big smile whenever he looked at me. His dark hair was as shiny as his dark eyes, and he was pleasant and likable, but I had no thoughts of him beyond that.

One morning, on a day too nice to descend to the basement— we enjoyed a rare day with sunshine and blue skies—the sirens went off as usual. Delayed by Mr. Ed's incorrect assumption and unconvincing argument that "if your name is on the bomb, there's nothing you can do," I happened to be the last person out of the office. Jim was standing by the entrance, slightly hidden behind he door. As I tried to pass, he stepped forward in a protective stance but, instead, pulled me back, and, enfolding me, gave me a passionate kiss—my first.

I was too shocked to feel anything except surprise. Since I had no romantic feelings towards him, his question, "Have you ever been kissed?" hurt my pride, and I would not admit that he had guessed correctly. What I considered my real first kiss occurred at another time with another man.

ONE SUNDAY AFTERNOON, I VISITED Mr. and Mrs. Schwarz, friends of my parents in Vienna, who lived a few towns away from Epsom, closer to London. I was standing at the bus stop, ready to go home. The sirens wailed, and I was toying with the idea of returning to their apartment when I spotted Eric running across the street towards me. "My mother sent me to take you back to our home, so let's go quickly before the planes get here," he said hastily as he took me by the hand, turned around, and rushed me across the street. What a relief. Eric, six years my senior, had helped me on the platform in London when I arrived three years earlier on the Kindertransport. He'd come to the rescue of a broken lock on my suitcase. Back at the apartment, Mrs. Schwarz said, "We'll telephone Mrs. Harter and tell her I want you to stay overnight. Even if the all-clear sounds soon, it will be dark and too late for you to travel by yourself."

After dinner, Eric played the piano for me, accompanying himself in songs he had written. He impressed me greatly with his talent, his charm, his big broad smile, and his little jokes. To me, he seemed worldly and sophisticated. His dancing eyes, under heavy lids, noticed everything. His parents went to sleep, and a bed for me had been made up on the sofa in the living room, where Eric continued to play the piano. As the evening progressed, he said, "We should be a little quieter. I'll put the gramophone on instead."

We started to dance. A waltz was difficult because there was too much furniture. We switched to a foxtrot. He stroked my hair, we danced cheek-to-cheek, ever slower, ever closer, until we stood enfolded in each other's arms. Then he kissed me. I was in heaven, feeling all the more romantic as all that was happening during an air raid. I savored that kiss for the duration of the war. We embraced and caressed, but he was careful to preserve my innocence and virginity by explaining that he was on leave from the army's Pioneer Corps and expected to be transferred to a special intelligence unit on his return, where he could not be contacted, nor did he know when his next leave would be granted. He was, in fact, integrated into the SOE (Special Operations Executive), a secret unit whose mission later in the war involved parachuting behind enemy lines, and, at great risk, inflicting as much damage as possible. His army job made it difficult to meet, but we corresponded.

The injunction "Keep calm and carry on" was adhered to by everyone, despite the daily bombardments. I continued working at Edwin Clark & Son, got along better with Minniehaha, and became more English in my attitude and thinking, perhaps, because, with very few exceptions, I knew only English people. Minniehaha suggested to me one day, "You mentioned you would like to help the war effort, Lisl. They are looking for volunteers in the canteen. It would be nice if you gave some time."

"Yes, certainly I'd be interested," I answered eagerly. I worked in the local canteen an hour or two every Saturday. My job in the church hall was to set the long tables for dinner, and help clear them after the soldiers had been fed. I was not assigned to serve them, which meant I had little contact with the soldiers.

In the summer, I spent a week of my vacation on a farm to assist the war effort. I arrived there on a pleasant English summer day, not too hot. I was handed a sack and told to fill it with peas growing in the field nearby. Sitting in and between them, I didn't have to move to reach out to that fresh, young, tasty vegetable—a rare gift in those days. One handful found its way into the sack, the next into my mouth, followed by the next, and the next, and the next. I stopped only when I started to groan with a stomach ache. I had to overcome it by working fast to fill the sack in time to turn it in.

The following summer, I again volunteered one of my two weeks of vacation. At that location, I was told, "Just climb up the ladder on that haystack. All you have to do is stand on top and catch a bundle of hay as the machine drops it off, roll it to the side, and stack each one in an orderly fashion." I did as I was told. Work proceeded quite well until, suddenly, one of my moccasins fell off.

The sun was shining in my face as the bundles kept coming—it seemed at faster and faster intervals. I didn't say anything, because I was sure I would locate and pull out the shoe from wherever it was, even as my back was being hit by the next one coming up, and then the next, which I was no longer able to arrange in any order. I turned around, and, to my horror, another—with long, sharp ends of hay—was coming right at me.

By then the real workers, standing at the bottom, had noticed something was wrong, and the very thing I had wanted to avoid inevitably happened. They stopped the machine, and one of them yelled up to me, "What's wrong? What happened?"

He climbed up, straightened out all the bundles, which by then were lying around helter-skelter, and to my relief as well as embarrassment, found my shoe.

I have in my possession a card from the Ministry of Agriculture and Fisheries, which made me smile when I read: *I wish to thank you for your help last year and wonder if you were paying us a visit this season. If so, do try and make up a party, because good workers are scarce.*

21

LEAVING MRS. HARTER

A S I GREW OLDER, I learned to get along better with Minniehaha, and, I suppose, she did with me as well. She allowed me to travel to London to visit Lottie, the refugee chambermaid who'd lasted just three weeks before she left Mrs. Harter's employ, and soon after married. I had such a good time meeting her husband and new baby that I stayed too long. I caught the last train leaving Waterloo Station that night, just before it was bombarded during one of the worst air raids on London.

The train stopped several times between stations. The antiaircraft guns thundered so loud, I thought surely they were mounted on top of the train. Dark green criss-crossed tapes covered the windows to prevent them from shattering. One of the windows had a note gummed to it with instructions not to tamper with the tapes, *because they are there for your protection.* Underneath the official notice somebody had scribbled, *I thank you for the information, but I can't see the bloody station.*

As passengers departed at their destinations, only a young Canadian soldier and I were left. He sat opposite me at first, then moved next to me and started to talk to me. Events outside were rather scary, and in my ignorance I felt anxious about his close proximity, intensified by the smell of liquor on his breath. I thought he might be drunk. The blue light bulb used for blackout in all train compartments gave him such a ghostly appearance that my imagination soared. He was nineteen, he told me; I was fifteen and a half.

The guns that sounded so close to the train roared again, which meant the German planes carrying bombs were overhead.

Looking straight at me, he asked, "Are you scared?"

"No, no," I stammered.

"Then why are your teeth chattering? Here, take my helmet," and without waiting for an answer, he shoved it on my head. It covered my forehead and half my nose. Gathering courage and throwing my head back to enable me to see him, I said, "Thanks, but what will you use as a cover?"

"Oh, I'll put my pack over my head, if needed."

The train stopped again. This time it had pulled into Wimbledon station. Without a word, he grabbed my hand, threw open the door, and pulled me along onto the platform, where I found myself standing next to him in utter amazement. The whole sky was on fire. Rubbing and clapping his hands, he kept saying, "Look, look, *wonderful!*" I had never seen anything like that. I watched in awe as a broad, brightly lit yellow-orange streak rushed down to earth in a wide curve. The soldier jumped up and down, yelling, "Just look at that! We got that Jerry.

Bravo!"

A few minutes later, the train started to roll again, slowly. An hour must have passed since we had left Waterloo Station, ordinarily a fifteen-minute ride.

He said he was stationed in Leatherhead, one stop beyond Epsom.

"I can get off at Epsom and walk you home. I know the town quite well from visiting my girlfriend there."

"Thanks very much. That's very kind of you, but I am sure I will be picked up at the station," I answered in all sincerity, trusting him by then but wondering if Minniehaha would really be there.

I decided I would have to take the chance of walking home alone, scared, twenty minutes in deepest blackout, rather than risk appearing with the soldier. That would have been the end of me.

She was at the station, having waited one and a half hours for me.

INEVITABLY, THE WAR IMPACTED OUR lives—and not always menacingly. After the American planes joined the British in bombing Germany, we could tell which they were by the formations of each. Usually, the Americans flew during the day, the British at night. When we heard the familiar, loud growling noise, we ran outside and counted the returning planes.

"Oh, how sad," said Shirin, "two are missing." Both of us hoped the British pilots parachuted to safety.

"No, look, they are in the back, limping in," I called excitedly.

We clapped our hands with joy. One emitted a thin streak of smoke, and the other accompanied him.

REGULATIONS FOR REFUGEES HAD BEEN lifted, so that Mama no longer had to work as a domestic. Her sister, Mitzi, asked her to join her in making eyeglass and teapot covers, as well as other small articles, which she sold to the better department stores. I remember Aunt Mitzi from Czechoslovakia as whiny and complaining, her shiny complexion often covered by tears. Maybe that's why she had never counted as one of my favorite aunts.

Mama and I viewed this arrangement as the longed-for, long-awaited opportunity for us to be re-united.

I left Mrs. Harter after having lived in her house for four years, not entirely without misgivings. On a warm Sunday in April, the sun actually shining, I packed my few belongings to meet Uncle Viktor, Aunt Mitzi's husband, who was to take me to my new home.

It wasn't too far from Epsom, which made the parting easier. I can't tolerate lengthy good-byes; since I can't always explain that and make them short, I often appear curt and uncaring. In keeping with that, all I said was, "Good-bye, Minniehaha, and thank you for everything. I appreciate what you did, and I'm sorry for any trouble I caused."

"Good-bye, Lisl. Stay well, and keep in touch. Good luck to you."

We hugged, and I was off.

Mama had found a furnished one-room apartment in the vicinity of where Aunt Mitzi and Uncle Viktor lived with their daughter, Erica.

Uncle Viktor, a broad shouldered, heavy-footed conniver, but very likable, helped us move in, meaning he carried two suitcases.

Mama was waiting as we climbed the stairs. She was obviously happy to see me as she advanced towards me with a big smile. We hugged and kissed, and I was glad, too.

I entered the room, took a quick look around, and froze. I was dumbfounded. The furniture was old-fashioned, the chairs upholstered in drab colors, a square table in the middle of the room covered with a tablecloth of dubious vintage, and off-white, cheap lace curtains hung on the two windows. The little heater placed between the windows had an attachment for coins to be dropped in before it gave any heat. Even that day's sun was unable to penetrate the dreariness, or take the chill out of the room.

My body language must have spoken louder than words. Mama of course noticed and said, "We're together now, and I am so happy. You'll see, Liserl, we'll make a go of it."

"Yes," I had enough sense to answer, "and to make up for the lack of heat, we'll eat better, because you're such a good cook. I won't have to eat rhubarb in all its forms and tastes."

Uncle Viktor put a shilling or two into the little heater, which kept it going for just a couple of hours.

Our new living quarters were in Kew Gardens, a little closer to London than Epsom. I continued working at the law office in London, and our combined earnings sufficed for our daily life together. Invitations to dinner at my aunt's house were rare. My cousin Erica, two years older, loved to tell us, "I met this very nice American officer."

"Where did you meet him?" I would ask.

"At the Cumberland Hotel. They have wonderful dances there."

Mama sent me to dancing classes and wanted Erica to take me along. It never happened. Mama had friends whom we visited together. We listened to the radio, we wrote letters, we read, I took Spanish lessons at night, and we had our own thoughts. I kept in touch with a couple of girl friends from school, but there had been no dating while I lived with Mrs. Harter.

One of my girl friends had joined the Auxiliary Territorial Service (ATS), the women's branch of the army. She was assigned as a telephone operator and took advantage of her position to make private phone calls. We had many lengthy ones in which she almost persuaded me to "join up." I was quite patriotic and of an English mind by then, and liked the idea.

After one of those conversations, I told Mama, "I am thinking of joining the ATS. Mary says it is really quite a good life, not hard to go through the training, and she has an easy job."

"If you join the ATS, we can't leave for America till the war is over, even if our visas arrive sooner, which I think they will," Mama answered in a calm voice.

I think it must have been that hope that kept us going. My dislike for our living quarters soon turned to hatred. I could freely talk to Mama, ask questions, and get answers, but I missed the life I had become accustomed to in Epsom. I had become quite English in my thoughts and behavior, unlike Mama, who did not feel British.

And something else irked me. Mama, who had been so

strong and brave in her stand against the Nazis, and managed to get my father, my sister, and me out of their clutches and to freedom, had changed. She was set on going to America to join Papa, but she relied on me to make decisions for her. Should she be business partners with her sister Mitzi, or get another job that was offered, or buy something for the apartment? I didn't like that. I was busy with my own teenage turmoil. I didn't want the responsibility of taking care of her.

One day, I was surprised to hear, "Henry offered to have us come and live with him in his house in Kingston-on-Thames." Henry was a family friend, a semi-retired dentist.

"Is that what you want to do?" I asked.

"Only if you come, too. I'm not quite sure about it. I want to discuss it with you and hear what you think."

I thought that getting out of those dismal rooms was a gift.

We moved to his spacious, lovely house. He was a nice man, not tall, a little overweight, about sixty. He had a square, wrinkled face, his kind eyes smiling approvingly whenever I talked to him, and he obviously liked Mama. There were enough bedrooms, but Mama insisted I sleep in the bed next to hers.

22

WAITING TO IMMIGRATE TO THE U.S.

WE SETTLED IN AT HENRY'S HOUSE, and Mama seemed to revive—though she was never the same person again after her internment, which included three wrongful months of imprisonment. That was such a shock and inflicted so much damage that she did not fully recover. She missed Papa terribly. He was in the U.S. by then.

Irenli, in Palestine, married nineteen-year-old Gideon from Vienna. He was a violinist; she played the piano. Her letters, which took weeks to reach us, sounded very happy.

Papa, in New York City, worried about us once more. When I was still at Mrs. Harter's, he had offered to send food, which she would not accept. At that time, even during the officially allotted period of two ounces of butter weekly, I mentioned to her one day, "My Uncle Viktor said he can get us butter and some extra meat."

"Tell your uncle, 'Thank you very much. We are managing quite well, and we don't need anything.'" Since those provisions would have been black market, she wouldn't touch them.

Papa was concerned about Mama and me because the bombings had started again.

They were different air raids from the ones during the Blitz. It was 1944, a cold, wet summer day, when the first V-1s, soon followed by the V-2s, came buzzing over from occupied France and Holland. They were pilotless flying bombs, launched shortly after the Allied landings at Normandy. The V stood for *Vergeltungswaffe*—"vengeance weapon." They were called "buzz bombs," also commonly referred to as "doodlebugs."

Those missiles made a distinct, rather loud noise since they flew at low altitudes. Their timing mechanism was faulty, which resulted in the noise stopping and an immediate plunge. They fell to the ground and exploded. That left just a few seconds to run to the shelter. There were no safe areas. They were deadly weapons—detonating indiscriminately, killing hundreds of civilians daily.

Between June 1944 and March 1945, more than 9,000 of these doodlebugs were dispatched. Only some 2,000 made it to their intended targets. The rest were shot down or caught in the barrage balloons that dotted the path to London.

In September 1944, over 3,000 V-2s were launched. They were rockets that flew so fast that it took only three minutes from launch to landing. There was no warning. Many thousands of civilians were killed by the V-1s and V-2s—more than by the traditional bombs. They did not stop until March 1945.

One afternoon, I was home alone in Henry's house, talking on the phone to my cousin Erica in Kew Gardens, several miles away. I heard the loud roar of a doodlebug; the noise stopped, and I quickly exclaimed, "Hold on a minute, a bomb is coming." Throwing the phone down, I ran to the cellar. Just as I reached it, I heard the deafening noise of the explosion. Back on the phone a couple of minutes later, my cousin said, "Boy, that was a close one. I could hear the bang through the phone."

I found some broken windows in one of the rooms later that day from the missile, which had landed across the street. I was not afraid but was careful to take shelter.

My friend, Mary, on leave from the ATS, invited me to spend the weekend with her at her parents' home in the country. Before I left, I suggested to Mama, "Why don't you go away, too?"

"No, I don't feel like it."

She sounded depressed, so I urged, "Yes, you should go. Call Aunt Rosl. She always wants you to visit. Henry already left to be with his son. It's no fun to stay in the house alone."

"All right, I'll call Rosl," Mama answered reluctantly.

We were thankful that we had left. On our return, we found both our beds covered with broken glass from windows shattered by a doodlebug that had landed nearby.

DURING ALL THOSE MONTHS, WE waited for my visa to make our intended trip to America a reality. Mama had already received hers, since she was on the Czech quota. I was on the Austrian one, which was much more in demand, and therefore took longer. Under no circumstances, however, would she leave without me.

"I did it once, when I sent you to Czechoslovakia, which I have regretted many times, and I will not be separated from you again," she said decisively. And so, we waited for weeks, then months, then years. When my visa finally arrived, we—that is, Mama—was elated. Stamped on it was an expiration date.

"Oh, good," Mama said. "Now we'll both apply for an exit permit, which we have to do by mail."

"Wouldn't it be faster to just go to that office and be done with it?" I asked.

"That's the regulation—by mail. The point is we had to wait for your visa because the reason—and proof—for leaving England has to be stated, and they want a copy of the visa," she told me.

She was happy at first but grew nervous as time went on, and checked each mail delivery only to be disappointed. When, after several months, the exit permit arrived, my visa had expired.

I made my way to the American Embassy in London to secure an extension. With that accomplished, we were ready to go, but, alas, there was no transportation available. From time to time, all departures were canceled until further notice. At other times, a small number of civilians was allowed on troopships that for various reasons were bringing soldiers back to the States. In the meantime, the exit permit expired. I didn't mind, because I would rather have stayed in England than immigrate to the U.S. If Papa could have come over instead of Mama and me traveling to him, I would have been much happier. Our friend, Henry, wanted her to stay; he liked her a lot, but she didn't feel that way. I found a letter recently addressed to my father, in which she wrote, *I can't wait to be together with you again. Except for being with Lisl, I am so unhappy here.* I had been unaware of that. *I was quite* happy. I worked, had my friends, and felt and sounded more English every day. I had become every bit as patriotic as Minniehaha. I had no accent and passed as English.

The day arrived when I turned to Mama and teased, "Well, we have our visas, the exit permits have been extended, the ban on leaving the country has been lifted—all we need now is a ship, Mama. Are you happy? Are you ready to go?"

"It's not as simple as you think," she answered in a melancholy tone. "Transportation is tricky. I can't go and talk to anybody to try and secure passage for us, because departures are kept secret, so we have to wait, keep our fingers crossed that all documents are still valid, and be ready to leave at a moment's notice."

"All right, okay," I said. "So we'll wait."

We waited two years for all documents, rules, and ship tickets to be in sync.

I visited and telephoned Minniehaha from time to time during those years, and, when we were advised of our departure date, I had enough time to go to Epsom to bid her a final farewell. I didn't have time to stay for tea, so we sat in the living room at 38 Ashley Road, the house we had moved to from Ingleside.

"I am glad your long wait has come to an end, Lisl," she said as she put a hand on my leg, "and I am sure you will be happy being re-united with your parents. I would like you to have a little keepsake, which I hope will serve as a memory of your time in England."

She got up, took a small box from the top of the piano, and presented me with a silver pin that had an oval jade in the middle and two little corals on either side.

"Thank you so much, Minniehaha." I opened it and sincerely said, "I love it, and I'm going to put it on right now." As I did so, I continued, "You know I am not really going to say a final good-bye. I intend to come back to England soon."

"And I will be happy to see you. Take good care of yourself, give my love to your mother, and thank you for coming to see me."

With a hug, and a final "and thank you again for everything," which came from my heart, I dashed out to catch the bus back to Kingston-on-Thames.

23

ARRIVING IN THE U.S.

WE FINALLY MADE IT," MAMA said, looking pleased as we boarded the *S.S. Aquitania,* surrounded by soldiers and other uniformed men.

This large ship, one of the "grand trio" express liners (the other two were the *Lusitania* and *Mauretania*), had four smokestacks, had been elegantly furnished before the war, and boasted many amenities, most of which had been removed for our crossing, since as much space as possible had been converted to accommodate returning armed forces from the European front. We were among the handful of civilians allowed to board.

The vessel was fast, enabling it to travel alone rather than in the protection of a convoy, which would have resulted in proceeding at a much slower speed. Instead, she zig-zagged across the ocean, thus making herself less vulnerable to German submarines.

There was some entertainment at night, but during the day we did not have the luxury of using the pool—I think it was boarded up—or lying comfortably and lazily in a deckchair on one of the decks. We were constantly on the alert for an emergency, but were fortunate in a smooth passage—courtesy of the calm weather, except for two rough days during which almost all, except my mother, became seasick. Strolling on the deck to recover in the fresh air, I became re-acquainted with some of the officers from the previous days, one in particular, as well as a girl my age.

The *Aquitania* reached Halifax, Canada, the closest point of land, without any incident. From there, we took the train to New York City, with a stopover of several hours in Montreal. We used that time for a little sightseeing and some window-shopping. My mouth dropped open, and my eyes grew wide, as we passed a grocery store.

"Look, Mama, just *look* at all the oranges and grapefruits on display, and all those vegetables. I've forgotten what they look like. It's not just one or two—they are *piled up*." Mama bought us each an orange—a delicacy after not seeing one for several years.

After boarding the train again, we prepared to meet my father. We did not talk much, each of us silent in her own thoughts about the upcoming meeting. I conjured up several different scenes: the three of us arms around one another, all talking at once. Or my parents hugging for a long time, with me standing next to them, wondering when my turn would come. In a third scenario, I imagined my father quite fat and not looking the way I remembered him.

When we actually did meet, my parents had no trouble recognizing each other instantly, and I was glad to see Papa was not fat. He was waiting at the gate as we walked up the steps, waving his hat held high before we reached the top. In fact, he was thinner than I remembered him, and I didn't think he looked older. The last time I'd seen him, I'd been less than thirteen. I was then nineteen. Both my parents were all smiles, eyes glistening with tears of happiness. Papa, in a suit and tie, was the first to speak. "It is so good to see you. I worried about the ocean crossing, but no more. Now we're all safe and together again. I can't tell you how I've waited for this moment."

"I can't believe this is real—it's too good to be true," Mama said, "I am so happy."

"It's so wonderful to see you again, Liserl. I've waited for this with longing," Papa said, turning to me with kisses and a hug. While I was also very happy to see him again—we had wished for just that for so many years—I didn't feel as exuberant as my mother. Those kisses seemed awkward and strange. I didn't feel quite as close to him at that moment as I had in my dreamworld while we had been separated.

Putting his arm around Mama, after hugging and kissing her repeatedly and reaching for me with his other hand, he chuckled and said, "I won't let go of you two again, so we have to get a porter for the luggage."

The sun managed to cut through the clouds between the rain showers that April day, but by the time Papa had hailed a taxi and we were driving up Eighth Avenue, it was drizzling constantly, not helping my mood. I didn't feel as cheerful as I thought I should. I was surprised to see papers and all kinds of garbage lying around on the sidewalks and in the street. Dirt and chaos surrounded us. There were so many people gathered at each corner, waiting to cross, that, at first, I thought something had happened for such crowds to gather in one place. I had seen photographs of Fifth Avenue and thought that was how all of New York City looked.

The living quarters Papa had chosen were the next shock. They were in a rooming house where I had my own room, and my parents shared another. Stowed away in a little alcove were a two-flame stove and a tiny refrigerator.

Papa had only recently found a job through a friend. He was fifty-one years old when he arrived in the U.S. and was considered too old for several job openings. Also, his English was passable, but not great. Mama's was much better. He told us that he had walked from the Eighties all the way downtown to the Hebrew Immigrant Aid Society (HIAS) for lunch to save bus fare— a nickel at that time. He had scrimped and saved over the years but couldn't afford a better, more expensive place to live.

For me, it was the third adjustment in six years. Although I had challenged Mrs. Harter's values and, often prompted by my teenage status, expressed my opposition to her preferences in speech, manners, and rules, I had internalized a great deal of her attitude and her ways. In some respects it was easier, and at times even satisfying, to act like a big shot, confronting her without bearing the responsibility of actually being one, in comparison to feeling that roles had reversed, which was the case when I first lived together with Mama again. She revived in New York, but I was still approached to make certain decisions.

ONE OF THE MEN I'D MET on the *Aquitania* was an American pilot whose job in the war had been to ferry planes across to England. He was fairly tall and very handsome in his uniform, and we made a date. When he came to take me out two days after our arrival, I introduced him to my father. They chatted politely for a short time, after which my father ended the conversation with, "It was nice to meet you. Have a good time. I want my daughter home by 10:30."

"Yes, sir," the pilot replied. I never saw him again. I should have realized right away that a gap existed between my father's values and mine.

Papa thought I was a snob. I felt he misunderstood me, because I didn't think I had anything to be snobbish about. I was far from feeling secure. He, on the other hand, had yet to move ahead six years, to come to grips with the fact that I was no longer the child he had known. That must have been hard for him. Of course, I made a big mistake when, during dinner one evening, as I brought the fork to my mouth, I declared, "You know, food does taste better when you use silver utensils."

He was furious. "Who do you think you are?" he raged at me. "I scraped and saved and counted every penny to buy the ones we are using. Is that what matters to you, rather than being together again?"

I apologized, feeling ashamed for my remark. Secretly, however, I still thought it was so. Furthermore, I hated the way we lived, wondering—sometimes out loud—when we would move to a decent apartment.

It took a lot of work, mostly on the part of my father, to

lessen the gulf between us. He did succeed—after months of trial and error. I was old enough for some reasonable talk, but mostly I came to recognize his love, his kindness, his patience, and his willingness to change. He learned to neither forbid something nor to give me orders, but he was protective when he felt it was necessary.

In the beginning, before I had formed other friendships, the only other young person he knew was Erica, the girl I'd met on the *Aquitania*. Compared to me, she was a *femme fatale*. About my age and height, her dark eyes and her thick black hair, combined with long red fingernails, gave her a striking appearance. She wore a diamond ring from her Australian fiancé (she was on her way to meet him), yet she was the one who suggested going to dances, club meetings, and other places where young people congregated. We had a great time together meeting guys, dancing, going out, and enjoying ourselves.

President Roosevelt died on April 12, 1945—two or three days after our arrival. Both Mama and I felt sad, but we were unable to share my father's profound grief. That, and our continued interest in the king and queen and their two daughters, the princesses, were incomprehensible to Papa.

Barely three weeks later, on May 8, V-E Day was announced. Erica and I found ourselves in Times Square. In the midst of the celebrations, I thought, *What am I doing here? I don't belong here. I should be celebrating in England. How I'd love to be on Trafalgar Square now. Except for those who have friends or family in the armed forces, people here don't know what it means that the war is over. No more air raids, no more blackouts, no more food rationing, and no more not having some provisions at all.*

Anybody coming from England found the food rationing in the U.S. was not really rationing by comparison.

24

LIVING WITH MY PARENTS IN
NEW YORK CITY (MY FOURTH HOME)

ALL THREE OF US—MY parents and I—did our best to adjust. To be reunited as a family was satisfying. To find a suitable job was less so.

Communication had its problems, even socially. Mama and I stopped at a Horn and Hardart automat one day, only to be surprised that the server behind the counter could not understand us, and we had difficulty understanding *his* English, which ended in our pointing to the meal we wanted. Since I was an immigrant, people were frequently surprised to hear me speak English without an accent. The very thing I had been so proud of in England—my flawless English—became a hindrance. Some guys I met labeled me conceited.

I found a job as a secretary in a small law firm shortly after my arrival. One of the partners was out of town when I was hired. Several days after his return, a loud commotion erupted in the next room, and soon I overheard: "Why did you hire her?

Was it because of her red hair? She can't get the dictation straight." He was yelling, and he was correct. I had trouble understanding the partners' rapid American speech, and had to interrupt frequently to ask him to repeat. I was fired.

Getting another job, and yet another one, before I ended at M. Lowenstein & Sons, a well-known textile firm that produced Wamsutta sheets, was not too hard. I did well in the nine or ten years I spent there, especially in 1952, on my return from my first trip to Europe.

Mama, too, found a job. Relaxing on the sofa in the living room one summer evening, she announced triumphantly: "I really like my job at Bonwit Teller." It was a high-class apparel store on Fifth Avenue. "I'm working in the corset department. Maria, a German woman, apparently likes me. She sits next to me and has befriended me, and she has taught me everything there is to know about making a garment from scratch."

"I, too, like it, Mama, that you are working there. I love the discount I got last week on the suit I bought."

Mama learned quickly. She was also good at picking up from just watching, so that by the time she left her employ at Bonwit's she was a proficient corsetiere. Papa encouraged her to open her own store on Columbus Avenue in the Seventies. She ventured into making special bathing suits, as well as garments according to medical prescription, all of which helped in attracting a great neighborhood clientèle. Not only that—my father gave up his job in New Jersey, to which he traveled daily, to do the bookkeeping and other tasks that needed his attention.

By that time, Papa had overcome the hurdle of the idea of

moving, but not before, some time earlier, in answer to my prodding, he admonished me with, "Be realistic. What are you thinking?"

"Well, Papa, I thought I was. After all, you are working now, so is Mama, and I am, too. I thought we could afford to move to West End Avenue. I visited someone there who said rents were affordable."

Instead, we moved to a five-room apartment on Ninety-first Street, near Broadway. I liked the location—close to the subway station, within walking distance of a European bakery where Papa frequently bought fresh bread, *apfelstrudel*, or Linzer torte, as well as close to stores on Broadway. I picked out one in particular that had dresses I liked.

It was no longer embarrassing to bring friends home. The living room's curved, light green sofa, and the matching striped arm chairs, looked good on one of the Persian carpets, enhanced by thin white curtains and heavier drapes on the windows. The glass cocktail table in front of the sofa, and a reading lamp next to another armchair, made it a comfortable, friendly room. The den/dining room next to the kitchen was cozy with a dark-red-and-brown carpet, which supported an early American wooden sideboard—Mama's pride and joy. The upper part had shelves on which she displayed plates of various origins—hand-painted Austrian designs, Hungarian and Czech patterns, some expressing national pride, others just colorful impressions.

MY GREAT DESIRE, ALMOST A need, to continue my studies brought me to the admissions office at Hunter College. The person who looked at my Sherwood School report from England suppressed a laugh when she read that I was being hindered in my tennis playing by an unsuitable racquet, or that I did well in French.

"With no grades, there is no way for us to evaluate where you stand scholastically," I was told, and was advised to take the high school equivalency test. While I prepared for that, I enrolled at City College, which offered a program of non-matriculated courses, which, if I maintained high enough grades, would later count towards a degree. By the time I married, I had accumulated two years towards my bachelor's degree by attending night classes.

I was lucky to have Erica, whom I'd met on the *Aquitania,* as my friend. She telephoned. "Can you meet me at the St. James Theater in twenty minutes? Let's try to see *Oklahoma.*"

"Yes, I'll be there," I told her. I picked up my sweater from the floor, gave Mama a quick kiss, and hopped on the subway. Erica and I attended many performances on the spur of the moment—standing room, if necessary. Living close to the Ninety-first Street subway stop made that easy, and if the show was sold out, I was home again in less than twenty minutes.

She had given up on getting married in Australia, and we spent more time together. She introduced me to Jerry, a German refugee she had met at a singles' function. He and I spent many evenings on the famous roof of the Astor Hotel on Times Square, dancing under the auspices of the then popular Big Bands— Tommy Dorsey, Xavier Cugat, Louis Prima, and others.

I wasn't ready for marriage, which he had proposed, but I recoiled from Irenli's remark. She was visiting from Palestine. One evening, we emerged from the subway as Jerry was approaching. Neither he nor I had a chance to say anything before she blurted out, "You can't come up for dinner. We didn't cook enough."

She visited again two years later. I was still wishing for a loving sister and was happy that we managed to spend two pleasant days together. She greatly admired a gold bracelet I was wearing, and mentioned how lucky I was to own one—that she didn't have anything like that. Since I had two, I gave her one. That did not stop her, a few days later, from asking with a smirk, "Are you going out tonight with Harry *mit der schiefen Goschen?*" (Harry with the crooked snout). His mouth turned up slightly on one side.

She returned to Palestine, which freed me of being judged in my choice of dates and of her constant put-downs. I had various boyfriends, which was perfectly acceptable in those days, as long as the relationship remained on a certain level.

Then I met Sol. It must have been through a friend's introduction, because my father did not check up on him. By and large, he had by then given up seeing me as thirteen years old (I was in my early twenties then), which greatly improved our relationship, so that we could like and love each other again. However, Papa wasn't able to judge a man's character, or understand his background, if he was American, the way he could figure out a European.

Sol's good humor and ready smile made him a welcome visitor. Several years older than I, he served as my mentor. His blue eyes followed me lovingly around the room.

There was talk of marriage. He was thoughtful, protective, and he loved me, but as time passed, I recognized that our likes and dislikes, as well as our values, were quite different. His background was Orthodox, to which he no longer adhered, he claimed, but when I heard mutterings about keeping a kosher home, and that he would want our children to attend a yeshiva (Jewish religious school), I knew it wouldn't work. However, as always, parting was hard and we still saw each other from time to time.

25

MEETING JACK

THE YEARS BETWEEN 1945 AND 1952 proceeded in a calmer and more predictable manner than the previous ones, after I had overcome the obstacles with my father. By the time we moved to the apartment on Ninety-first Street and I started work at Lowenstein & Sons, life was pretty normal. I had a decent job, had achieved a good relationship with my parents, had received my high school equivalency diploma, and was enrolled in evening classes at City College, studying for a bachelor's degree, and concentrating on my social life.

Early in June 1952 I received a phone call from my friend Renee, whom I had known for some years. Her big nose and poor skin texture did not detract from her overall attractiveness, because she was bright, vivacious, and her throaty, quick laugh made her eyes twinkle.

"Please come up and keep me company," she pleaded. "I had to dance with the busboy last night, because there's no one here."

She had gone to Young's Gap, a hotel in the Catskills, for a week's vacation.

"I can't come," I told her. "I'm working."

"Come for the week-end at least. You don't have to worry about clothes. All you need are shorts and a dress for the evening."

"Well, I'm not——-"

"Oh, come on," she interrupted. "If you're a good friend, you can do it."

She expounded some more on being friends and the meaning of friendship in her frank, forthright manner. I knew my parents would agree with her—they, especially my mother, had formed a close relationship with her, maybe because she had lost her parents when she was young.

When I tried to enter the dining room at the hotel in the morning, wearing shorts, I was stopped by the maitre d'.

"That's all right. Come upstairs, and I'll lend you a skirt," Renee said, standing next to me. I felt embarrassed all during breakfast and afterwards, too, walking around in the lobby in a skirt that was quite long on me.

The afternoon of that very warm day, crowned by glorious sunshine, passed much better. We spent most of the time in the pool or lounging by the side of it, where a lot of the other newly arrived guests had also congregated. Among the newcomers was a foursome: Rose and her boyfriend Manny, and his friends Rudy and Jack.

Rose and Manny were both good-looking and tall, and it soon became apparent that they had been together for a long time.

Rudy, incredibly thin, and Jack, not so thin, were somewhat shorter. Rudy engaged me in conversation after my swim, and the four of them and I arranged to meet in the evening. Renee was off somewhere talking to another guy.

After dinner, we gathered around a little table in the night-club, ordered drinks, and listened to the music. Although Rudy was talking and looking at me, Jack asked me to dance. We had spoken briefly at the pool in the afternoon.

Jack made some uncomplimentary remarks about my rumba, possibly because *he* was not very good at it. We laughed about it and continued dancing. I felt I had enough practice in dancing from the days at the Astor Hotel. The following day, he approached me in the dining room at breakfast, and we made a poolside date for the afternoon.

Before I left New York City, I had asked Sol if he wanted to drive up with me.

"I'm very busy in the shop right now. Have to finish an order I promised a customer. Tell you what—I'll come up Sunday and take you and Renee home."

He arrived around three o'clock, scanning the scene. I waved him over to join us and introduced him to Jack and his friends. Even Renee had decided to be part of the group. The foursome left to drive home after about an hour.

The ride back later with Sol and Renee was pleasant, because they didn't spar with each other the way they sometimes had in the past.

Two days later, I met Renee. We usually dropped in at a little luncheonette near school after class, to exchange news over a cup of coffee, before heading home.

"That guy Jack really liked you," she said as soon as we sat down.

"Don't be silly," I answered. "He didn't even ask me for my phone number."

"I can't believe you're so naïve. I heard him talk about your father—he found out you lived with your parents, and he asked whether you lived in Manhattan. You mentioned your street."

I SAW SOL AGAIN. HE mentioned Jack briefly but also talked about the others he'd met. During a disagreement at dinner, we decided not to see each other for a couple of weeks.

Jack *did* call me, and, under the circumstances, I made a date with him. On our third date, as we drove to an outdoor concert at Lewisohn Stadium on 138th Street, he felt compelled to say, "I really like you a lot, but I feel I must tell you that I'm not interested in marriage."

I liked him, too, and although I did not expect a proposal, I was surprised by the statement, and answered, "Well, I guess that leaves me free to date others."

We met again before I left for Europe on July 3. I liked his sense of humor, his looks, and his intelligence. His glasses sometimes slipped down his small nose, which made him look like the proverbial professor. I also liked his decisiveness. His car radio was tuned to WQXR, the classical music station, which started to play as soon as he turned on the ignition. He did that to impress me—and he succeeded. I found out later his appreciation of classical music was, in fact, not great.

26

BACK TO ENGLAND

THE NEWSPAPERS WERE NOTING THAT the newly built *S.S. United States* would soon take off on her maiden voyage to England and France. Even more important was its aim to become the fastest ship to cross the Atlantic.

I wanted to go to England on that ship in the worst way. I had become a U.S. citizen the previous year. I was in the possession of an American passport, and I had saved some money. There was nothing to stop me. Besides, my parents were supportive, saying, "We are willing to subsidize your trip."

"Oh, that's great, but I can't accept that."

"Yes, dear, you can." My mother sounded convincing as she continued, "Papa and I put the money aside that you contributed to the household, and we'll be glad to give that to you." I looked over at my father, who was nodding in agreement, smiling at me. I gave them both a hug and thanked them. They, especially Papa, were happy to do that. He was acting on his values—to support your family in every way—and it gave him a chance to take care of me.

Supportive as he was, however, Papa felt I needed some advice: "If you really want to get on that ship, you'll have to give something to that Mr. Johnson at the shipping company."

"I don't think that's necessary, Papa," I answered, fumbling through some brochures on Europe. "He guaranteed me a ticket, and I have a feeling I can trust him. I've been calling him every other day, promising a gift from Europe. If he doesn't sell me a ticket by a certain date, I'll go and see him." His office was downtown on Broadway.

He came through with a cabin space in third (tourist) class at $170.00. I was thrilled.

I had mapped out my itinerary, but only in a vague fashion: England; a stop-over in France; meeting my aunt Lore and her husband, Edgar, in Italy; meeting my aunt Poldi (now living in Sweden) in Austria, where she'd gone to a spa; and meeting Lottie (the refugee chambermaid at Mrs. Harter's in England) in Switzerland, where she was vacationing with her husband and two children.

I had no fixed return date or any exact dates to meet those people either, except Lore and Edgar in Italy. My aunt Mitzi in England was going to be my coordinator and official news anchor.

AT THE TIME, I WAS still working at Lowenstein & Sons. I had been employed there for more than three years when I planned my trip. I told my boss, in confidence, that I might be gone a couple more days than my two-week vacation, because I had to take care of some business in Austria. I didn't think at that time that the extra couple of days would stretch into nine weeks.

"I'll keep your secret," he answered, smiling. "And don't forget to send a postcard." After all, *he* was not paying my salary. He himself was an employee in that vast machinery.

The previous week, at 9:15 a.m., Mr. Lowenstein's secretary (he was chairman of the board) summoned my boss to his office. I'd answered the phone, saying, "I'm sorry, Mr. K. is away from his desk."

Mr. K. had been late that morning and was grateful that I hadn't divulged it. The firm had stiff rules, even for executives. He might very well have been reprimanded. People like me had to punch a time card. Mine was equally sprinkled with blue and red ink (for being late, though I tried to be on time). I got away with it because they needed me and liked me. I was a good, reliable worker. Before there had been a permanent opening for a secretary to one of the more important executives, I'd worked for minor ones and, whenever necessary, been called to fill in when a secretary was sick, including the higher-up executives. My shorthand was good, so that at the end of the day the letters I returned to the boss for signing were correct. In contrast to some of the other young women, I was also able to handle phone calls maturely, make appointments while the man was out of the office, and deliver proper messages. In that way, I got to know most of the higher-up executives.

I had decided earlier that I had perfectly good reasons for making the trip. I liked New York City, but I was homesick for England. My relationship with Sol had practically ended, and as far as Jack was concerned, I knew I was taking a chance. "You know how I still feel about England," I told him. "I have the opportunity to go there on this maiden voyage, and I wouldn't want to miss it. I feel our relationship is grounded well enough to continue when I return."

He agreed, adding, "I'll be green with envy." I was relieved and also thought that, since he was not ready to get married, there was nothing wrong with what I was doing.

ON JULY 3, 1952, A beautiful summer day, Jack saw me off as I boarded that grand ship for my first return trip to Europe. "I'm sorry I can't stay. I must get back to work. Have a great trip and don't forget to write," he said, hugging me. He kissed me good-bye and vanished into the crowd.

I was directed to my cabin by a good-looking young attendant in bright-white starched pants and shirt. He was friendly, not quite sure of the way, and he smiled apologetically every time he took the wrong turn. The cabin, when he finally located it, was furnished with three berths, a sink, three chairs, a little table, a closet, and a small bathroom. I was traveling with a lot of luggage and had to figure out what I would wear on the crossing and have the rest stored. My roommates were two German women, which troubled me somewhat. At the time, I was not kindly disposed towards anybody German; but they were pleasant enough and our paths rarely crossed.

As I started to explore the ship, I met another young woman from New York. We teamed up. She asked, "Have you seen the lounge yet? If not, you must see how big it is, considering this is

Tourist Class." We marveled at the large oval windows, the many sofas, armchairs, and the concert piano. We continued our exploration. This time *I* noticed a theater, lots of small rooms that were really not so small, a library, and, as we continued into First Class (my first of many visits there), the beautiful ballroom with its crystal chandeliers, and the dining room, all done in modern furniture; the movie theater, reading rooms—one set up for chess games—and the paneled library with its leather sofas, easy chairs, and tables with straight chairs, as well as countless other rooms. It left us both breathless.

At one point, I commented to my new-found friend, "Have you noticed the sense of gaiety and excitement on the ship?"

"Yes, I have," she said animatedly. "I must say, I didn't see a single tear coming from any of the seventeen hundred passengers crowded at the railing of the deck as they waved good-bye to their friends and relatives."

"On the contrary," I answered. "There were hordes of curious onlookers gathered at the pier, including the ones hoping for a cancellation. Maybe *they* shed a tear or two." There hadn't been a single cancellation.

The ship was escorted out of the Hudson River and into the open sea by a whistle-blowing tugboat plowing the way in front and others accompanying us on both sides. She returned the salutes with short, booming blasts.

As I headed back to my cabin, I had no idea which of the nineteen elevators I should take. I asked the first guy in uniform I met, "Would you direct me to the tourist class?"

"Not quite sure, miss, but if you go down a flight of stairs, you should see an elevator that will take you there."

After inquiring three more times of one of the almost one thousand crew members and receiving similarly uncertain answers each time, I made it back to the cabin in about twenty minutes. It really did not matter. It gave me a chance to see the swimming pool, cross the layout for shuffleboard on one of the decks, and as I stopped to look around on yet another one, a crew member in his white, starched uniform approached me, "May I reserve a chaise for you, miss?" I was thus introduced to the good life. The passengers, as well as the crew, all seemed to be walking around with smiling faces.

At dinner, I asked the waiter, "Are you expecting bad weather? I see you're filling the glasses only half full and pushing the plates and cutlery towards the center."

"Not at all, miss. It's a precautionary measure, because there are a couple of flaws on this ship. One of them is that they overlooked putting an edge around the tabletops to prevent plates from falling off if it's stormy. The other thing," he continued, "is that the swinging doors in and out of the kitchen move in the same direction. We have to be careful carrying trays full of food out of the kitchen not to bump into returning waiters. I apologize for any delays this may cause in serving you."

There was another flaw he did not mention: The doors between classes were left unlocked. I took full advantage of that. When I returned to my cabin after the first evening's dinner, one of my roommates was in the room. Watching me, she commented, "You're taking off your clothes. Are you going to bed early?"

"Good heavens, no. On the contrary, I'm changing into something more formal, and I'm going over to first class."

That's where all the action took place. There, I found myself face to face with Margaret Truman (Harry Truman was president at the time), friendly, sweet, smiling, and, to the relief of many, not singing. She did complain, "I can't go anywhere without being followed by secret service men." I also met Commodore Manning, decked out handsomely in his dark uniform, medals on his chest and gold epaulets on his shoulders, as befit the captain of the ship. He approached me. "I'm sure we've met before. Just tell me your name again." He introduced me to some old ladies sitting at his table. They stared, trying to figure out who I was. He was about to sit down, after motioning me to sit at his table. In the few intervening seconds, as I was secretly hoping he would ask me to dance, Miss Truman passed by and he made his way over to her.

Evenings were filled with fun. Dinner in tourist class, a quick change of dress, and music and dancing in first class, accompanied by aimless, easy chatter about the excitement of the ship's speed. The anticipation of achieving her goal did not evaporate in the daytime, either. There was no sign of sea sickness, no bad moods, no complaints. Everybody was clearly in a jovial, accepting, happy frame of mind.

DURING THE DAY, I RELAXED on my assigned chaise on the deck, wearing a turquoise nylon dress and half-covered with a thin blanket to keep the breeze off. I sipped a cold drink, which the steward had just served me, and marveled over my good luck as

I looked at the never-ending blue ocean, its glistening waves topped by white foam, and the almost cloudless sky, from which the sun was shining its blessing on all of us. I felt content and peaceful, and was actually glad to be alone for some time to allow the serenity to sink in. *Returning to England,* I thought happily. *What a different crossing this is from the one when I left there.* I read for a while, then got up to join my new friend for afternoon tea served at another part of the large deck. We snacked on finger sandwiches filled with egg salad, ham, cheese, fish salad, cookies, and a choice of cakes and drinks.

In the evening I met Mr. Taylor, a man in his fifties. A first-class passenger who always wore a suit and tie, he was an executive at Westinghouse. He sometimes kept me company when I went to first class.

The last two nights on board were sleepless. The night the ship broke the speed record, I stayed up late, dancing until the orchestra stopped playing. After that, most of the passengers drifted out onto the deck. Some of the musicians followed and continued to play for us. I went to bed at four in the morning. At 6:30 a.m., when it became official that the ship was breaking the speed record, I received a phone call from Mr. Taylor. "You must come at once to the Navigator's Bridge to celebrate the historical event of passing Bishop's Rock."

"What did you say?" I asked drowsily.

"Come quickly. Just come as you are. She is making history."

Indeed, she was. She reached Bishop's Rock on July 7, after three days and ten hours.

Passengers congregated on the deck again. Some were still in their evening clothes, others in their pajamas, and still others (and I belonged in that category) had a coat thrown over a skirt and blouse. It did not matter; we were all too excited with what was happening, which made us very accepting of each other. Nobody cared or looked or made comments on what each one wore.

She was very important to Mr. Taylor. He had been in suspense for three days. He explained, "Much of the ship's equipment has been manufactured by Westinghouse. It's machinery, and you never know what may happen." He was at that moment the proudest, most excited, and happiest of men. I, too, felt proud and excited to partake in that history-making event.

The musicians were still on the deck, and as we passed Bishop's Rock, they played "The Star Spangled Banner," "God Save the Queen," and the "Marseillaise," followed by "Yankee Doodle Dandy," "Tipperary," and other American songs. Passengers were dancing, at one point forming a conga line, laughing and shouting all the way. Skipping, jumping, or hopping around was also acceptable. The prevailing mood was to celebrate. Standing still was out of the question.

The following night also called for celebrations; it was the last night on board. We had been lucky with good weather and smooth sailing, which helped to keep passengers in a continuously festive mood, able and ready for anything as long as it was fun and exciting.

The day we neared Southampton, a great reception awaited us. We were met by tug boats, fire boats, excursion craft, and small vessels, as well as planes flying overhead. Welcoming whistles sounded everywhere, coming from all sides and all around us. The deep-throated steam whistles of the big ship responded. Crowds of people, who had gathered on the shore, were waving frantically, and we were waving back.

27

MY SUMMER IN EUROPE

TIRED AND WORN OUT AFTER two busy, sleepless nights, I reached Aunt Mitzi's house in the afternoon. Uncle Victor greeted me: "So glad to see you again, Lisl. I cooked a wonderful dinner for you."

"Glad to see you, too, Uncle Victor. I think I can smell a goulash. Is it all right if I just take a nap for an hour first? It's only five o'clock, so I have time before dinner." My nap lasted until the following morning, and I missed my uncle's special dinner.

The newspapers were full of descriptions of the maiden voyage, and I was bubbling over with my own tales. The British *Punch* magazine dryly remarked, "After the loud and fantastic claims made in advance for the liner *United States*, it comes as something of a disappointment to find them all true."

AUNT MITZI HADN'T CHANGED MUCH. She still had short black hair, liquid, teary eyes, and wore what I considered an unfashionable dress, but she was nice to me and interested to hear about

Mama—her sister. She put me up in a small room on the second floor. There were several bedrooms in that ample house, which had had refugees lodged there during and after the war, all of whom had left, and only my aunt, uncle, and their daughter Erica remained. They ended up owning the house. The furnishings were old and unimaginatively placed in a utilitarian manner, but comfortable enough for three people.

Erica, too, still looked the same—very pretty, her black hair in a pageboy, but somewhat heavier than she'd been seven years earlier.

The following day, during lunch, when they had heard enough about the crossing, I was surprised to hear Uncle Victor's suggest, "Why don't you and Erica go to the tea dance at. . ." or, another time, "You should take Erica along with you when you go to the museum." I was not at all interested in going to a tea dance to meet a man, but the idea of taking her was puzzling. When I was still living in England, I remember my mother wanted so much for Erica to take me to meet one of the many "boys" she had boasted of meeting and knowing. She'd never invited me. I'd had no boyfriends then.

Uncle Victor, too, appeared unchanged. I knew him quite well, but, for some reason, I had retained an image of him as I watched him bend down, a little clumsily because of his weight, to throw a couple of shillings into the little stove to produce some heat in the room Mama had rented after I had left Mrs. Harter's house. He was a good cook, and enjoyed making the food as long as we appreciated his Austrian cuisine—although he was Czech. On my last evening with them, just as we were enjoying the schnitzel he'd made with *nockerln* (small dumplings) and cucumber salad, he put down his knife and fork, gave me a sideways glance, and earnestly said, "You've changed, Lisl. America has changed you."

"What do you mean?" I asked.

"You are now an attractive, self-assured young woman," he continued, nodding a couple of times for emphasis.

Oh, little does he know, I thought. I was far from self-assured. My appearance may have undergone a change. I had started to apply lipstick and mascara, and my extensive wardrobe included some newly bought dresses, one made of nylon—the new wonder fabric.

I had expected to stay in England three or four days, then continue to Rome to meet my aunt Lore and her husband Edgar from Pittsburgh. (Lore, Mama's youngest sister, was the one who had taken me across the border into Czechoslovakia in 1938.) Aunt Mitzi, who served as liaison between Lore and me, told me at dinner, "I had a telegram from Lore. She and Edgar are delayed, and they won't be in Rome until the fourteenth. Of course, you'll stay longer with us."

"Good, I'd like that. Also, it'll give me a chance to make a leisurely visit to Mrs. Harter, rather than rushing it."

I dialed the never forgotten telephone number—Epsom 1104—and when I asked, "Minniehaha?" I heard her familiar voice, "Lisl, is that you darling?" Half surprised to hear "darling," but one-hundred percent pleased, I arranged a date and took a bus to visit her. She was in her seventies by then, still good looking, still standing erect. After an early tea, she suggested,

"Shall we drive up to the Downs for old times' sake?"

"Yes, I'd love that," I answered, careful not to add that I hoped it wouldn't be too much for her.

We retraced our steps where we had exercised the dogs during the War, but now the racetrack was smooth, kept in shape for the big derby.

"How nice of you to think of me, Lisl, and how kind that you made the trip to visit me," she said as we strolled along.

"But of course, Minniehaha," I replied. "I wouldn't come to England and not see you." We chatted more easily than in the years when I lived with her.

She continued, "And, tell me, darling, how are your parents, especially your mother. Is she well?"

"Yes, she is, thank you. She sends her regards to you."

After some more polite conversation and inquiries about various people, I took my leave, Minniehaha saying, "Thank you again, darling, for your kindness in coming to see me." What I wouldn't have given ten years earlier to be addressed as "darling" several times in one conversation.

There was time to plan one more activity before I took off for the French Riviera. Shirin and Unity had arranged a party in my honor in the home of their mother, Hilda, who lived in Hampstead. Besides Hilda, their grandmother, and several other relatives who attended, their father, Stanley, took the train from Wales where he was living then especially to see me.

At the party, Shirin asked to talk to me privately. We withdrew to another room, where she immediately turned to face me and said, "I wanted to tell you something. When we were both living at Minniehaha's, I was quite deceitful with you. I made things up so I would also get the shoes or dress that Minniehaha was going to buy for you. I did not need the things, and if you went somewhere, I found some reason why I should go. I think it was terrible of me, and I want to apologize to you."

What a surprise! I was dumbfounded. I did remember how deceitful she had been, and that I had recognized it at the time. I did not tell her that. Instead, I said, "I think you are very brave, Shirin, and it is big of you to admit that to me. I want to thank you. It means a lot to me to hear you say these words, and I think it is wonderful that you did. Not many people would. Thank you again." We hugged and returned to join the others, both feeling happier for this revelation. We are still friends and in touch with each other.

THE NEXT DAY, I FLEW to Nice. One week of my vacation was gone by then.

On the plane, an elderly gentleman started a conversation during which he told me, "I'm excited and eager to get to my hotel, because I'm expecting a telegram from my daughter to let me know that I've become a grandfather." His receding hair elongated his long face, and behind his glasses a contented look was visible. Wearing a suit and tie, combined with his kindly, polite manner and speech, made him unmistakably English. Learning that I was traveling alone, he addressed me just before we landed.

"I am staying at the Grimaldi. Give me a call if you need anything."

I didn't bother writing down the name or the telephone number of this man in his sixties, thanked him, and left for my hotel.

When I woke up the next morning, I was itching all over. I didn't know what had happened. I sat up in bed, worried, as I watched something small and black crawl on the sheet, then quickly disappear under the mattress. I had never been on my own like that before and didn't know how to handle my predicament. After much deliberation, I telephoned the Grimaldi.

The man listened to my worried tale, then said, "Well, you are in France now, you know, and it sounds like you had a visit from bedbugs. If you like, I will help you find a better hotel, but there's no guarantee that you won't find bedbugs there, too."

I felt disgusted, but since I couldn't afford a more expensive hotel, I asked to have my room changed. I closed my suitcases to make sure the little beasts wouldn't be transported, dressed very quickly, and left the room.

Just a few blocks from the hotel, the Promenade des Anglais came into view, lined with shops, cafes, and hotels on one side, palm trees and the scenic Baie des Anges on the other, the Mediterranean glistening in the usual hot July sun. I took in the view and meandered for a little while before catching the bus to Cannes, glitzy and glamorous, and more carefree than Nice. I could only experience the restaurants facing the water from the outside and try to imagine life on one of the sailboats, painted in lovely rainbow colors, or on one of the luxurious looking yachts anchored in the harbor. The streets were filled with women in shorts and halters of all colors, and men casually dressed, strolling in loafers or sandals under awnings of expensive shops. To me they looked glamorous in their wide brimmed hats and dark sunglasses.

The following day I went to the beach in Nice. I was in search of a sandy spot—all I could see were little cobblestones that served as the beach—when I spotted a girl I knew from New York. We didn't know each other well, but we hugged like two old best friends, lost and found. We watched the topless women parade in front of us—all shapes, sizes, and ages. I stared in admiration of their confidence; even old women, who, I thought, would have fared better in full bathing suits, strutted with utter self-assurance. Nobody besides us stared.

My newly found companion (I don't even remember her name) and I had such a good time talking and looking that, by the time I got back to the hotel, it was late and I'd missed the plane to Rome.

The concierge made arrangements for me to take the night train instead. He even procured a seat in a compartment. The train was overcrowded, mostly with young people, some of whom had to sit on their backpacks in the corridor for lack of seating space. The smell of food and crumpled paper from hamburgers, French fries, sausages, and pizza was only surpassed by the singing and loud talking, which, in turn, was interspersed with shouts and laughter. I don't think anybody slept or wanted to. If you had to go to the toilet, you literally had to step over legs, climb over squatting bodies, suitcases, and try not to land on uneaten packages of food and backpacks strewn on the floor.

ONCE IN ROME, SLEEPY AND bedraggled, I took a taxi to the Albergo Santa Clara, a small *pensione* located near the Pantheon,

and asked for Professor and Mrs. Foltin. I had been looking forward to seeing Lore again and, with some trepidation, Edgar. I'd liked her as a child, and we had grown closer as adults. She had met Edgar when he was her law professor at the University of Prague. She'd fled to England after Hitler's invasion of Czecho-
- slovakia, and he, although Catholic, also had to escape. He had voiced his liberal views too openly and had defended one of his Jewish students once too often. Somebody had come to his house one evening to warn him to leave right away, because he was about to be arrested. He left for England in 1939. Franziska, who was his wife at that time, did not want to go to England, and she returned to their house in Innsbruck, Austria. (He was Austrian).

Edgar and Lore immigrated to the United States, and after the war he divorced Franziska and married Lore. I did not see them in England, but we got together in the United States.

I knew Edgar primarily through Lore. She boasted of the books he had written, the important people he had met during his appointment to a special committee in Vienna after the war, his time as Dean of the University in Prague, his intellectual prowess, his popularity with students, and his reputation as an excellent teacher of criminal law, as well as his charm, his sense of humor, and his good looks. I used to wonder if she had left anything out. Here was a genius on a pedestal. I had met him only briefly once or twice. On one of those occasions, my sister had been eager to be engaged in conversation with him, and, frankly, although it was not her motive, I had been relieved to stay in the background.

The summer of 1952, quite unexpectedly, starting with the ocean crossing on the *S.S. United States*, turned into the most exciting one of my youth. It had another aspect, one that had a profound influence on me to this day.

28

MEETING EDGAR

WHEN EDGAR ENTERED THE LOBBY of the Albergo Santa Clara, where I had been waiting, my first question after a cordial greeting was, "Where is Lore?"

"My dear, young girl—" an expression he would often use during our next three weeks of travels— "that's a long story. Have you had breakfast yet? If not, allow me to invite you to have a bite to eat." I was speechless. The last thing I wanted was to be alone with him. Everything Lore had said about him raced through my mind as I found myself vis-à-vis this genius. *What will I talk about, and will I understand what he is talking about?* Maybe, he sensed my discomfort, standing there close to the front desk in the modest lobby. Tall, good looking, and dressed casually, he steered me into the little breakfast room next to the lobby. We chose a table between two windows, through which the July sun brightened up an otherwise uninteresting interior.

He lit his pipe, pushed some hair off his high forehead, a gesture I noticed often repeated, and, his eyes shining intelligently, explained, "Lore went to a university in Germany to do research for the book on Kafka she is writing." She was a professor of German at the University of Pittsburgh (she could not practice law in the U.S.). He continued, "I did not accompany her, because I refuse to set foot in Germany. The three of us—you, Lore, and I—will have to get together at a later date." He, too, was a professor at a university in Pittsburgh.

He asked, leaning towards me, "Well, now, what would you like to eat? Not that they have much choice in this place. You'll have to tell me about France, and the train ride you mentioned. You must be tired, so I hope a little food will refresh you."

All during breakfast he was friendly, interesting in his descriptions of what he'd been doing so far, charming, and low-key. I was pleasantly surprised that I did not find it difficult to be with him at all. Before we'd finished our continental breakfast of juice, coffee, and a roll, he wanted to know how long I intended to stay.

"Three, maybe four days. I'm not sure how long it will take to see what I had in mind."

"In that case, would you allow me to be your guide in Rome?" he asked. I felt flattered.

He waited while I quickly showered and changed my clothes and we set out on our first sightseeing trip together. On that hot, sunny day, already late morning, we took the bus to the Catacombs at his suggestion. From the last stop we still had to trudge for ten minutes, sweating as we proceeded along the Via Appia, a long, straight thoroughfare lined with poplar trees on both sides of the road, which afforded almost no shade. When we reached the Catacombs, we chose the German tour rather than the English one, since no waiting in the sun was required. Edgar fell into conversation with the guide, and that was the first time I heard that Barbara was the name of his guardian angel. That was also the name my aunt Lore had chosen when she changed religions, without ever commenting on it. At one point, I am not sure when, my aunt had converted to Catholicism, claiming it provided her with more meaning and greater satisfaction than the Jewish religion.

The Catacombs, dark and musty, were of greater interest to Edgar than to me. He knew the names and attributes of the various saints and sages entombed there, and stopped frequently with explanations to me.

When we emerged from the cool underground, the sun felt even hotter than before. We stopped for lunch at a little restaurant nearby at an outdoor table, shaded by an umbrella. It was so hot, and the flies gathered on the food as well as on my hands and face were so annoying and numerous, that I declared my intention of leaving Rome immediately. Before leaving, however, I mentioned that I needed to stop at the American Express office to pick up my mail.

"My dear young girl, this calls for a little advice. Do I have your permission?" Edgar asked.

"Yes, of course."

He warned, "It isn't really necessary to be in a hurry to go for the mail. If, however, you feel compelled to do so, I suggest you go on the last day of wherever you happen to be. Under no

circumstances should you run there every single day for the simple reason that very often disappointing or unpleasant news
awaits you. After all, a vacation should be fun and interesting
and why spoil it? Furthermore, usually nothing can be done
about the disagreeable communication."

He was right. That was the first thing I learned from him.

A letter from my mother was waiting for me. She wrote, *Sol
called and complained that he hasn't heard from you. If it's your
intention to break up with him, you should be forthright and tell
him so.* Edgar received letters from Lore that she would be in a
certain city until the fourteenth, in another one on the fifteenth,
and here we were on the fifteenth, too late to reach her. We never
did catch up with her.

LATER, BACK IN THE UNITED States, Edgar recalled that he'd had
to wine and dine me to keep me in Rome. He'd accomplished
that by calming me down as we left the restaurant with the flies,
reminding me that, "When in Rome, do as the Romans do,"
which meant it was time for a siesta. "After that," he suggested,
"you'll feel like a new person. Rome is very beautiful at night.
I'll show you the Capitole. The lit steps there are quite a sight.
And we'll have a nice dinner." The steps, shining in full glory as
they reflected the lights emitted by old-fashioned (but electrified)
iron lamps on either side, were indeed a sight—majestic, and so
romantic as I stood there and envisioned slowly descending in a
long, flowing gown.

Back at the hotel, after dinner, he asked, "What would you
like to see tomorrow?"

"Maybe the Colosseum and the Trevi Fountain?" I answered in a questioning tone.

"That sounds good," he said, smiling. "And, if I may, I'll add some other sights you might enjoy." He jotted down all my suggestions and looked at the guidebook to figure out distances, entrance times, the best way to reach the places, and other necessary or interesting information.

"All that needs to be done the night before, so as not to waste valuable time in the morning, when it's important to get an early start before it gets too hot," he explained, his voice warm and soft. This, too, was a learning experience for me, because I'd never bothered doing that before.

At the Colosseum, Edgar led me up some stairs and, standing on a stone that had once been a seat, he waved his right arm as he exclaimed, "This giant amphitheater of stone and concrete was built in 82 AD and seated up to 50,000 spectators. In later years, imagine yourself sitting here and watching thousands of hand to hand combats between gladiators and the famous contests between men and animals."

"I don't think I would have watched that," I contended. "But it certainly is impressive. Do show me where they kept the animals."

"Follow me. Be careful, the steps are steep and uneven."

Back outside in the street once more, I mentioned that I had to find a place to change some money.

"Never mind searching around. I see some people are getting their money changed right here." At that moment we, too, were approached by a couple of young men. Edgar changed fifty dollars, receiving in return thousands of lire. The exchange rate at that time was fifteen hundred lire to the dollar.

"Would you mind holding the guide book while I count the money?" he asked. "Those damned guys cheated me!" he realized, too late. They were gone. While I was sympathetic, I also derived some comfort from the realization that he was not infallible after all.

My admiration for Edgar grew daily. Everything Lore had said about him was true, and I came to understand, even if I did not agree, why she had changed religions. Ironically, he did not like the way Catholicism was practiced in the U.S., and he had by then become interested in Eastern religion—Taoism, to be exact.

I threw pennies into the Trevi fountain, and followed the custom of making a wish. Mine was to return to Rome one day. I thought it was a great city. To me, the beautifully laid-out piazzas, with the fabulous fountains, represented an outdoor museum, eliciting feelings of pleasure and wonder.

"Just look, Edgar," I pointed out, as if I'd been the first one to discover it, "Each piazza is showing off a grand fountain spouting water out of the mouths of sculpted animals or mystical figures in its midst."

"My dear young girl," by then a familiar phrase, sounded in the back of me. "How would you like to sit down and relax in a café with a cold drink or ice cream? We can watch the fountain, and also see the other tourists plod by in the sun while we sit in comfort."

"That's a great idea, Edgar," I admitted. Service was slow

which gave us a chance to relax. After half an hour or more, he asked, "Are you ready now to climb the hundred-and-thirty-nine Spanish Steps? It sounds like a lot, but it's a shortcut to where we want to go."

When we arrived there, I asked, "Do you mind waiting a minute? I have to look at some of these gorgeous flowers." They were displayed at the bottom of the steps.

We not only looked, but we felt compelled to smell as many of the variety of species as we could. The vendors boasted every conceivable color and type—roses, carnations, violets, as well as others—the names of which we didn't even know—in that sea of floral glory.

The days passed and we visited every church, it seemed, the Vatican, and other important sights. I liked all of it, including the pastas, the wine, and the afternoon stops at cafes. Most of all, I learned to enjoy Edgar.

On our way from the hotel one day, a priest passed us. As soon as he was out of sight, Edgar commented, "I hope he says at least ten Hail Marys the way his eyes moved from your neck down to the opening of your dress. Oh, that reminds me of a joke." He told me of an arrangement he had with his colleague at the university. In order not to bore each other with their little stories, which both knew quite well, they'd listed them on a chart and numbered them. Then they'd refer to a number and laugh. The priest we had just passed would have fallen into category number five. Since I could not go by the numbers, he recounted many of his little anecdotes. I was a captive audience, laughed at each one, and he was glad to have a chance to tell them, embellish them, or otherwise shape them any way he felt at a particular moment.

He was not always funny intentionally.

In a restaurant one evening, we ordered pasta. The waiter had brought the wine and, white napkin thrown casually over his arm, stood by the table, waiting for our order. Edgar ordered my dinner, adding, "*E per mi pasta sensa olio, sensa burro, sensa formaggio, sensa*— oh," he struggled, mumbling, "without anything" and translating, announced out loud, "*sensa, sensa.*"

"In other words, sir, just plain," answered the waiter, not flickering an eyelid. While Edgar was working his way through the ingredients that waiter had given no indication that he understood perfectly what was being said.

NOT EVERY PIAZZA WAS LIKE the Piazza del Popolo or the Piazza Navona, which I liked so much, or the streets leading to them. We ambled through alleys full of beggars, and Edgar dispensed coins freely to them. When I questioned his generosity, mentioning that I had heard many of them were faking their poverty, he said, "Maybe that's true, but if I give them the equivalent of fifty cents or a dollar, it doesn't make that much difference to me. I prefer giving to some who don't need it rather than withholding from those who do. If I can spend a few hundred dollars on this trip, the ten or twenty I give away won't kill me."

Forty years later, I traveled to Indonesia, which harbors many beggars. I walked around, keeping coins in my pocket. Frequently, I dropped some into their cups or hats, each time mumbling to myself, "You can thank Edgar for that." It gave me satisfaction when I learned that a quarter bought them a week's supply of rice.

It did not take long being with Edgar to find him more interesting, more appealing, more charming, and funnier every day. Lore had not exaggerated. I felt I was in the company of a genius. I marveled at his knowledge on many subjects, history in particular, became aware of his humility, appreciated his sense of humor, learned that it was possible to have a conversation with the simplest person as easily as with the most educated, and I appreciated his genial company.

He, in turn, complimented me frequently. When he said, "You catch on quickly, you are smart," I just dismissed it at first. Nobody had ever said that to me, except perhaps my mother or father, and they didn't count. On the contrary, I was used to Irene's put-downs, which I had internalized. After a little more than a week had passed, he said one day, "My dear young girl, I will also call you 'Copperhead,' if I may. I must tell you that I really enjoy your company, and it's a pleasure to have you as my traveling companion."

I was able to answer, "Yes, I know, Edgar. I feel the same way about you," in a normal voice, no longer shy and timid.

29

CAPRI WITH EDGAR

A FTER ALMOST A WEEK IN Rome, I told Edgar that I had planned a visit to Capri. I had wanted to see it for a long time. He must have guessed the answer he would receive, but he was diplomatic enough to ask if he might accompany me. We took the train to Naples and from there a ferry to Capri.

I had already boarded the train when he decided to go back to buy a bottle of soda. The conductor stood at the next coach, whistle in hand, ready to blow it, but there was no sign of Edgar. I was craning my neck, standing on the steps of the carriage, when I caught a glimpse of him in the crowd on the platform as he sauntered towards me. I waved him on; his pace did not change. He barely made it, pretending (I thought) he did not know the time of the departure. There were one or two other incidents when he played the absent-minded professor, if it was convenient for him.

We reached Naples in the late afternoon, and we decided to

sit on a bench by the beach and watch the sun set, its reflection waltzing over the water in different shades of orange. He started to talk to other tourists, also Americans. Soon the conversation turned to books. It became obvious that neither the woman, in her fifties, nor her male companion of about the same age, had read too much. Nonetheless, the chatter flowed with laughter and little jokes. His animated remarks kept them interested enough to want to meet us—Edgar—again. After they left, he commented, "Nice people, but I don't think they read a book beyond second grade." I noticed again how he was able to talk to anybody at all.

Earlier, I had suggested, "Why don't we look for a better hotel than the one in Rome?"

"My dear young girl, dear Copperhead," he answered, as he slowly turned his head towards me and said, "I think I am traveling with a spendthrift."

I knew that remark contained a reference to the taxis we'd had to take because of my heavy and numerous pieces of luggage.

At any rate, something was being celebrated or convened in Naples, which made hotel rooms very scarce, and we were fortunate to find a vacancy in a *pensione*, where the owner behind the desk told us he had just one room left as he flipped the pages of the registration book, nearly losing his thickly framed dark glasses as they slid down his thin face. He showed us the room. Its light blue walls served as a friendly background for the painting of a seascape. It was a simple but pleasant room—the big bed, covered with a white bedspread, its outstanding feature.

"But we need two single beds," I blurted, blushing from the

chin up (later reported by Edgar).

"It *is* two beds, miss. I move apart and put night-table between," the owner smiled, barely concealing a sly grin as he pushed the glasses up his nose. We took the room.

AFTER SPENDING ONE NIGHT IN Naples, we took the ferry to Capri. It was everything, and more, that I had envisioned: white-washed houses; small, narrow alleys; donkey carts; blue, sunny skies; beautiful walks; and the Blue Grotto in the Mediterranean. It was on the main piazza in town, enclosed all around by restaurants, cafes, and shops, and on one side by the church, where I sat with Edgar one afternoon, enjoying coffee and cake, while I composed my letter to Lowenstein & Sons. By then I had been gone far longer than my two-week vacation. It took some discipline to remember to write. I had conveniently forgotten the United States and its residents—one and all. I lived happily in my present state only.

Circumstances beyond my control are keeping me here, and I am not sure how much longer I will have to stay. I will call as soon as I am back, I wrote, in part. Prior to my departure, I had told my boss that I had some business to take care of in Vienna.

"I am not supposed to be in Italy, Edgar," I remembered. "I'm supposed to be in Vienna. They'll be able to tell from the stamps."

"Well, my dear Copperhead, I have an idea. I will forward your letter to Franziska" (his first wife) "and ask her to mail it for you. She may not go to Vienna, although sometimes she does, but it will be sent from Austria."

I was relieved. "Great. Thank you, and thank her, please. I don't think they'll realize that the postmark is not Vienna, as long as the stamps are Austrian."

With that obstacle out of the way, I could devote my time, my thoughts, and my feelings to being with Edgar. His mild prodding, his genuine appreciation of me, and his compliments—dismissed in the beginning, but which by then I knew were honest and from the heart—did wonders for my self-esteem and confidence. In turn, I sat in awe and wonder, with respect and admiration, looking up to this master and guru.

He had to leave for a long-standing appointment in Venice with an old friend, nicknamed "Knight Pumpus Le Grand." Neither of us wanted to part. I wanted to see Florence, as did Edgar, but he didn't have time before meeting his friend.

We took the ferry back to the mainland, standing in the back of the boat under the usual blue sky, as we watched the foaming white wake and the waves jumping in the sunlight. His arm around my shoulders, wind blowing through our hair, we looked up from the white and blue water at each other, smiling—no words necessary. We'd arranged to meet in Venice.

Florence by myself without Edgar, even for three days, seemed like an eternity, but I could not help but take pleasure walking around in that beautiful city. I was thunderstruck by Michelangelo's *David*—the sculpture was stunning, standing there in the museum. I gazed at it from all sides, walking around it, marveling at each muscle he had sculpted to look real.

On another day, at the Uffizi, I climbed the steps to the next floor, and gasped in astonishment and pleasure at unexpectedly finding myself face to face with *The Birth of Venus*, by Botticelli, which until then I had only seen in reproductions. My sightseeing included a walk across the Ponte Vecchio, which took me an hour to cross because of all the stores on either side.

I missed Edgar but managed quite well by myself. I knew I would see him soon.

WHEN I APPEARED AT THE pre-arranged date at the hotel in Venice, more like a small inn tucked away in one of the side streets, I was told there was no Professor Foltin registered there.

"That's not possible," I said. "I know he must be here."

"No. He not here," answered the old man. He had been standing by the desk during that part of our conversation but went behind it to bring out his guest book after I said,

"Check again, please. There is a mistake somewhere."

"I tell you, no." He scratched his bald head. "Oh, I see here—he check out."

"When did he check out?"

"Two days ago."

"Did he give you a forwarding address?"

"What you mean?"

"Did he say where he was going?"

"No."

"Are you sure he is not here?"

"Yes."

As I turned away from the desk in utter disbelief, trying to figure out what to do, I looked up, and there was Edgar standing in the doorway, with Pumpus just behind him.

Poor Pumpus looked much older than Edgar (then in his early fifties), frail and sickly. Although not Jewish, he had been in a concentration camp, and it showed in his thin, wrinkled face.

At the earliest opportunity of being alone with Edgar, I wondered how the threesome would work out.

"*No problema*, as we are told so often here. He can tell that we're close, and he'll just come along and join us wherever we go." So it was. The three of us rode in a gondola—Edgar and I sitting together on one bench, Pumpus opposite us. I had hoped Pumpus hadn't been disappointed in making the trip to meet Edgar and finding me there, too, but he seemed quite content.

VENICE, OF COURSE, WAS BEAUTIFUL—all the more so because I was with Edgar again. I confessed to having missed him in Florence, and he admitted, "Oh, and how I've missed you, Copperhead." I had heard of some of his escapades, which didn't allow me to believe that he loved me. On the other hand, I remembered how jealous he'd been in Capri when he found the hotel owner's son in an animated conversation with me. He had burst out, "Should I return to the room to give you a chance to make a date?" When I became aware that his compliments and appreciation had not been mere flattery but had come from the heart, I'd been ecstatic. It was even more satisfying to realize that he'd already felt that way in Capri.

There was nothing (except the *grappa*) I did not like in Venice—the Grand Canal, the smaller ones, the many steps up and down bridges, all the sightseeing, including numerous visits to churches—big ones, small ones—the frequent and various smells of fish, or pizza, or the aroma of freshly baked bread and rolls wafting towards us through the open door of a bakery, even the heat—it was all great in Edgar's company.

The smaller side canals with their twists and turns, and the gondoliers who maneuvered their slender vessels around those curves in such a masterful way, were more intriguing than the Grand Canal, which shared *its* beauty with the palaces and the big, white Santa Maria della Salute church, as well as the Piazza San Marco bordering on its shores. Taking the vaporetto for a few lire served as a tour boat, and I had my own guide in Edgar, who commented with historical flavor on most sights as the vaporetto sailed past them.

It was very hot in Venice, which made us stop for refreshments more frequently than in Rome. Edgar usually drank his grappa in the afternoon, and persuaded me once, "Try a glass. It's great." One sip was enough to feel it going down my throat and I knew exactly where it was in my body at a given moment. He loved it. Fortunately, we were in a café bordering one of the canals, which received the rest of my drink when he wasn't looking.

Edgar had two days left of his allotted stay in Venice after Pumpus' departure. We relished our time alone. On our last evening together, Edgar took me to dinner in one of the better restaurants, where, over a glass of wine, we recounted our favorite days and moments, expressing our appreciation, fondness and love for each other, the pity of parting, and making vague plans for a reunion.

It was August by then, and I had already been away from my

job and my home for five weeks, three of which had been spent with Edgar in Italy. We had expected to meet again at my aunt Mitzi's house in London, but that did not materialize. We had to wait until we had both returned to the States.

I MADE MY WAY BACK to London via Bad Gastein, a small, pretty resort town; a has-been spa in Austria but still known for skiing, it lies almost in a straight line north of Venice. I had originally wanted to travel to Vienna from Venice, but Edgar had told me, "If you do, you have to cross through the Russian zone, and I'm not sure if you want to do that." At that time (1952) Vienna was occupied by American, British, French, and Russian troops, each allotted one sector.

"Do they interrogate people?" I inquired.

"I've heard rumors to that effect. You may want to avoid that."

"I certainly do. I'll scratch Vienna."

I made the trip to Bad Gastein solely to meet my aunt Poldi from Sweden, formerly from Vienna. She was another of my mother's sisters, easy to talk to, an eager listener to my stories, and helpful in her answers. She hadn't always been well, and the treatments in the spa soothed her. Her short brown hair, with a wave on one side of her forehead, gave her a 1920s look, just like the spa, I thought. It had been several years since I last saw her in Vienna, and I spent a few very pleasant days with her before continuing on to Switzerland and Paris.

I wanted to meet her again because I had always been family conscious and missed the closeness, both emotionally and geographically, of our extended family, now lost due to Hitler. He had not succeeded in the Final Solution to exterminate every single Jew from the countries he had occupied, but those of my family who survived had scattered all over the world. My relatives had immigrated to Sweden, England, Canada, U.S., Mexico, Australia, and Israel. All of them had lived in Vienna or the Czechoslovakia, a mere few hours apart, in close proximity to each other.

I WOULD PROBABLY NOT HAVE gone to Switzerland except that Lottie was expecting me. She had been the refugee chambermaid at Mrs. Harter's thirteen years earlier when she became my friend and confidante. Her family was vacationing and she had wanted me to meet her two children.

"Wait till you meet Peter. He's about the same age you were when we first met at Mrs. Harter's," she'd explained eagerly.

It was a short, happy reunion for the two of us as we'd always had a lot to talk about. Her daughter, a pretty eleven-year-old, and her son, were not as impressed as she had expected them to be. They went off to do their own thing. Lottie, her husband, and I did get together again several years later on a skiing trip in Switzerland.

They all came to the station to see me off on my way to Paris—my last stop on the Continent.

ON FRENCH SOIL ONCE MORE, I remembered my stay on the Riviera, when I'd thought, *I could live here; I like their lifestyle.* At lunch, by myself, I chuckled when the waiter took for granted, "White wine or red?" I loved Paris, inhaled its ambiance, but its citizens, individually, were very often rude if I spoke English. They responded more kindly when I used my poor, halting school French.

In London, I picked up some clothes I had left with Aunt Mitzi, and caught a plane back to New York City. By then, I'd been gone nine weeks from my job.

30

NEW YORK CITY AND BACK TO WORK

I T WASN'T EASY WAKING UP to face reality and putting aside such an idyllic dream of the time spent in Europe. Knowing I'd have to look for a job was too tough for a wakeup call, so I turned around and tried to go back to sleep, but the thought nagged me. There was no choice. Slowly and reluctantly, I got up.

Before starting a serious search, I thought I'd give M. Lowenstein & Sons—my previous employer—a call. I talked to the personnel manager and was surprised at his cordial manner. "Welcome back! Glad to hear from you. I hope everything worked out all right for you." And even more unbelievable, "Would you like to come back to work?"

My previous boss, Mr. K., one of the department heads, also greeted me warmly. Barely a week after my return, the Chairman of the Board, Leon Lowenstein (referred to as Mr. L.L.), had me summoned to his office. His secretary was out sick, and he wanted me to take minutes at a board meeting. I was not thrilled at the honor. His reputation as a diamond in the rough, a product of his frequently curt manner (although approachable in many instances, as I would later learn), fit that no-nonsense man. He was in his seventies then, fairly tall, a big man who stooped slightly when he walked, which did not diminish the impression of physical strength.

It was raining hard that September morning. I had worn my old green-and-brown outfit with matching low-heeled green walking shoes, and was thinking I should have dressed more stylishly as I made my way to the conference room. "Sit down next to me," he ordered in his low, loud voice, "and take down everybody's name." Since I had been in the firm several years, I knew the names of the twenty men sitting around the large table in the paneled room. Each, in turn, gave me a sympathetic smile as my eyes moved from one to the next. Every once in a while during the meeting Mr. LL stopped addressing the participants, turned to me, and said, "Did you get that all right?" Or he would interrupt a speaker: "Wait a minute. I want to be sure she gets that."

His English was known to be atrocious; he mispronounced names (I was always Elizabeth; his Dictaphone operator, named Norma, was always Norman; and Miss Perlmutter, his senior secretary, Miss Poilmudder). His grammar left much to be desired.

I returned to my office to type the minutes and, after I finished, asked my boss, "Would you mind reading what I typed? It doesn't sound quite right to me."

"Sorry, Lisbeth, I don't know what L.L. meant. Why don't you go to his nephew, Bob B.? He's the vice-president of the mills down South, and he'll be able to figure it out." What that smart, friendly man figured out was quite different from what I had written. I knew my shorthand was correct, and I had no trouble reading it.

I left my typewritten notes exactly as my shorthand read in L.L.'s office. Returning from lunch, my boss asked, "What are you doing? Why is all that stuff on your desk?"

"I'm cleaning out my desk, taking my personal belongings home, in case I get the pink slip over the week-end."

The following Monday, Mr. L.L. called me to his office. Smiling, he told me, "I want you to work for me. I've finally found someone who wrote what I said instead of people trying to improve my language and writing something I didn't say and didn't mean."

So that diamond in the rough, in the end, was always more diamond than rough with me, and I was glad whenever he was in the office, feeling protected from his senior secretary's jealousy.

He spent the winter months in his Miami Beach home in Florida and, one year, decided we had to take a winter vacation, because we did not have enough work while he was away. He must have discounted the large packages of mail and phone calls that went back and forth between New York and Miami daily.

When he heard that I would be going to Miami, he immediately told me to call him so he could send his chauffeur for me to give me some work. "But Mr. L.L.," I protested, "I'll be on vacation."

"Never mind. A little work won't hurt you. Give me a call when you get there. You hear me?"

Chauffeured in his big black Cadillac, I arrived at L.L.'s

home, and found him at his desk in the den in front of French doors that led to a garden where a birdbath stood close to a little waterfall. A couple of books were scattered on the leather sofa, no doubt belonging to the bookcase on the opposite side. As soon as he got off the phone, he said, "Something's come up. I'll be busy on the phone. Go talk to the missus for a while."

I looked for her and noticed the mid-sized house was not as big as I had expected it to be. His tastes were simple enough, but the lifestyle of his wife and her grown daughter from a previous marriage had led to a more elaborate manner. I never did meet her that morning because she was upstairs, suffering from a migraine hangover. Whenever he mentioned his missus, a bill for a dress costing $1,150.00 that had been sent to the office for payment conjured itself up in my mind. I used to think of Belgian lace, fur, and imported silk, and make up all kinds of dresses, but I was never able to imagine anything that added up to that amount of money. The year was 1953.

After alighting from the Cadillac at my hotel, various young men whom I had never noticed before, or they me, showed a keen interest. That gave me a chance to find out what Collins Avenue, known as The Strip, was about. I was introduced to Wolfie's, the Jewish delicatessen, serving their famously piled-high pastrami and corned beef sandwiches, accompanied by free pickles and cabbage standing on the counter. Vast hotels, one after another, greeted me, many in Art Deco style. Street vendors sold freshly squeezed orange juice, others sold hot dogs, to noisy crowds in a hustle and bustle during the day, a street awash in neon lights at night.

Before I had left his house that morning, L.L. had invited me to the fashionable, newly opened Fontainebleau Hotel for the afternoon the following day. The hotel—glamorous, glitzy, garish, and glowing—not too far from where I was staying—had an entrance under a canopy on Collins Avenue, and fronted the Atlantic Ocean in the back.

Young men, one after another, in sparkling-new white uniforms, greeted me politely and asked if I had a membership after I announced I was on my way to the terrace. Upon mentioning L.L.'s name, I was escorted in style down a red-carpeted foyer, able to catch a glimpse of bars, clubs rooms, restaurants, shops, smaller halls, and rows of elevators, all brilliantly lit by luxurious chandeliers. The veranda, where I had my rendezvous with L.L., was no less lavish, furnished with comfortable white lounge chairs and chaises in high-quality, expensive fabrics, the accompanying tables well appointed. The awning, which provided shade for the entire length of the terrace, displayed the same pattern as the fabric on the chairs. Not far away, an unusually long swimming pool, surrounded by grass, stood unused in the sun. In the distance, the ocean was visible, waves of the incoming tide audible as they roared in.

The uniformed young man took me right to L.L. and quickly found a chair for me. Within seconds, a waiter was at my side, ready to take an order for a drink. L.L. sat surrounded by his cronies, smoking and sipping their glasses of whatever. They all wore shorts and colorful shirts, relaxing in the big, comfortable chairs, which surrounded a small, glass cocktail table. I recognized the dark-haired one from New York City, but did not know any of the others. L.L. wasted no time coming to the point: "Do any of you know a nice man for Miss Elizabeth?"

"Yes. What about Max Cohen?" offered the blond-haired guy as he took off his sunglasses and slowly puffed on his cigarette.

"No, no, no. He's a ladies' man. No good. Object: matrimony," L.L. hurled back in his usual clear, loud voice.

He was more successful in another matter back in New York. My sister had come from Palestine for a visit and run into difficulties securing an extension to her visa. I mentioned this to L.L. one day. He told me, "I have to leave the office now. Call me at home tomorrow at eleven o'clock and remind me." To call him at home was unheard of—a no-no. I did, and he said he would call his good friend Senator Lehman. The extension was granted post haste.

I had a chance to meet Senator Lehman once briefly when he attended L.L.'s annual luncheon, hosted in the conference room next to his office. Other attendees included Cardinal Spellman, Rabbi Marks, Judge Schwarz, David Rockefeller, and several other men. In L.L.'s opinion, it was important for these personalities from various factions to meet. I am not sure what he tried to accomplish, but I know he got a kick out of those meetings. Cardinal Spellman must have liked them, too. His St. Vincent's Hospital and Fordham University were endowed with enormous donations, worthy for each to have a wing named in Leon Lowenstein's name.

On the other hand, I admired L.L. for turning down an invitation for lunch at the Merchants Club. He telephoned its president and, in his forthright manner, declared, "You won't allow Jews to be members in your club, and until you do, I'm not going to set foot in your place. It's a disgrace that you refuse to let Jews join." He followed that up with a letter in the same vein.

I have never forgotten another letter, on a different subject. He had visited one of the firm's mills in South Carolina and, on his return, wrote to the foreman in part:

I also want to thank you for inviting me to your home for lunch. I have been thinking and admiring what a nice family you have. Your wife is a good cook, and so pleasant. You are a lucky man to have such an intelligent, hard-working son. I hope you appreciate that. Good luck to you. Both L.L.'s wife and step-daughter had a drinking problem.

Working for L.L had its perks.

He passed my desk, just outside his office, on his way home. (Miss Perlmutter had strenuously objected to having my desk in his office next to her, although that had been his intention.) He stopped and asked, "You'll be on vacation next week, right? Here, have a good time." He dropped a fifty-dollar bill on the desk and continued on out. Miss Perlmutter, returning from lunch, noticed, and wanted to know, "How much did he give you?"

"Twenty dollars," I lied, to ensure her jealousy would be somewhat restrained and not manifest itself in too mean a way. She liked to keep information from me, discussing it instead with the Dictaphone operator, so I would appear ignorant should Mr. L.L. refer to something I should have been aware of. Sometimes he said to me, "Oh, just write the usual letter." For that, it was necessary to know what it was based on, and that's what she kept from me.

In one of those "usual letters," I made a typing mistake—I wrote $100,000 instead of $10,000. He caught it, and all he said good-humoredly was, "Hey, you got one zero too many here."

My Christmas bonus amounted to six weeks' salary. I received the summer bonus retroactively after having taken nine weeks off for my European jaunt. I did not have to go through the personnel office for anything. Rosh Hashanah was coming up, and as he left the office he told me, "I'll see you Wednesday."

"Mr. L.L., I won't be in till Thursday. I observe both days."

"You'd better be here Wednesday, if you know what's good for you." I did not answer. I returned on Thursday, and not another word was mentioned. You could answer him once; after that, he needed to have the last word.

If you worked hard—and he made sure of that—and showed some common sense and some initiative, he wasn't hard to get along with. On the contrary, he spoke his mind but he was kind, and I liked it much better when he was in the office rather than out.

31

A DEATH AND A WEDDING

FTER MY RETURN FROM EUROPE, Jack and I spent more time together than before, often teaming up with Manny and Rose. Manny was Jack's best friend. I'd met him and Rose in the Catskills the same weekend I'd met Jack. Manny, who was handsome, smart, Harvard educated, and so low-key and anti-work-oriented that it chagrined Rose throughout their whole marriage. She was attractive, vivacious and ambitious. Each a wonderful person in many ways, their different sense of values and goals didn't make for an ideal marriage.

We all loved the Italian festival held in Greenwich Village every fall—invariably a sunny, balmy day. The four of us pushed, or were pushed, through rowdy, happy throngs, salami in one hand, a cold drink in the other. If we were jolted and spilled some soda, it turned into a joke.

"I like the pattern the sugar made on your shirt," Jack teased as he took a bite of a freshly baked piece of pastry.

"Oh, it's worth it, don't you think?" I countered. "It's so

crunchy and delicious. Nobody makes these pastries the way they do down here." We joined the singing of Italian folk songs at the next street corner, Jack next to me happily belting out the tune off key.

On weekends he and I enjoyed drive-in movies, kissing between scenes, and bemoaning the fact that one or the other of my parents always seemed to be home at the wrong time.

Since I lived in Manhattan, he drove in from New Jersey in his two-seater Plymouth to visit museums together, join friends for dinner, or attend outdoor concerts in the summer. We got along well, shared a lot of laughter, the same values as well as a strong physical attraction. I valued his decisiveness (barring marriage), a welcome contrast to Mama's indecisiveness. We'd soon been together for two years, I loved him, and if he had suggested living together without marrying, I'd have done it (rare in 1955).

Later that spring, on a clear, moonlit night, we strolled by the Hudson, sat down on a bench, and he finally popped the question, "I'm not very romantic," he started, "but I would like to marry you. What do you say?"

"I thought you'd never ask," I answered in the same vein, "but yes, it makes me very happy."

We kissed and hugged, and he promised to give me his mother's engagement ring. "That's an honor," he emphasized, when a couple of days later he proudly slid it on my finger.

We made no particular wedding plans at the time. He was a frequent visitor in our home after our engagement, and the two of us continued happily getting to know each other better.

PAPA HAD BEEN DIAGNOSED WITH colon cancer—in addition to the heart disease he had acquired in the concentration camp. His condition grew worse each month. Mama had taken care of him, with the exception of administering injections for pain. I'd offered to take over, asked the doctor about it, who explained, "I'll be happy to teach you how to give an injection, if you come to the office. I won't be making house calls any more." The first, and only, injection I tried to give my father turned into a fiasco—the needle got stuck.

Mama bought a television set for him, still somewhat of a novelty in 1955, and I checked in during my lunch hour whenever I could. I continued my college studies at night after work, curtailed my social life with Jack, and tried to give moral support to Mama.

Soon it became necessary to transfer Papa to the hospital. We all knew it was terminal. I dreamt he died on a holiday, and dreaded the upcoming July 4. It came and went. Labor Day also passed. We buried Papa on October 11—my thirtieth birthday. He never complained about an earlier operation or pain or any discomfort. I missed him. He was gentle, patient, humble, and his sense of humor never left him. I knew he loved me dearly.

THINKING OF HIM NOW MAKES it clear that, of the four of us (Mama, Papa, Irene, and me), he suffered the most during the Holocaust years, as well as a result of them. He spent four months in a concentration camp and was released from Dachau in March 1939, suffering from a heart condition, with the stipulation that he leave the country within two months. He was hiding in Vienna for fourteen months, twelve of them alone because Mama, Irene, and I had already left. He'd become a fugitive and, if located by the Nazis, arrest was certain, followed by a return to Dachau ending in death. He was silent about that period. I don't know where he lived, except I've gleaned from letters I found recently that, on several occasions, he sought safety in lengthy stays for minor injuries in at least two hospitals—apparently a secure hiding place from the Nazis, but those hospital stays accounted for only a few weeks, at best.

He could not go to his favorite café, or to another coffeehouse, or to a movie, or to the opera, or sit on a park bench, which had *Juden verboten* (Jews forbidden) warnings, or even just walk through the park. He did have to stand in line at the Finance Ministry to prove he owed no taxes, at another office to declare any real estate and other assets, and finally at a third to buy his ship ticket. The SS patrolled these lines, which created panic and fears in people of being taunted and arrested. He received his visa in 1940 and embarked in Italy just days before Mussolini joined the Axis, and he arrived in New York in May. Then *he* worried about *us* in England. He waited until 1945 for Mama and me to arrive.

JACK HAD BEEN SUPPORTIVE DURING the sad period of Papa's illness. We wanted to get married, and I opted for a small wedding. Even so, Mama was not overly involved in helping to prepare for it. She was too burdened with losses she'd recently suffered— the death of her husband, the closing of her store, and she worried about getting ready for a forthcoming trip to Palestine for an extended stay with Irene and her second husband, Rudy. In addition, she had on her mind that I would move out, leaving her to cope with an uncertain future alone.

It was spring 1956, six months after Papa had died. We wanted to marry before Mama would leave for Palestine, but conservative rabbis did not perform weddings between Pesach and Shavuot, whereas some Reform rabbis did. We located Dr. Marks, Chief Rabbi of the Reform Temple Emanuel in New York City, who agreed to marry us in his study.

I found a tight-fitting, light-blue-and-white silk cocktail dress, cut low in the back, adorned with a large bow in the back at the waist. It looked good on me. I weighed ninety-five pounds to which I had dropped during my father's illness. White shoes, short, white gloves, and a hastily bought little white hat with a veil completed the outfit. The day before the wedding, I chose a small bouquet of white flowers at the local florist.

As we entered the rabbi's study, he greeted us, "I thought you were going to be five or six people. I am counting twelve." I remember nothing of what he said to us during the ceremony.

The guests included only the immediate family—both our mothers, Jack's two brothers and their wives and little Avram and Rachel (their children), my aunt Rosl, who had flown in with her son, Frank, from Toronto, and a couple of cousins. We married May 10. Mama left the next day for Palestine to visit Irene.

Irene's mother-in-law chose not to attend the ceremony but insisted on holding a reception for us. She had an elegant luncheon prepared for all the guests in her equally elegant large house on Long Island. Jack and I both worked, and decided to take a short honeymoon, motoring through New England.

MARRIED LIFE IN OUR NEW one-bedroom apartment in West New York, New Jersey, was fun and easy. The fairly new building on Boulevard East at Sixty-second Street overlooked the skyline of New York across the river. After dinner, Jack would suggest: "Let's go down and sit by the river and enjoy the city lights from there," or, "How about the main drag?" We'd amble up the few blocks to join other strollers in window shopping, stopping for ice cream, or buying a few groceries. There was time to listen to the radio, read, play Scrabble, buy furniture, and visit friends. We enjoyed each other's company, laughed, teased, and gave each other moral support when one or the other had a complaint about co-workers. Sometimes we'd eat out, when Jack often said, "Eat some more. You are not eating enough." I got so used to following his advice that a year later he teased, "Boy, you eat like a truck driver." We have retained that remark in the family, making use of it to elicit a smile. Happy and carefree, we were ready to face the future with confidence.

My mother spent six months in Palestine. She had always emphasized her independence. Nonetheless, we asked on her return, "Would you like to live with us instead of being all alone? We would look for a larger apartment, of course, but it would be in New Jersey, not in New York." Her unambiguous acceptance came as quite a surprise.

We rented a comfortable older house on Jefferson Avenue in Cliffside Park, its kitchen and bathrooms remodeled, which fit our needs. Of the three bedrooms upstairs, Mama had the use of one for a sitting room.

32

RICHARD

I N 1957 I BECAME PREGNANT with our first child. I felt fine and continued working until the end of June 1958. I did faint once in the kitchen while Jack was frying bacon for breakfast. Then I knew what food and smell to avoid. We attended classes together to prepare for natural childbirth. My little overnight bag was packed, ready to accompany me to the hospital at a moment's notice. When the contractions drew closer at increasingly frequent intervals, I telephoned the doctor, then Chief Obstetrician at Englewood Hospital, who advised us to wait, which turned the next two days into a frenzy of anxiety and much discomfort.

When he finally admitted me, I still had to wait several hours, during which Jack kept telling me, "Breathe. Take a deep, slow breath," as we had learned in our preparatory classes. The crescendo of his reminders culminated in what seemed like shouts.

"Don't be so nervous, Jack," I said between contractions.

"You don't have to shout."

"I'm not nervous, and I'm not shouting," he answered, smiling, trying hard to sound calm. "It's your imagination. Breathe."

Idealistically, I was prepared to do whatever it took to stay with natural childbirth. The next thing I knew, a spinal injection entered my body—no questions asked or explanations given, and with no permission on my part. Fortunately, I suffered no side effects and gave birth to a healthy baby boy. *I* had no gender preference. When the doctor announced, "It's a boy!" I thought, *That'll please Jack.*

The baby was born with a lot of dark hair, large round eyes, and weighed close to seven pounds. I nursed him for several days when, just before being discharged, one of the nurses informed me, "It seems your milk supply is inadequate. He's crying. You'd better feed him from a bottle."

"I don't understand that," I answered, perplexed. "It doesn't feel that way to me."

"Well, he's crying."

The next day, I made an appointment with a woman physician who was very supportive, encouraging and, best of all, assured me that my milk supply was fine and I could nurse for as long as I chose. Everything went well from then on. He was an easy baby, ate and slept well, and he was healthy. He didn't even have a cold.

He was born July 14, 1958—Bastille Day. "Shall we give him a French name?" Jack threw in as a joke. We had already decided earlier that we would call him Richard, after my father.

We did not have a traditional *bris* ceremony. We'd asked the doctor to circumcise him in the hospital on the eighth day.

Little Richard cried when I took his clothes off to lift him into the tub for his first bath. I didn't know whether to hold him in my right arm and wash him with my left, or vice-versa, or how to stop his crying. Luckily, Emma was in the house that day. She had come to clean and looked just like Mammy in *Gone With The Wind*. "Here, let me help you, Mrs. Maklin," (that's what she always called me), she said softly as she took over. When she held him, wrapped in a towel, in her ample arm close to her even ampler bosom, he calmed down instantly, looking contentedly into her eyes. In the future, too, he would always be happy to see her, often asking, "Where's Emma?"

He was a delightful little boy, smart, happy, quick to learn. He walked and spoke early, and for me it was a joy to spend time with him. Sylvia, our neighbor, also liked him. She used to bring her small poodle over to keep him company. Sitting next to each other they were the same height. To complete our happiness, Jack presented me with a gift in honor of the baby's birth—a gorgeous gold bracelet set with sapphires. He continued to shower me with gifts over the years, alternating between jewelry and paintings.

Shortly before his second birthday Richard started to vomit. It continued for several days. The doctor could not find a cause, and called it a virus, although Richard neither coughed nor sneezed, nor showed any other symptoms of a virus. Since he did not improve, we took him to Babies Hospital at Columbia Presbyterian in New York City. Even there it took several weeks to reach a diagnosis. When they did, finally, they thought it might be a brain tumor. Jack and I sat in the waiting room rather than leave the hospital after they'd taken him to the operating room, taking turns calming each other down during the longest two hours I'd ever spent. When the surgeon returned from the operating room, he announced triumphantly, "It's not a brain tumor. We don't know yet what it is, but anything is better than that." We were relieved, of course. We thought at that moment that the happiness we had experienced with him since his birth two years ago would continue. It didn't occur to either of us that another demon existed.

Richard had to stay in the hospital for further tests. After a few days, as I was standing next to his crib in the private room he had been assigned, six doctors entered. One was the surgeon who made his rounds in the teaching hospital wearing just a white jacket; the others, interns, residents, and students, in full white coats, had stethoscopes slung around their necks.

"We have news for you, Mrs. Malkin. We have a diagnosis," announced the surgeon. He was so earnest, business-like, and matter-of-fact, I felt it couldn't be anything good. "What your son has is called 'neuroblastoma.'"

"What's that?" I asked weakly, expecting the worst.

"It's a form of cancer that attacks children, usually under the age of five, and. . . ."

His words trailed off as I squeezed out, "Could you get me a chair? I think I am going to faint." I did not faint, because he pushed my head down so hard, my neck felt as if it was about to break.

I closed my eyes, swallowed a couple of times, and asked,

"What are the chances of recovery?"

"The younger a child, the better. At his age—two years— it's fifty-fifty."

The doctors left the room abruptly, and I just sat there.

I looked at that beautiful baby, a handsome toddler by then, my little Richard, lying quietly in his bed, in utter disbelief. *How can this be?* I thought. *No, it can't be so. They must be wrong. He's always been so healthy. He'll get better—I'll see to that.*

Dozens of conflicting thoughts drifted through my head. I felt dizzy and thought I'd vomit.

Hours passed before Jack arrived in the evening after work. In the meantime, I paced up and down the corridor, at the end of which was the large, airy ward full of sick little children, many ill with leukemia. It was a busy floor, some kids running around—two boys on crutches in a race—and nurses moving swiftly in and out and between them. I moved from one chair to another in Richard's room, which was a good size, with a window that allowed the afternoon sun to shine in. I tried to get him and the new, stuffed dog I'd brought, into a conversation. When Jack finally came, I burst out with the news. He was stunned; at the same time he tried to calm me, adding, "I'll come earlier tomorrow and make an appointment to talk to the doctor. Let's go for dinner and talk more."

The closest restaurant—there weren't many to choose from— was across the street, a small, dark Spanish eatery, which became our haven on many evenings during the following months when-ever Richard needed to be hospitalized.

Usually, since I spent the days at the hospital, it was I who received whatever news there was, and I relayed it to Jack in the evening, but that day, as planned, Jack spoke to the doctor, in my presence. Dr. A. had a serious and efficient manner about him. In his late fifties, fairly tall, Jack mentioned towards the end of our conversation that I was pregnant with our second child.

"That's good." He grinned, and turning to Jack, continued, "Your wife should have this child, plus others."

Although he hadn't addressed me, I replied, "If I can't have Richard, I don't want any other children," and I stomped out of the room.

Jack told me afterwards in our Spanish hideaway that the doctor had warned him to watch me.

"Why?" I asked

"He thought you might throw yourself down the stairs."

"He's an idiot. I have no such intention. I was just angry at what he'd said. Of course, I want to have the new child, but I want Richard to get well, and I can't think about future children now."

The need I felt to get angry at various doctors occurred frequently. During the course of the next ten months, Richard had to be hospitalized several times. More than once, I was told, "Unfortunately, Mrs. Malkin, the medication we have been giving your son hasn't worked. We'll try another one, or increase the dosage of the present one, but there's a danger to that."

"You mean danger of an overdose?"

"Exactly."

"Well," I started, trying to formulate what I wanted to say without sounding too accusatory, but without success, "You are always behind the eight ball, it seems to me. I'll take him to Europe, where they'll probably have a remedy that hasn't yet been approved here."

"You are certainly free to do so, but it would be stressful, and with no better results."

Another day I came to the hospital armed with newspaper clippings, and told them of cases I'd heard of on the radio in which the doctor had claimed a cure. When they heard that, they warned excitedly: "Whatever you do, do not believe those ads, and do not, under any circumstances, take Richard to those doctors, who are nothing but quacks. If you want to take him to Sloan-Kettering, we will send his file along to save him from having to go through all the tests again. It is not necessary, however, because we have no doubt about what is going on with him and we are doing all we can."

Jack agreed with the doctors and did not think taking Richard to Europe would be wise.

I lived on an emotional roller-coaster. When Richard had a good day, I was elated, still thinking the doctors—there were several on his case—were wrong. (They'd predicted a four-month span and we were well past that). When he was limp and without energy, I felt the same way.

I went through my second pregnancy against all the rules and advice to mothers-to-be. I did not exercise, and I did not rest as much as I should have or eat the right food. On the contrary, when Jack came to the hospital in the evening, we would dash across the street to the little Spanish restaurant where, famished and upset, I would gulp down all the spicy food, not giving a

thought or care about nutritional value. On many days, I was so
hungry and frustrated that I ate what Richard had left on his dinner tray, which they served around five o'clock. Later I learned
that his chart read he had a pretty good appetite. The nurses
were glad for any parents present to help out at dinnertime. They
were acutely under-staffed and didn't ask any questions.

My frustration was not only caused by his disease and the
doctors' decisions or what I at times considered absence of decisions; some of that strain stemmed from inhaling the unique hospital smell, the odor of the mix of ammonia and cleanser from
wiping the floors, as well as the waiting around—for Jack to
show up, for the doctor to give me an answer to a question or
suggestion—and, not least, watching the unsettling and disturb-
ing hustle on the floor outside Richard's room as the frequent
news of another child dying reached my ears.

I got to know the doctors, who, as time progressed, became
quite approachable and cooperative, especially Dr. Sitarz, a young
woman physician, empathetic, friendly, and someone I could talk
to and learned to trust. If her schedule allowed it, she'd stay
sometimes for a few minutes, not rush in and out like some of
the other doctors. She had a slight accent—she was Swiss—and
she was reassuring yet honest.

I did my share of complaining, but felt I wasn't forceful
enough or taken seriously enough by some of the doctors to protect my little son. I was his spokesperson and had failed him.
When they took him to an examination room to do spinal taps,
and I heard his loud, long, piercing screams of pain, I wished afterwards I had just rushed into the room, snatched him and said,

"Stop that. I won't allow you to do that again." Jack soothed me, and sometimes he had to come to the hospital during the day to talk to the doctors, if I thought they were negligent.

As my pregnancy progressed, I turned to Jack one day. "It's becoming increasingly cumbersome to first lift Richard, and then the stroller, onto the bus when I take him to New York. Maybe I should ask Ellen next door to help? She offered, you know." We had only one car then, which Jack needed for work. After talking it over, he said he would call the Cancer Society to ask if they had suggestions.

"I called them," he told me the next day, "and they'll provide us with a volunteer to drive you to New York whenever necessary."

The unassuming, kind, talkative woman who showed up to help me had herself lost a child to cancer. On one of our rides to New York she asked, "Don't you know that there have been many children in our area who have died from this illness?" How on earth, I wondered, could she bear to be involved in that particular volunteer work?

It wasn't necessary to go to the hospital every day, but little Richard had reached the point when, on awakening, he'd ask, "Do we have to go to the nurse's today?" The word 'hospital' did not yet exist in his vocabulary. There was a period when he received chemotherapy as an outpatient, for which I was grateful. I tried as much as possible, especially on weekends, to keep him at home. Sometimes they'd allow it, instructing me how to administer his medication. We were discharged with these words "Mrs. Malkin, be sure to cut the pill we are giving you to take

home in half, so as not to overdose him. We don't have the correct size right now. And you know about the other medication."
Suddenly, it became scary to leave the hospital. I was in complete charge, responsible for doing the right thing at the right time. What will I do if he won't swallow the pill? Just skip it? Try again later or wait until it is due again, and then give a double dose? Will that overdose him? Just the same, I waited for Jack to drive us home that night, glad to have Richard with us.

He lost his hair while he underwent chemotherapy. His pillow needed to be changed several times a day from sweating. Mealtimes turned into a long, drawn-out process. Encouraging him to eat, and feeding him, if necessary, doing the laundry, making sure he received the medication on time, and his naps left only short periods of time for playing with him. I did talk with him as much as possible, especially when he had to be hospitalized.

The next time that became necessary, I informed the receptionist at the desk, who was sitting very straight, her blonde hair pulled back, eyes cold, looking me over, "I would like to get a room this time where I can stay with him."

"That's out of the question. Those rooms are reserved for people from another country or, at least, from out of town."

"I won't leave him, then," I insisted. After some back and forth, and a telephone call by her, she found a room for him that also had a bed in it for me.

That was a period when he wasn't too bad. On good days I grabbed one of the strollers standing around and took him to the playground a few blocks from the hospital. I made an effort to normalize his life as much as possible and decided it was best that nobody on the staff knew about our little outings to avoid being told it wasn't allowed. I put him on the swings, he puttered around in the sandbox for a few minutes, and we played ball, throwing or rolling it back and forth three or four times. Then he was tired, and we'd sit and watch the other kids.

The next morning he was scheduled for a test to be performed without eating. A nurse entered the room carrying his breakfast tray. I moved towards her to explain the situation, adding, "Would you mind taking the tray out and bringing it back later?"

"No," she answered snippily, "I can't do that. You can put it on the dresser and tell him he can't eat it now."

"I'll do no such thing. I'm not training a circus dog here!" I was furious and added, "Just take it out. He's not allowed to eat now, and you should have known that." I held the door open for her and waved her out before she had a chance to put the tray down.

Labor Day weekend approached. I knew no tests would take place, but none of the doctors I approached was willing, or empowered, to sign him out. Dr. Lowe, a neurosurgeon, passed by. He had been on our case earlier and would stop by from time to time to inquire about Richard's progress. He not only signed us out, he drove us home. (He lived near us.) I had to promise to be back Monday night—like a prisoner out on parole.

My little Richard, which I frequently called him so that he, in turn, called me, "My little Mommy," had changed from a friendly, outgoing, happy toddler to a whining, introverted child, even crying when a neighbor he liked stopped us while I took him for a walk. He started clinging to me, rebuffing other people.

I used to wonder why he should be so sick while I was well. Perhaps it should be the reverse. Death was on my mind. What I dreamed that night was startling but not surprising.

God was sitting in a big armchair, looking exactly like the statue of Lincoln in Washington, D.C. There was a long line of people passing before Him, and when it was my turn, He said to me, "Are you willing to die for your son?" I was going to say, "Yes, I am," but God said, "It took you too long to answer. That means no. Your son must die."

Richard needed to be in the hospital for longer stays, and I had learned the routine. It was spring 1961. Whenever a child died, a nurse would hurry in with a little cup in one hand and a bottle containing red liquid in another, and pass it to the mother of the child. I'd watch, and on bad days thought, I guess we are — next, but we weren't, not until the evening of April 19. I had heard from other parents that the doctors ask permission to perform an autopsy. I was unable to reach a decision while thinking about it.

That evening I did not leave when visiting hours were over. In the past, during the winter, Richard would start to cry when it turned dark, because that coincided with the end of visiting hours. That night he didn't; he mostly slept. A nurse reminded me that visiting hours were over, but I refused to leave. She summoned the head nurse, a friendly, middle-aged woman, who, I felt, put on a stern mien as she very seriously told me the same, and also, "I have to warn you, we have to enforce the rules."

"I can't," I told her. "I have to wait for my husband, and it's different tonight. I can't explain, but I can't leave."

When Jack came I told him what had transpired, adding, "They'll have to drag me out." By then, two supervisors had appeared, one tall and thin, the other short and stocky—a ludicrous-looking pair under any other circumstances. Jack told them, "We both want to stay tonight."

"That's not possible, it is not allowed, and it is against regulation," the tall one said. I had never before refused to leave, but I was adamant.

"I just cannot leave tonight," I repeated. The short one glanced at me, then at her partner. The two of them conferred, a few paces away out of our hearing, then the tall one said, "We'll have a cot put up for you in the sun-room, and you'll have to take turns sleeping there one at a time." The sun-room was adjacent to the ward. I did not use the cot at all, but at one point I suggested that Jack lie down. I stayed in the room with Richard. I bent over the crib to look at him every few minutes. Something was very wrong, I felt later during the night. I called the nurse and asked her to wake Jack. The baby was in a coma then, because he did not react to voice or touch.

We were both with him when he died a short time later. A nurse came with two cups of the red liquid and made us drink it. When we came home in the morning and told my mother, it was the only time I ever saw Jack cry.

When the doctor called regarding the autopsy, declaring, "It's important to us, especially in Richard's case, because the illness didn't manifest itself in the usual way. That's why it took so long to diagnose." I listened and had not yet answered when he pleaded, "If you give permission, that's the surest way for us to learn what to do for the next child."

That convinced me to say, "All right, go ahead."

33

MOURNING

NOTHER OBSTACLE REMAINED TO BE overcome. At the cemetery Jack and I met with the man in charge, who sat behind a large desk in a faintly lit office, which made me uncomfortable as soon as we entered. Jack explained that we wanted to buy a grave.

"You can't buy one grave," we were told in no uncertain terms. "It's either two or four." Two didn't make sense, so we agreed to buy four.

No sooner was that unpleasant task settled than an argument about the gravestone arose. The rude, overbearing guy presented us with the dimensions of the stone he suggested we buy.

"That's a very big stone. Wouldn't a smaller one be better?" I asked.

"Sorry, those are the ones we use here. Those are the rules, and I'm the one who makes them." I was ready to punch him.

"Look here," Jack put in. "He was only a young child. Let's

talk about that." Jack managed to get him to agree that we could have a foot-stone erected instead.

IN THE WEEKS AFTER RICHARD'S death, I sat in the room he had shared with Debbie (my mother occupied the other of the three bedrooms), and thought about him while Debbie was sleeping in her English-style baby carriage in the sun on the front lawn. She was four months old then, and slept soundly. All I had to do was to check every fifteen minutes to make sure she was covered and comfortable in the spring weather.

After checking, I returned to the room. It faced south, catching the afternoon sun, which reflected on the glass of one of the pictures on the wall, creating little patterns. A slight breeze coaxed the small, lightly colored spider up and around the frame. I watched, making no move to disturb it. I was fixated on Richard. I ruminated, playing scenes over and over in my mind. *Why did I not take him out of his crib on that last night and let him die in my arms? Why was I so obedient to the nurses' warning not to do it? And, most of all, why did I allow them to perform those painful spinal taps? Why didn't I just burst in and snatch him away from the doctors' eternal need to do research?* I became consumed with guilt. I had borne the responsibility, been — his spokesperson, and failed him. I was beginning to be afraid of losing my mind if I continued that way.

Then it struck me that there was nothing I could do. It was finished, and he was gone. I didn't cry; I felt my throat tightening, making it hard to breathe. Other times I felt a pain, an emptiness in the stomach, or, often, as if I'd lost one of my limbs.

Usually, after somebody's death, you hear, "He had a good life, and he was quite old when he died. He accomplished so much," followed by details of what the person had done that was of consequence, but Richard had not yet reached his third birthday when he died. Then it occurred to me that *his* accomplishments were that you could have a conversation with him because he spoke in full sentences early, that his happy personality was like a bright star shining in our midst.

Dark thoughts returned from time to time, so that, six months after he had died, I called Dr. Sitarz, the female physician who had been one of his doctors.

"Did the team do everything they could for Richard?" I asked.

"Yes, I remember him well, and please rest assured, Mrs. Malkin, we spent a lot of time discussing his case, and we made sure we left no stone unturned."

"Dr. Sitarz," I continued, "I feel terrible that I allowed the team to administer so many painful tests to my little son. Was it really necessary?"

In an empathetic tone, she answered, "You know, Mrs. Malkin, one often feels guilty when someone near and dear dies. It happened to me when I lost my father, and, being a physician, I felt I should have done more for him."

That helped a little, not too much. Jack also tried to reassure me that I had done more than necessary for the child. He was being kind to me, I felt, but going through his own grief, I wasn't sure of his objectivity.

Jack and I had talked about getting rid of the sandbox he had built in the backyard for Richard, where he used to play with his neighborhood friends, but we had never gotten around to doing it. One evening, in the early summer, I reported to Jack, "Guess what?" I looked out the window, and there was Donna and a couple of other little kids playing in the sandbox in the backyard.

"Oh, that's good. I'm pleased," he answered. "When I re-membered that we didn't get rid of it, I was hoping that would happen."

"Yes," I answered, "and the best part was that I'd been afraid of feeling sad and also jealous if I watched other people's children play there without Richard, but I was surprised to find myself smiling. I actually felt glad to see them. They even stopped in for a cookie and a cold drink, just as they had when he was there with them."

THE NEIGHBORS, ALL YOUNG WITH small children, were very nice to me. They invited me to play mah-jong with them, which they did daily. One of them told me, "It's great. We have a lot of fun, and I've formed a wonderful friendship with one of the women." Two weeks later I learned that this bosom-buddy friend had turned into her arch-enemy.

I wasn't interested in learning to play mah-jong or canasta. Instead, I decided to go back to school, knowing that, once I was enrolled, I would take the time to do the homework, and it would provide a focus.

My guilt and anger subsided, helped by the summer months, which made everyday life a little easier. I made a point of recall-ing the happy times we had spent with little Richard, instead of the terrible months during his sickness. I was able to concentrate on a vacation we had taken on a farm, and remembered his joy as he became acquainted with some of the animals. Talking about him to whoever was willing to listen also helped. Our next-door neighbor, a charming, supportive woman, asked what she could do. "If you just let me talk about him, that would be nice," I answered.

"Yes, of course," she said, but she was visibly uncomfortable listening, although I did not harp on the worst parts of his illness. She didn't know what to say, so I changed the subject. I wasn't looking for her input or sympathy. I just needed to vent.

IN THE FALL OF 1961 I was ready to register at the local university, Fairleigh Dickinson, which gave me credit for most of the courses I had taken at the City College of New York (CCNY) before my marriage. It counted roughly for two years. I started taking just one course once a week in the evening. Later, I took two. Doing the reading—I liked literature courses—and writing papers for two courses was all I could manage besides running the household and (later) bringing up two children. At that rate it took several years to get my B.A. in English, with a minor in Psychology. By the time I graduated, both my children, Debbie and Bradley (who had not been born yet when I returned to school), and my mother, attended my graduation. It was held outdoors on a lovely sunny day. Jack was not present—he had a business appointment. He was proud of me, but he was never really happy that I had returned to school. In some respects he acted more European than the American-born man he was. When I distanced myself from the proverbial housewife, it spelled an underlying threat to him.

I was glad to have my mother around. She had been so helpful during Richard's illness, and after he died she provided Debbie with the loving attention I was not yet able to give her. However, the night I attended school we used to get a baby sitter. My sister Irene made a fuss and insisted that we do that. Her reason was that it was too much for Mama, who did not mind, because Debbie was in her pajamas by the time I left the house.

34

DEBBIE AND BRADLEY
(MY FIFTH HOME)

E HAD LIVED IN THE rented house in Cliffside Park for nearly three years when the landlord told us he needed it for his newly married daughter. That meant house-hunting for us.

We were ready to buy, and we looked in several neighboring towns, choosing Tenafly for its excellent school system. We saw a house I liked. The real estate agent, visibly embarrassed, said in almost a whisper, "I don't think you'll be happy in this house."

"Why not?" I asked. "I like the little brook."

"It could overflow and cause problems."

She mentioned another flaw and quickly added, "Let me show you another house before you make a decision," and ushered us into her car.

Jack later explained that she'd made an excuse because people were not selling to Jews in that area. It worked to our advantage. The house with the brook was situated on a hill, a drawback for my mother, who suffered from heart disease. The location of our future home seemed ideal. My mother was still working, commuting to New York City every day. The bus stopped two short blocks away on even ground, and the supermarket was within walking distance—good for me since we only had one car, which Jack used for work. The school was also very close.

The house had not yet been built when we first stumbled upon the model. We had a choice of three styles, and we picked the plot with the biggest backyard. I did not like the idea of living in a development; the sameness of all the houses repelled me. It reminded me of my sister-in-law, Thelma, and her family, who lived in a development in another town—I'd been invited for lunch one day and I gotten lost because all the houses looked the same.

Our new home was at the beginning of the development, opposite larger homes that had been built by a different builder, which eliminated the development look. It happened that one of those other houses was for sale at a considerably higher price. "If we buy that house," Jack announced, looking somewhat troubled, "then we can't take vacations summer and winter."

"In that case, let's not get it," I was quick to answer. "I don't want to become a slave to the house."

In retrospect, the higher price spread over a thirty-year mortgage wouldn't have made that much difference, but Jack was afraid to venture further beyond our budget, already stretched, and I, taking for granted that he was smarter and knew more than I, accepted his decision.

We moved to our new home between Christmas and New Year's Day in 1960.

Bundled up to resist the chill, I carried in boxes and containers, some quite heavy. Jack had a chronic back problem, but despite the pain, he staggered into the house, schlepping packages. I didn't know I was pregnant (I had forgotten the date I was supposed to get my period) and soon after had a miscarriage, which had supposedly been caused by the lugging and lifting. It wasn't too bad, and since I hadn't expected to be pregnant, the emotional as well as the physical effects were minimal—no need to be hospitalized.

The split-level house—three bedrooms, two and a half bathrooms, and a den—was well constructed. We opted for an extra window for my mother's bedroom to make it as light as possible, something she craved. Debbie and her future brother, Bradley, shared a room.

A day did not go by when one or another of the neighbors, who themselves were newcomers, just walked in unannounced. I despaired, wondering if that was what happened when you own your own home—a complete lack of privacy. The visitors, and their curiosity about us, lessened after two or three weeks though, and it actually gave me a chance to become acquainted with all of them, making friends with some of them.

The various new owners were all young, with small children, and we grew into a little community as the years passed.

New York City, always a strong draw for me, was an easy commute, too. I liked the idea of looking for furniture there.

I was busy the first year, decorating and taking care of the baby.

By the time the following winter arrived, I was pregnant again. Early in the pregnancy the doctor had given me DES (diethylstilbestrol), the drug that was used widely to prevent miscarriages. He did not ask if I wanted it, nor did he discuss the pros and cons. "Here, dear, this will prevent you suffering another miscarriage," and, whoosh, the needle went into my tush. I hadn't had any problems in my first pregnancy, nor did I anticipate any in the second. The DES had little effect on the mothers. The offspring was the sufferer. Years later, surveys revealed that the daughters often had trouble conceiving and were almost never able to carry the baby to term, and that the sons likewise encountered their share of problems.

By late December, my gynecologist determined it was time for the baby to be born, and on my last office visit that month he asked jokingly, "How would you like to have a New Year's Day baby?"

"Sure. I'd love it. I've gained so much weight, this baby must be huge," I answered, after making sure he wasn't joking.

When we woke up on January 1, 1961, heavy snow had fallen during the night. Jack prepared to take me to the hospital around lunchtime to have the baby induced. In the excitement, the car got stuck at the bottom of the driveway, where the snow had been piled up by the town's plow trucks. Jack, angry, started to shovel, but progress was slow.

A patrolling police car passed by and stopped. I had stepped out of the car and was standing near Jack. One of the policemen took one look at me and asked, "Can I help?"

"Maybe you can," Jack said, and explained the circumstances, whereupon the policeman turned to me and said,

"Come on, ma'am. Get in the car. I'll be glad to drive you to the hospital."

Jack arrived later, squirming in the chair next to me because of his back pain (and my contractions!), and before long I was transferred to the operating room. I hadn't chosen natural childbirth for this delivery. I was too tired and worn out—physically and emotionally—from Richard's illness. It was an easy birth—I was anesthetized.

Our little girl, Debbie, was born January 1, 1961, with a head full of dark hair, and was pretty and serene from day one.

By all accounts, she should have been a difficult baby, because of my unorthodox, unhealthy, and highly emotional pregnancy all during Richard's illness, but we were truly blessed. Debbie ate and slept well, and she was very easy to take care of. When the nurse brought her to me for her mid-day feeding, we snuggled, I, slightly propped up on the pillow, Debbie nestled in my arms. I looked at her, very tired but smiling happily as I inserted the bottle in her mouth. Two minutes later I was fast asleep, totally worn out from Richard's illness, followed by giving birth. She drank to the last drop without any encouragement from me. She was bottle-fed rather than nursed, to allow me to be with Richard, especially for unplanned hospital stays.

Mama was wonderfully helpful during that critical period of the first three and a half months of Debbie's life, which coincided with Richard's last. We had hired a baby nurse for the first two weeks, and after that Mama would get up at night to give her a bottle, and she also took care of her during the day while I was at the hospital with Richard. Fortunately for us, she had retired by that time.

Mama would look at Debbie and say to me, "You are so lucky; she's a wonderful baby. You'll get a lot of pleasure from her." How right she was! We soon recognized how bright she was, pretty, imaginative, and so content, and later, so flexible.

Debbie was easily toilet trained—too easily. She used to take off her wet diapers while playing in the backyard. One day, she couldn't have been much more than two years, I received a phone call from a neighbor, "Your child is running around naked again."

All went well. She spoke early, and she grew and behaved normally—with one exception. I worried about her and frequently called the pediatrician during his early morning phone-in hour. "I think she's overweight," I'd report, or, two months later, "I think she's underweight, she has a vein across her eyelid" (something that concerned the doctors in Richard's case), and, "Something is very wrong—she's not walking." I was terribly worried that Richard's sickness might be repeated.

"Bring her in at ten o'clock, if you like, but I can assure you she is fine." Those last three words were what I needed to hear each time I telephoned.

Twenty-two months later, while I was busy in the kitchen, I heard a clear little voice calling, "Look, Mommy, I'm walking." I dropped everything and ran to the living room to watch a miracle unfold. Debbie was holding onto the cocktail table for dear life, taking her first steps. What joy! I think I was more elated than she. Clapping hands, laughing, and singing, we danced around the room together, ending with a big hug.

She grew up to run in several marathons.

Gradually I started to pay more attention to her, and, once I'd begun, I quickly became immersed in her, loved her fully, and reaped the rewards of my mother's earlier prophecy.

We talked a lot to Debbie about getting a new baby brother or sister, and she eagerly awaited the event.

Her little brother arrived September 10, 1963, when she was a little more than two and a half years old. Born in New York City's Columbia Presbyterian Hospital, he—like my other two children—arrived in the world healthy, with a full head of dark brown hair and big round eyes. All three children looked very much alike on the one-day-old photographs. It was more or less natural childbirth, which I had asked for, but they gave me oxygen to ease the birth. He was circumcised in the hospital. I did not nurse him, but he did very well on the bottle. I do remember that no DES was administered while pregnant with him.

During my hospital stay I contacted Dr. Sitarz once more. By then it had been five and a half years since she took care of Richard. She remembered me and was glad to hear of Bradley's birth. She even came to visit for a few minutes.

He was not at all a replacement for Richard, but we were overjoyed to have a boy. I did not want to call him Richard, though it is customary in the Jewish religion to name a baby after a deceased, close relative. Baby Richard had already received *his* name after my deceased father, and no way was I going to repeat that name. Jack came up with the name "Bradley." Irene heard of it and immediately commented, "Bradley, Jr., Bradley III." It sounded alien to me, too—I didn't know anybody by that name—but Jack liked it. I chose Robert as his middle name, should he prefer one day to have the choice of a more common identity.

Bradley suffered colic attacks as a baby, making the first few months difficult for him. The pain usually started around five o'clock in the afternoon, and I remember carrying him a great deal. In time he outgrew it. When he was two years old he needed a hernia operation. I could not stay in the local hospital with him, but he did not seem unhappy when Jack and I picked him up the day after the operation. He was cuddly, like the many stuffed toys lining his crib; he liked to sit on my lap and liked being carried, and I liked it, too.

He adored Debbie, uttering, "Dubbie," as his first word, and later expressed his wish to marry her—never me. He became my mother's sweetheart. Nothing he wanted was too much, or out of bounds as far as she was concerned.

His kind and good-hearted nature showed early. One afternoon he was eating a piece of chocolate while waiting with me in the street for Debbie to come home from school. She noticed it and said, "I want some, too."

"That's the last piece, dear, but—"

Before I had finished the sentence he took the chocolate that was on its way to his mouth and handed it to her. They were unusually close as children. Bradley's adoration of Debbie and her sense of protectiveness worked wonders when they were little, very much the envy of our neighbors and friends.

For me, Jack's comment one day, "You really enjoy the kids," rang true. Why not? Bradley was an adorable, cuddly baby, and later a lively, smart toddler. His life was harder than Debbie's due to my inexperience. There was a time I got angry at my mother for interfering in the upbringing of my children, but instead of taking it up with her, I got impatient with little Bradley. He was loving and forgiving, and if he got his way he repaid it tenfold.

They played well together until Debbie reached her tenth or eleventh year. Then trouble started. Donna, Debbie's friend from across the street, spent all day, every day, at our house. I had the feeling I was bringing her up. She was thin, and taller than Debbie. She used to stand by the door, her big, brown eyes peeking insecurely, waiting to take her cue from Debbie. During the months she spent with us she managed, with a little encouragement from me, to overcome her fear of dogs. We took care of our neighbors' dog for a couple of weeks while they vacationed, and it was by far easier, and more preferable, to get Donna accustomed to the dog than to worry whether they needed to be separated.

By the time the girls had reached twelve years they wanted to be by themselves. They would go to Debbie's bedroom and shut the door in Bradley's face. "Let me in, I want to come in," he yelled, banging on the door. It was incomprehensible to him to be excluded from Debbie's company. Bradley had to find his own friends and learn to tolerate Donna.

Our children continued being close, and now, in their fifties, they still enjoy playing April Fool's jokes on each other all the way from Georgia to California.

35

REVELATIONS

THE SCHANZERS, WHO LIVED ACROSS the street in 1970, became our friends. Walter was from Vienna; his wife, Trudy, was American. One day she mentioned that they were foregoing a vacation because they couldn't take their dog. I told Jack, adding, "That doesn't make sense."

"I hope you're not going to offer to take Monty," he answered quickly.

"Well, I already have."

The little schnauzer enjoyed living with us, and the children loved having him. The result was they wanted a dog. We promised one by the time Debbie reached fourteen, thinking she'd have forgotten by then—five years hence.

The following year, Jack and I traveled to Israel for ten days. In exchange for having boarded Monty, Trudy offered to take care of our children. They were almost as happy with her and Walter as Monty had been with us. Her attentiveness knew no bounds, but they never forgot that "Mrs. Schanzer made us eat lima beans before we got dessert."

Jack had done some work for Histadrut (Israel's Federation of Labor), which afforded us the free trip.

Climbing Masada was on the agenda. It is a fortress situated on top of an isolated rock plateau, overlooking the Dead Sea. The Israelites defended it to death against the Romans in 74 C.E.

Nowadays, it is possible to ride up in a cable car, but we had to start the ascent before five in the morning, on foot, to avoid the mid-day heat and sun. The pleasure of seeing it rise behind the Masada rock, and watching as the darkness of the night slowly receded into the light of day and the rock formation began to glow in the sun glistening on it, more than made up for the early start.

We started to lag behind the group until we were the last ones, far behind everyone else. Jack was huffing and puffing, and had to stop several times to catch his breath. The group leader stayed with us, and asked, "Are you okay? Would you like some water? You don't have to do this, you know, we can meet you later."

"No, no, I'm fine, thanks," Jack answered, breathing hard and heavy, but he decided to continue.

Word reached us that, once you were on top, there was a cup attached to a chain from which you could drink water that trickled into it from a nearby cistern full of stored rainwater.

"No way am I going to drink from the one cup that everybody's using," I muttered to Jack. He didn't bother to answer. An hour later, hot, tired, and thirsty, we reached the top. Jack wasn't talking. I called out, "Where's that cup with the water?"

We thought Jack was out of shape. We had no idea that his difficulties stemmed from the sickness that would eventually kill him.

Our guide, young and enthusiastic, proudly pointed out that the orange groves all around us had been swamps and marshes only a few short years before. He showed us pipes carrying water winding through the bushes and around trees. "We planted those trees and bushes, and made that soil fertile." His eyes beaming as he made the announcement. He mentioned Israel's Nobel Prize winners in Medicine and Science, referred to other accomplishments and advances, and described how the country had defended itself against overwhelming odds when attacked by surrounding enemies. By the time I left Israel, I felt proud of being Jewish for the first time in my life. That came as a revelation. All my life I had adhered to what I had been taught: Don't flaunt being Jewish, and don't be loud.

JACK WAS HIS OWN BOSS but claimed too much work was waiting for him, and he returned after ten days. I stopped in Sicily on the way home. I had always wanted to see beautiful, old Taormina. The dining room at the small hotel became overcrowded at dinner. I was asked to join three other guests at a table for four—a young couple and a man, approximately my age. They all spoke German, and I fell in with them, which aroused the older man's curiosity. Sizing me up as an American tourist, he commented, "You speak German well."

"Thank you," I answered.

"Well, I mean, you didn't learn to speak like that at school," he pushed.

"Perhaps I did."

"So where did you go to school?" he asked, leaning towards me with a smirk.

"I went to school in Vienna, where I was born and lived until I was thrown out when Hitler came. I was twelve then."

He did not reply. There was dead silence at the table. It felt as though many minutes went by without a word spoken by anybody. I relished the moment. My newly acquired pride in being Jewish had made me hold my head high. In the past, under similar circumstances, feeling embarrassed, I would have broken the silence. This time I waited. After all, I hadn't left my home voluntarily, and I had nothing to be ashamed of. I hadn't killed anybody or done anything wrong. I left it to one of the others to start conversing again.

He tried to ingratiate himself with me a few days later, when our paths crossed again. On an evening tour to Mt. Etna, the temperature fell. Halfway up, old army coats were distributed to the tourists. He ran back and forth to find one small enough to fit me, but back in those days my philosophy held that a non-Jewish German my age or older was guilty till proven innocent. He fit into that age category. I thanked him for the coat, but avoided him rather than engage in conversation.

JACK AND I HAD A SECOND opportunity to go to Israel the following year. The plan was for him to pick up Debbie and Bradley at the Schanzers (they took care of them again) as soon as he returned from Israel and to put them on a plane to Switzerland. I had flown there from Israel to meet them. My mother, who was vacationing in Wengen, invited us to spend a week with her. They loved their first plane ride. The flight attendant—called "stewardess" in 1972—fed them can after can of Coca-Cola, all kinds of sweet goodies, gave "wings" to Bradley, a stack of cards to Debbie, and nonchalantly handed them over to me in the hall where I was anxiously waiting. "You're their mother, right? They were great." And she was off.

In the hotel we met Mama, and the following day we took our first hike—riding up the mountain in a cable car and hiking down—not as easy as it sounds. Our calves hurt plenty the next day. We inspected the town, which did not allow cars, and went to an indoor swimming pool the day it rained, but mostly continued the hiking. After a week, my mother left to meet her sister, Mitzi, in England, and I took the children to Bern, afterwards to Holland, where we rented bicycles in the country and did some sightseeing in Amsterdam.

Both children moved from nursery school to elementary school, from day camp to sleep- away, from swimming lessons at the local swim club to special, beloved vacations at Mr. Muller's farm. He was a Gentile who had escaped the Nazis. He had been the editor of an anti-Nazi underground paper, and had landed on the Nazis' blacklist. A charming, soft-spoken man, he led interesting after-dinner discussions, which the adults enjoyed, and he allowed the kids to ride on the tractor with him, which was a treat for them. In the winter, there were ski lessons, which Debbie had asked for and Bradley shunned. He was athletic; she profited from the lessons. Both became excellent skiers at Burke,

Vermont, where even my skiing improved to the advanced level so I could keep up with them.

In pre-school days, I had befriended most—and became good friends with many—of the neighbors. I socialized with bright, intelligent women day in, day out, while the little ones had fun on the playground. The conversations, however, centered on diapers and baby food, and, in later years at the swim club, the emphasis was still on kids. I contributed as much as anybody, yet something was missing for me. I couldn't quite describe or pinpoint it until I stumbled on Betty Friedan's *The Feminine Mystique* in the early Sixties. What an eye opener! She wrote about *me*, the suburban housewife, unfulfilled in one area of my life and feeling guilty about it. I wasn't a freak after all!

Before I had read Friedan's book, I hadn't realized that my restlessness had a name. On the contrary, I worried that I was ungrateful. I had a husband who loved me and two healthy, good-looking, smart children; we enjoyed summer as well as winter vacations, but she reassured me that there was nothing wrong in pining for more intellectual interaction and wanting to continue my interrupted education, and that I didn't have to feel guilty.

I personified the suburban housewife. I did some volunteer work for National Council of Jewish Women, helped my mother in various ways, and attended the local university one evening a week, all of which filled my time, but not my needs.

Socially, I gave up the Monday night opera subscription I'd had for years, because the late hour was rough on Jack. We changed to Friday nights; we relinquished that after a while, too, because he really was not an opera buff. It took two years to find a friend interested in opera who was willing to drive to the city with me.

We arranged few dinner parties. We sometimes socialized with friends on the weekend, or we went to a movie. Many weekends were spent at home. We patronized few restaurants; the stores, Bloomingdale's and Alexander's on Route 4, and a movie theater in town showing run-of-the-mill-films made for pretty dull suburban life in the Sixties. I found it hard. I had always been a city woman. Jack was in contact with people all day during the week. He was happy just being with the family on weekends. To pep up suburban life, some of our neighbors' pastimes consisted of parties. The focal point was gossiping, drinking, and playing games during which husbands and wives exchanged partners. We did not participate.

When, in later years, he chose to go into private arbitration, he had an office built in one part of our unfinished basement. It turned into a pleasant room. The paneled walls housed an air-conditioner in one of the windows, and a heater, a large desk, wooden cabinets as well as metal filing cabinets, and our old kitchen table for extra papers filled the space. Built-in bookshelves, a big fluorescent light that covered most of the ceiling, and a beige carpet thrown over the linoleum floor gave it a finished look. Later, he bought a special rug to fit under the desk, where Ginny, our dog, slept while he worked. He spent evenings, and a great deal of time on weekends, down there. He was a workaholic, and I missed his company.

During the course of our marriage, he had moved from being

Director of the Schiffli Association (representing owners of Schiffli firms, which had machines that produced the Swiss type Schiffli embroidery) to teaching at Fairleigh Dickinson, and later at Newark College of Engineering, where he lectured on labor relations, to being the head of the National Mediation Board in Newark. He was also president of the American Arbitration Association in New York City, where his photograph hung with others in the conference room. His work as a private labor-relations arbitrator would have constituted a conflict as head of the Mediation Board, so he resigned.

Jack loved his work as arbitrator. I felt trapped in the suburbs.

Luck turned my way. A friend put me in touch with Dr. Constance Sutton, a professor of anthropology at the uptown campus of New York University. She offered me a job as secretary of her department. The school was in the Bronx, off Fordham Road, which made it possible for me to drive there in twenty minutes. The job was part-time—just right. I could be home at about the same time as the children. They were under orders to come straight home from school—just a few blocks away—and to take the same route every day. Should they be home before me, they were to go to a specific neighbor. Jack did not want me to work, but the opportunity at NYU, he agreed, was too good to pass up.

My boss was the department head, Professor Charles Leslie, a handsome man with a gray-black beard and dark, deep-set eyes. The old building in which the Anthropology Department was housed had once been a private home. The furniture was sparse and worn. A short hallway led from the outside to the room I occupied. Next to my desk and typewriter stood a table against the wall, large enough to accommodate at least half a dozen people. There was a cupboard on the opposite wall, adjacent to a staircase that led to the upstairs room, which was used by the three or four other professors who made up the staff, hardly a matter of consequence since they were rarely there at the same time. Charles and Connie shared a room. They had to pass through the one I occupied to get to it.

The atmosphere was open, friendly, and congenial, and we were soon on a first-name basis. Before long, they decided to let me run the whole department, coordinating everybody's schedule, and whatever needed to be done to have it run smoothly. Sometimes they discussed school problems with me.

Charles, as the chair of the department, had received a grant to teach a 'bridge' class for disadvantaged students who had been pushed through high school and graduated, but had been found unprepared for college. None of the professors in the department had the time or the inclination to teach the course. Instead, Charles asked me to teach the class, which coincided with my working hours. One of the students, after placing his shiny knife on his desk, usually took a nap in the back row. Another one was on drugs. Most, though, were motivated. When I asked one of the girls one morning why she hadn't done her homework, she said, "When I come home, my mother leaves for work, and I've got two younger kids to take care of. By the time they go to sleep, I'm tired, and I want to watch TV. I don't feel like doing homework then."

I couldn't very well reprimand her or tell her that education was important. I thought I would leave that for a later opportunity and just said, "I can understand that. If you want to come in early and stop in my office before class, I'll help you with your homework or any questions you may have regarding the course." She did not come.

"How's the class going, Lisl?" asked Charles after a week, When I told him, he shrugged and, with one hand brushing back his hair, exclaimed, "Better you than me! I wouldn't have the patience." Then he invited me for lunch in the faculty dining room. Shortly after lunch it was time for me to go home.

On a Wednesday, I approached him. "Charles, I won't be able to come in next Monday. I have to go to a teacher's conference in Bradley's class."

His answer amazed me: "Well, just call in sick."

Thinking of the days I had worked in a commercial office, I wondered how that was possible.

The following term he left for India on a year's sabbatical.

CONNIE—TALL, BLONDE, BLUE-EYED, AND very attractive—took over as Chair. She became very busy with her teaching schedule and administrative tasks, so that time passed before she had a chance to keep Charles abreast of what was happening in the search for a new Chair at the downtown campus, and of the political intrigues in progress. I used to think intellectuals were above such pettiness. I reminded her that Charles had written to me that he was worried about his own situation. She suggested I inform him of whatever news there was, with which she entrusted me. That's how our regular correspondence started. He asked my help in having certain books and office materials sent to him, doing some research for him, and assistance in getting one of his books published. Apart from these requests, his letters contained interesting reports of his life in India.

Soon after Connie took over the department she called me into her office and invited me to sit at the old, wooden table next to her. The sun was shining through the two windows on the opposite wall, which made the room bright. It reflected our mood. Turning to me, she said, "Lisl, I want you to help me decide what title to use," and we bantered: "Chairwoman," "Chairperson," "Department Head," "Chair," and a couple of others. It was exciting. In no time at all we were talking about women's issues. She had always been "liberated," perhaps because of her profession as an anthropologist. We became close friends, discussed our private lives, and she took it upon herself to be my mentor. I needed support, she decided, to become my own person, which for her meant taking care of my own needs much more than I had done in the past. She started out, "If you want to go to graduate school, Lisl, do it. (I had my bachelor's degree by then). You don't have to ask anyone for permission. You have a right, as a person, to do what's best for you and to do what you need."

She continued supporting and encouraging me in my endeavors to free myself from the suburban mindset, and her interest in me, her patience, her nurturing, her knowledge, and her skill in guiding me were invaluable in moving me in that direction. She would easily spend an hour talking to me on a personal level before switching to women's lives in general. That's when I learned that the women professors' pay was, maybe, only three quarters of the men's, although they carried the same course load. She was popular with her students, who considered her an excellent teacher. She was extraordinarily smart.

Prior to his sabbatical, Charles spotted me in the faculty dining room with Connie one day, who treated me several times. He made his way to our table, and, facing me, said teasingly, "I bet Connie's giving you an earful about Women's Lib." Although he was broadminded, he was conservative. His family had originated in the South, and as he once explained to me, the slaves his ancestors owned hadn't had a bad life at all.

I left my job at NYU—my shelter—to enter graduate school. I was grateful to Connie. I owed her much.

36

SEVERAL SURPRISES

THERE WAS ANOTHER WOMAN IN my life who was a free spirit. In the fall of 1972, I enrolled in Columbia University for a master's degree in the department of "Family and Community Relationships." The program was structured around inter-disciplinary courses in psychology, anthropology, and sociology, leaving us free to choose. My interest had always been psychology, which made up the bulk of my classes.

Early in the semester, one of the students and I gravitated towards each other. She was tall, broad-shouldered, and beautiful. Her blonde hair and blue eyes, as well as her name—Ingrid—and her accent meant she was from one of the Nordic countries. We would meet in the cafeteria before or after class to chat.

One evening after class, as I was sipping a cup of coffee, I was struck speechless. She was not from one of the Nordic countries at all—she was German. As soon as I collected myself, I said, "Sorry, Ingrid, I have to get home early tonight."

I grabbed my notebook and purse and left without offering

to drop her off on the way home, which I sometimes did. As I drove to New Jersey, that was all I could think about, and not only then. The subject occupied my thoughts for several days. How could I like a German so much, feel so warm towards her, and, most important, how could I be friends with her, or even *want* to be? This question twisted and turned my mind in various directions till I became dizzy thinking about it.

At our next meeting, I made sure to let her know I was Jewish, partly to test her reaction. It helped to hear her say, "I've given up my religion. I'm Bahai now." We talked about our backgrounds. My concern that she might have been a Nazi was somewhat assuaged—she was thirteen at the end of the war. I reminded myself of Romeo and Juliet's "What's in a name?" Thinking she was Swedish or Danish, I'd liked her; I decided I would continue liking her as a German.

A second surprise awaited me. I was to pick her up one day, and I volunteered to bring lunch, which we were going to eat on the way to a special lecture. I parked the car on East Ninety-fourth Street, walked to her house, and rang the bell. The sandwiches for our lunch were packed in a brown paper bag. A good-looking man in his early sixties, his gray hair combed back, opened the door. He introduced himself. "You must be Lisl Malkin. I'm Dr. Rollo May. Please come in." Smiling at me, he motioned to let me pass, adjusting his horn-rimmed glasses as I gripped the paper bag to stop it from slipping through my fingers. I was shocked to find myself face to face with the well-known writer and psychoanalyst.

They invited me for lunch—the first of many more.

Ingrid and I became close friends, and I was at their home frequently, and also at their summer house in New Hampshire. I enjoyed being with them. Rollo was friendly and courteous to me, and Ingrid and I always had a lot to talk about. At dinner, celebrated guests—psychologists, writers, actors, and other notables sat to the right and left of me. Nobody ever refused an invitation to their home. When I told her that Jack was not available for a dinner invitation, Ingrid replied, "Oh, fine, then you can come by yourself." She cooked great meals in their duplex apartment, which consisted of a small kitchen, a large living room furnished with a black leather couch facing the fireplace, a couple of big black leather chairs on either side, and on the side closest to the kitchen, a long table with eight chairs around it, which served as the dining room. May's office and study were downstairs.

Jack regarded my friendship with Ingrid with some alarm. He referred to her as "unfettered," and we had several discussions about that. He was right, of course, but that was what I found so fascinating. Not necessarily what she *did*, but the idea of possessing the ability to be unfettered or, at least, *inclining* in that direction, seemed liberating, and that appealed to me.

Ingrid and I attended a workshop featuring Virginia Satir (a sought after family therapist) in a hotel in Massachusetts that provided an indoor, glass enclosed swimming pool. Ingrid decided to take a dip—naked. The hall was dimly lit from the fading sun as evening approached. Somebody turned the lights on, and, quite unperturbed, she called, "Please turn them off," as she slowly covered her breasts. I, fully clothed, sitting on a chair by the pool, had accompanied her at her request. I felt like an old chaperon—only in my forties, and just a couple of years older than she.

Her talent in nurturing and being supportive was equaled by her gift for networking. She started a consciousness-raising group for which she gathered several able women. At its high point we must have been eight or nine, ranging in age from a twenty-year-old single woman to a married one—a writer—in her early sixties. Helen Iglesias, an author, was in the group for a while, until she left for Maine to shut herself in her cabin to write another book. Happy, the wife of one of our professors, was a teacher at Banks College. Another woman, also a writer, who spoke so beautifully that I just sat and listened to her words without hearing the contents, once reported on her frustration over having an article turned down by the *New Yorker* magazine only to have it accepted when her husband submitted it under his name at a later date. Two lesbian women, who were partners, attended our weekly sessions several times. We had to ask that one of them leave—their choice—because their arguments with each other caused disruption, and it was not our task to deal with that. All of us either had been, or were then, in therapy.

We were very strict about the rules. You could only talk about yourself, your own thoughts, even better, your own feelings—not what your husband, partner, or boyfriend thought. One of the goals was to make us more assertive. That's how they found out I didn't have my own checkbook.

"It doesn't really matter," I said. "I have a signature on my husband's, and I can write a check whenever I want."

"Do you carry the checkbook around with you?" asked Happy.

"No, I can't. It's too big. It has three checks to a page."

"Well, there you are. You need your own, so you don't have to go running to your husband to ask for the checkbook," one of the other women told me, looking straight at me, just short of pointing a finger at me.

I realized they were right, but I needed to present the idea to Jack so he didn't feel threatened by the various ideas I brought home concerning Women's Lib.

They obsessed over making me more assertive. One of my assignments was to stop at a gas station and ask for just three dollars' worth of gas. If the attendant made a face or grumbled, I was to stick to my guns and repeat, "Yes, just give me three dollars' worth." That was an unwelcome request in those days.

Between my therapy and the consciousness-raising group, I was forced to look at my life—my actions and reactions, and where I was going. This inward-looking needed time and had to be balanced with homework for school, taking care of my mother's needs, running a household, and spending time with my husband and children. Also, there was often something exciting brewing with Ingrid that I didn't care to miss.

As we left an afternoon class one day, she said, "Bye, I'll see you tonight at the Everett's party."

"What are you talking about?" I asked. "I wasn't invited."

"Oh, I forgot. It'll be fine. You'll be invited," she called, running for the bus.

I had hardly stepped into the house when the phone rang

with an invitation. The party was hosted by the president of the New School.

As arranged, I arrived on time at the apartment on Twelfth Street opposite the New School, where Rollo was to speak later that evening. The maid took my coat, and I introduced myself to Dr. Everett, who, in turn, introduced me to two elderly ladies sitting next to each other on the sofa. I took my seat on a sofa opposite them. We were the first ones, each sipping wine served by the butler. When two more people arrived, one of the women got up, came towards me, and said, "I heard your name is Lisl. I suppose that means you speak German. Do you mind if I sit with you?"

She was tall, her gray hair combed back into a bun, and as I glanced up into her long, narrow face, I answered, "Please do. I'm delighted to talk to you." I had no idea who she was, but was glad to have company. She was Hannah Tillich, the widow of the German theologian Paul Tillich. Not long after we started to chat, I made a faux-pas of which I was unaware at the time. I had noticed two books in an open bookcase nearby. Prominently displayed were one by Rollo May and another by herself, on the shelf above his.

"How nice to see your book, Mrs. Tillich, and Rollo's sitting there close together," I said. She just smiled.

Soon the room filled with people. From what I heard, I realized that each of them had written a book, was about to publish another one, or had been asked to write a foreword to somebody else's. At that moment, I decided I would stay put; I would make no attempt to mingle or start a conversation with anybody, hoping that Mrs. Tillich would stay next to me to chat, or just smile.

Ingrid and Rollo arrived late and noticed me right away—she with a smile, he with a puzzled look. Ingrid, in her absent-minded fashion, had forgotten to tell me the purpose of the party. Apparently, quite a tiff had erupted between Rollo and Mrs. Tillich. One of them had written something in one of those books that the other objected to violently, which had led to a strained relationship between the two former friends. I was sitting in the enemy camp. Dr. Everett had arranged the party to bring them together, hoping they would make peace with one another.

AS FAR AS MY NEWLY earned master's degree in Family and Community Relationships was concerned, I found the best part was meeting Ingrid and attending the consciousness-raising group. I liked some of the classes. While it wasn't easy to find a job with that degree, something interesting occurred.

I received a phone call one afternoon from one of my professors at Columbia who, in addition to teaching our class, also taught at Lehman College.

"I can't teach the course at Lehman this term, and I was wondering if you would be interested in doing it."

"Why," I blubbered, "this is kind of sudden. I don't know if—"

"If you decide to do it," she interrupted, "I will lend you my notes. I will go over them with you and you can call me. The books should be in the bookstore soon."

"I do appreciate your offer, but can I think about it?"

"Yes. I'll be in my office till five."

It was five minutes after three. Jack was not home, and I didn't know where to reach him to talk it over. I decided to give it a try, feeling pretty sure of his support.

I telephoned her and heard that classes were scheduled to start the following week. I would have to meet her, and also the department head, before then. When she handed over her big file of notes, she also lent me the textbook and gave me some hints about what to do, and what not to do, adding, "It's okay if you just give them a true-or-false test."

The 101 course I was to teach was in family relationships, similar to one I had taken recently myself. I had no teaching experience (except the "bridge" class at N.Y.U.), and the books for the students did not arrive until three weeks into the term, which made for frequent nightmares. I was one chapter ahead of the students. Fortunately, I was familiar enough with the subject to answer questions, and whatever little experience I had with this course was still more than the students'.

The head of the department came to observe me. I had just divided the students into groups in accordance with their family ranking—oldest, middle, and youngest. They were to discuss their roles in the family positioning, how they perceived their place, treatments by other family members, special names and/or expectations assigned to them, and afterwards compare similarities or differences. This innovative teaching appealed to the department head. I was asked to come back the following year, which I declined because I wanted to get my degree in social work.

I ENROLLED IN ADELPHI UNIVERSITY'S School of Social Work, which worked out better than Columbia as far as my family obligations were concerned. I had done some volunteer work in the mental health department at the Bronx hospital, which, however, did not give me any hoped-for credit. It did provide some insight, though, into people's lives suffering from schizophrenia or paranoia, and I benefited from lectures held for employees by staff doctors.

The scheduling of courses at the school made life complicated. While it was not difficult academically, the timing was. I was assigned an internship one evening a week at Jewish Family Services in the Bronx. Late classes were held the next morning, which did not help me, because I had to get the children off to school.

My mother fell in the street and broke her pelvic bone. Hospital visits created a backlog in my homework and put a severe strain on my timetable, which did not allow for such intrusions. I complained to Jack, "I can't do it all. I'm going to drop out, although I know that means I'll never go back."

"Just hang in there, Lisl," he reassured me. "Christmas vacation is approaching. Tell you what. I'll take the kids and the dog skiing, and that will give you time to catch up. How about it?"

That was a big favor, because he did not like skiing, and he did not like the cold. But it gave me the time I needed to write overdue papers, and my only remaining obligations were to visit Mama in the hospital and feed the cat. That was a success for all concerned.

IT TOOK ME AN HOUR to drive door to door to Adelphi University in Garden City, Long Island, the same time as driving to New York City and looking for a parking spot. Once, as I drove past

Long Island Sound, I noticed several sailboats anchored in the water. The weather had been warm all along, and on that particular day the sun was shining in a cloudless, blue sky. The water sparkled like a mirror. I felt content, counting my blessings. Then I remembered the date—April 20, the day our little boy died. Instantly, I rebuked myself. How could I feel so good on that day? It was then almost fifteen years after his death, and I thought about him—smiling as I recalled some of his words and sayings, and feeling sad when I pictured a potentially exceptional life that had been lost. By the time I entered the school parking lot, I decided that remembering him was the right, as well as the good, thing to do, but it was also acceptable to be able to enjoy the sunshine and warm feelings, and it was healthy to move on with my life.

I graduated in 1977 (with my second master's degree) and received my license as a Certified Social Worker several months later. New Jersey did not require a license, but I had studied in a New York school, and everybody registered for the exam, so I did, too. The license enabled me to practice therapy in New York, but I preferred a job in a school in New Jersey—easier for the family.

Apart from the mandatory work required of a N.J. school social worker, which involved interviews with teachers and parents, and a class observation, all of which needed to be documented and written up to meet deadlines, I held workshops for teachers and for parents. Counseling of children turned into the major part of the job (by choice). I took a course at the Behavior Institute in New York City to become familiar with cognitive therapy, which I felt was necessary in school counseling, and sought supervision on my own with a child psychiatrist. Working in a school meant no evenings, that I was home when the children came home from school, and that our vacations coincided. It also became inevitable to spend less time with Ingrid and Rollo, and eventually none, at least in New York, because within a few months they moved to California, where they subsequently divorced.

37

BAT/BAR MITZVAHS
AND OTHER EVENTS

O MI," AS MY CHILDREN CALLED my mother, created no problems during the early years of the twelve she lived with us, but as they grew, I was relegated to being a child again, and she liked to be in charge. If Bradley asked, shortly before dinner, if he could have a cookie, she answered, "Yes, of course, sweetheart," before I had a chance to say no. If he did not like what I had cooked for dinner, she offered, "Would you like scrambled eggs instead? A hot dog? A hamburger?" She suggested another dish each time he refused the last. The dinners I cooked consisted of food both children liked, and her offers of different foods developed into a game that I didn't like. I felt she was spoiling him. She reprimanded me once in front of Debbie: "I don't know why you let her wear that dress. It's too short for her."

"What's the difference, Mama? She's only in first grade, and she loves that dress." Debbie never wanted to wear it again.

When Mama lived with us I dreaded the winters. One of the children would have a cold, she'd catch it, and it would turn into strep throat. Every winter, it seemed, she suffered a major physical catastrophe. Once she visited Irene, fell down some steps in her home, and broke a couple of ribs. She came back to our house to recuperate. When I carefully turned her in bed, she screamed, causing Bradley to shout, "You're hurting Omi."

On the other hand, when she felt well, she made breakfast for Debbie and Bradley and took them to the playground on a Sunday morning to give Jack and me a chance to sleep late.

She made Chanukah cookies with them. I supplied all the ingredients and then left the house, but not before I offered to clean up. The three of them needed the whole kitchen. Everything was covered in flour: the table, the counters, the floor, the stove, and even places where you did not expect to find flour. It was worth it. All three loved it.

Making Chanukah cookies with Omi became a ritual, and more than a happy memory years after her death. Debbie now makes the same Chanukah cookies with *her* children.

One evening during dinner, Mama was criticizing Jack, and the children, catching the prevailing mood, said some unkind words to her. Jack immediately cut in, "That's no way to talk to your Omi. Apologize right now, and don't talk that way to her again." I always admired him for that. His insistence on the children being respectful to her was very influential in the wonderful relationship the three enjoyed—a deep, lasting love for one another, as well as happy, loving memories.

Jack drove Mama if necessary, lent her money at a moment's

notice to save her a trip to the bank, and even found her a boyfriend, which added some pleasant hours to her life. What she enjoyed most was to be with her grandchildren, both of whom she loved dearly. It didn't occur to her that she was usurping my role as mother. This was the woman who had been so brave years earlier when she rescued my father, my sister, and me from being killed by the Nazis, sacrificing and accomplishing endlessly unselfish tasks to bring it all to fruition.

One day she was angry at me. We had a disagreement concerning the children, which was the sole point of disputes between her and me, at the end of which she said, "I think it's best if I move out," throwing me a stern look. In a flash I was the little girl in Vienna hearing her threat to leave the family. This time, I was able to answer calmly, "Perhaps, Mama, that would be best. We'll get along better that way. I think we'll laugh again instead of squabbling. I'll help you find an apartment." She was taken aback, surprise written all over her face, and her body stiffened as she stood straight. It was not the answer she expected. And she felt hurt. However, she found an apartment in a town nearby.

We missed her, especially Bradley. He was six years old and memorized her telephone number so he could call her unaided. It took several weeks for her to become accepting, but it was the right action to take. She became a frequent dinner guest during the week and also visited on weekends. I drove the children to her for breakfast. They loved eating cake early in the morning, I found out later. She and I did in fact laugh again, and we developed a trusting, loving relationship.

There were also happy times Mama shared with us—both the children's bat and bar mitzvahs. Debbie announced one day, at age eleven and a half, "I would like to have a bat mitzvah."

She had not attended Hebrew School because we hadn't belonged to a synagogue. We joined Temple Sinai, a Reform congregation, which happened to be close enough to our house for her to ride her bicycle there for weekly lessons. A teenage friend a little older than she had offered to tutor her in addition to the formal classes. She managed to be ready by age thirteen—a mere eighteen months later—and looked lovely in a short pink and white dress, her hair falling loosely over her shoulders. She chanted her Torah portion beautifully. How did we get away with not renting a hall with caterers, musicians, a photographer, and large baskets of flowers? The social part of the ceremony was partly held at the temple, and later we enjoyed a great party in our home with relatives, friends, and neighbors.

Two years later it was Bradley's turn for *his* bar mitzvah. Newly installed Rabbi Pinsky was young, bright, and enthusiastic. One day Bradley came home after his lesson, threw down his books, and said, "The rabbi said I have to make a speech after I'm done reading from the Torah. I'm not doing it."

Jack tried to appease Bradley, but his argument reached such proportions that Jack said to me, "They can't reach an agreement. I hope this doesn't mean that Bradley will decide not to go through with the ceremony."

"But we already made a reservation at the restaurant and invited people!" I cried in utter disbelief.

"Honey, I'm just telling you this, so it won't come as a shock.

I hope they'll work it out. Just be prepared. The restaurant is the least of it. We may not have a bar mitzvah." He sounded both sad and angry, despite trying to appear calm.

The day of the Bar Mitzvah arrived. Bradley, handsome in his first blue three-piece suit, did a superb job chanting from the Torah. In his speech of just a few words, he thanked Jack and me, and the rabbi.

The party was held at La Petite Auberge restaurant in Cresskill, to which he invited his whole class. Music, food, and drinks flowed, and the kids could make their own ice cream.

Mama felt proud and was happy to show off to her sister Rosl, who had flown in from Toronto with her son Frank. Attractive as always, Rosl was fashionably and tastefully dressed. My friend Renee made the trip from Chicago. She and I had been at the Youngs Gap Hotel in the Catskills, where I met Jack.

Irene, of course, was at the restaurant also. I was smiling happily when she approached me. "I need to talk to you," she said, and took me aside. "How can you let Renee stay with Mama?" She started to scold me.

"What do you mean? Did something happen? I know they like each other a lot," I answered in surprise.

"It's too much work for her. Mama just had to sit down, because she had trouble breathing. You have to make Renee leave."

I was sure Renee wouldn't let my mother do anything that was too much for her. Mama's condition at the party was based on lack of fresh air, but Irene was insistent. As soon as the party was over, I drove Mama and Renee to the apartment and passed on Irene's orders, adding, "Rosl and Frank are staying with us, but Trudy Schanzer, our friend across the street, kindly offered to have you stay with them. Of course, Renee, you'll be with us and share all meals with us." Always forthright, Renee commented on Irene's meanness in spoiling my day.

Lore—my aunt, who had taken me across the Czech border in 1938—was unable to join us. Her cancer had metastasized. I made several trips to Pittsburgh to visit her in the hospital. Edgar was not well either. His Parkinson's disease had worsened, making his walking unsteady, sometimes resulting in a fall.

When I visited Edgar after she died, his greeting, "I suppose you've come to get me to live with you," hit me like a deep stab in the stomach. I had to tell him I couldn't do it despite my love. I explained why, and promised, "I'll look for a nursing home nearby so I can look in on you every day."

Edgar didn't hold it against me.

My inability to take him into our house was based on a recollection of a recent day. Mama was complaining of chest pain. (She had a heart condition.) Jack suffered from emphysema. I was waiting for a call back from each of their doctors as I ran from Jack in the kitchen, as he was battling to catch his breath during an attack, to Mama in the living room, where she was lying on the sofa quietly, eyes closed. The prognosis was not good for either.

Before I left Pittsburgh, I asked, "If it's all right with you, Edgar, and if you don't need it, can I take Lorly's portable typewriter?"

"Of course. It isn't being used here. Go into the bedroom and take anything you want of Lore's jewelry. Don't be disappointed, though. I don't think you'll find much—unless she had a lover I didn't know about."

Edgar didn't verbalize his thoughts, but he must have made up his mind not to go on living. Communication became problematic. He was unable to write to me—his hands had grown too shaky. We tried telephone conversations, which were only partially successful. The woman who had been hired to take care of him informed me that he ate sparingly. He fell frequently. He was sixteen years older than Lore; he died six months after her.

I inherited some money and their cat, Mosey, who adopted Bradley as her favorite. She sat next to him while he did his homework, and she slept with him.

Mama fared well in her apartment, where she lived quite contentedly for many years. When she fell again, Irene said, "Mama can't be alone any more. If she can't move back with you, she can live with us." Mama knew that Jack needed caretaking, and that to also take care of her was more than I could handle, so she reluctantly agreed to accept Irene's offer. They did not get along well, and during their time together—a little over a year—the relationship went from bad to worse. Mama was relieved to usually spend weekends and one day during the week with us.

My sister's disrespect towards my mother was surpassed by her outrageous verbal cruelty towards her, like calling her an old witch, cursing her, and when she asked Irene where she was going, she was told, angrily, "That's none of your business." Tearfully, Mama recounted each incident. When she asked if Irene could cash her a check for ten or twenty dollars (which Jack had always done when she lived with us), my sister told her that she needed to let her know a couple of days in advance, so she could go to the bank. Crying, Mama reported that, if she wondered aloud that Irene didn't have ten dollars available, she became angry and yelled that Mama should stop pestering her. Jack considered Irene's behavior so abusive that we seriously considered taking Mama back to live with us.

MAY 10, 1981, MOTHER'S DAY, WAS also my wedding anniversary, and Mama spent that Sunday, as usual, with me. Jack was in the hospital, and I remember saying to her, "Not much to celebrate, Mama. I'm going to the hospital now to visit Jack, but we'll make up for it next week."

The next day I received a phone call from Irene that Mama had fallen and had hit her head against the wall. She was unconscious and was being transferred to Holy Name Hospital in Teaneck. I rushed to the hospital, took a look at Mama and waited, stunned and shocked, for Irene to arrive. When she did, fifteen minutes after me, she told the attending nurse not to use heroic measures—without bothering to check with me first. Mama never regained consciousness. She died while we were outside her room. I went to look at her again, stayed a few minutes thinking about her, and then bent down to give her a last kiss. After I came out, Irene decided to go in, too.

Mama was eighty-four when she died. I telephoned Debbie at Cornell to come home (Bradley was still in high school), and we had a small family funeral with Jack's brothers and wives in attendance besides Irene and her husband. We buried her next to my father in a section of the Austrian temple at the Fairlawn

Cemetery.

Jack was released from the hospital two days later, which gave my family a chance to talk about Omi. That eased the pain. I couldn't believe she wasn't with us any more—she had played such an important role in our lives.

Several months passed. Jack's emphysema worsened so that he was no longer able to sleep in bed and he needed to be more upright to facilitate his breathing. My mother's lounge chair, which could be elongated to provide a footrest, seemed the perfect answer. She had left it to me, but it was in Irene's house at the time. I called her, explained Jack's condition, and added, "I would like to come over for Mama's lounge chair for Jack."

"You can't pick it up. I won't give it to you. Rudi takes naps on it." Rudi was her husband.

It was the culmination of a history of HER mistreatment of me.

38

A TRIP TO VIENNA

JACK'S ILLNESS HAD PROGRESSED, WARNING me not to leave
him alone. But Debbie was home with him, which gave
me a chance to fly to Sweden and Vienna after Mama
died. I went to persuade Cousin Henny in Sweden to sell the
apartment house in Vienna, of which she was the principal owner.
She agreed, and I left for Vienna to talk to the manager of the
house. Mama, who owned a small portion, had left her share to
me.

As the plane started its descent into Vienna (it was a clear
day with good visibility), I craned my neck to see if I could detect
any landmarks, like the Riesenrad, the famous huge ferris wheel.
I wondered how my life would have turned out if I had stayed
there. Would I have attended university and received three degrees (which I had here), and would I have pursued a career the
way I had here, or would I have concentrated instead on marrying a "nice" man, as I had been brought up to expect. Inevitably
my thoughts turned to my parents, grandparents, other relatives

and friends no longer alive, and I compared how I had left on a train, with one suitcase, alone, some forty years before, to how I was returning, alone, on a plane. Then I spotted a motorcycle with a sidecar driving on the tarmac, the driver and passenger wearing helmets just like the ones the Nazis had used when they cruised the streets to find Jews to molest. Suddenly, I burst into tears, crying violently and, hard as I tried, was unable to stop my sobbing. By then the plane had almost reached the gate, and I became alarmed, worried that I would be pointed out as some undesirable, unstable person trying to enter the country or, worse, be taken off the plane by paramedics. What finally stopped the crying was an overheard discussion between the driver of the airport bus into the city and a passenger. A woman mentioned a destination as she was boarding the bus.

"I don't go there. Take bus number ten."

"Can I take this bus to—"

"No. Please get off the step. I have to leave."

"But I thought—"

"I *told* you, I am *late*. I have to leave."

"Just a quick question."

"I'm not going to answer any more questions."

"Don't get so uptight."

"How many times do I have to tell you to get off the step?"

The argument continued in that fashion, and I was able to smile.

IN THE HOTEL LOBBY, A young woman who had been a passenger on the plane recognized me.

"Would you like to walk around a bit while we wait for our rooms?" she asked.

"Yes, I would love to," I quickly answered, feeling relieved, and explaining, "I'm not crazy. I am sorry about making such a spectacle of myself on the plane."

She was Swedish—tall, blonde, attractive—and as we traversed some cobblestone streets in the old part of the city, she asked a little about my past.

It was she who explained, "I can understand how you felt. My father came to Sweden as a refugee, and he had a hard time the first time he went back to Austria."

Greatly relieved, I found she was not only willing to listen to me but seemed to empathize with my teary behavior. She understood why it had occurred better than I did. I was more concerned with the episode than the reason, worried that the sudden outburst had been so uncontrollable. Obviously, it had not occurred to me that I would be that vulnerable, or that my first return trip to my hometown would be so traumatic. As I remembered my past life there, it caused me to mourn my lost childhood and early youth, my lost home, my lost beloved relatives and friends, and a lost way of life.

There would be worse to follow, which I hardly expected.

THE NEXT MORNING I TELEPHONED the manager of the house, told him why I was in Vienna, and asked what would be involved to change the percentage of the apartment house that was in my mother's name to mine. Not much information was forthcoming, and he asked that I call back in the afternoon.

In the second conversation, I mentioned again that I needed to change my mother's name, as owner of a share, to mine.

"That's not difficult. We can do that," he answered.

"Fine. Would you mind telling me what it will cost?" I asked.

"Not too much."

"I would like to get some idea, Mr. Roth."

"I don't know exactly."

"Oh. Then just give me a ballpark figure."

"I told you, not much, especially if you pay in dollars." His voice rising, he added, "Besides, there is a written tariff for that."

I felt he was hedging (he'd had time to prepare), and, somewhat annoyed but still calm, I pushed, "In that case, would you mind looking it up and telling me the amount?"

With a sigh, and in an angry tone, he said, "Just a moment." Then I overheard, "The American Jewess is on the phone, and she wants. . . ." He had chosen not to mention my name, which he knew.

I was furious, and stunned, to still be confronted with anti-Semitism (it was 1981), and I struggled to think of a suitable response—in vain—so I thought I'd just let it go. That was unsatisfactory, because I remembered that's what we Jews had always done, and I would never forgive myself once back at home if I just kept quiet. By then he was back, so I simply said, "I heard what you said, and I'm surprised-"

"What did I say?"

I repeated his words. He did not apologize in any way. Instead, he ended the conversation politely before hanging up on me. He used an archaic German business expression that translates to "I kiss your hand, madame, good-bye."

As I shut my door to the hotel room that evening, that scenario replayed itself, and a scene flashed through my mind: *He was angry, which means he will go to the police to make a report, and they will pick me up and interrogate me, just as the Nazis did in Brno when I was a kid.* I understood then what "breaking out in a cold sweat" meant. I was sweating without feeling hot. Standing behind the locked door, I was close to shaking all over. Just in time, I managed to remind myself, *It's now, it's not then. You have an American passport. It's okay.*

The following day Mr. Roth sent a young man from his office to the hotel. He brought a bunch of papers for my signature, including one authorizing him to do what I hadn't asked, and nothing to do with changing the names of ownership. I didn't sign, and promptly received a phone call from him. He sounded anxious. I had recovered my strength, and I told him, "I'm taking the documents back home to the States with me to show to my husband. I will contact you."

39

JACK'S LAST YEARS

THE BOMB FELL IN 1975. Jack was diagnosed with emphysema. He had been smoking three packs of cigarettes a day. Trying to break the habit—which had become an addiction—was futile. Hypnosis did not help, nor did other strategies. Two years before his death, he quit cold, and at the end of those years, he once said, "I still miss that cigarette first thing in the morning."

He loved his work as an arbitrator, loved spending hours on each case before reaching a decision that he considered fair, legal, and in accordance with the prevailing contract between labor and management. His rulings were final. His work kept him going, and he continued in that capacity until his last hospital stay, notwithstanding that he was no longer able to bend down to tie his shoelaces. I spent more time trying to alleviate his embarrassment than tying the laces, which didn't bother me at all. Mornings were hard for him, but since he was in charge, he set the starting time for the sessions—usually 10:30 a.m. He would not have been able to work a 9–5 schedule.

One day he said, "I've been thinking, Lisl dear, that it might be a good idea for you to take a leave of absence so you can accompany me to hearings and be more available."

"I know, Jack," I answered gently, "but remember last week, when I couldn't lift the wheelchair out of the trunk of the car? Let's see if we can find a driver, and I'll be available for you when you get home."

When necessary, I did accompany him. At one session he fell asleep (due to lack of oxygen), and I pushed the attaché case, lying on the floor under the table, against his leg to wake him up. I learned to anticipate his needs. Usually I was at the front door when he returned, ready with a chair and medication.

When climbing the stairs from his basement office became too cumbersome, he moved to the den, one flight up, and worked late into the night. There was a large enough table, good light, and a bathroom. After that staircase proved too difficult, he continued working at the kitchen table. Eventually, it became so hard for him to tackle the six stairs to the bedroom that I stood behind him and pushed him up.

He was sick for six years, progressively getting worse. Although he finally gave up smoking, it was too late. Three or four times a year he had such severe inability to breathe that we ended up in the emergency room at the hospital, where he would stay for a week to ten days. Sometimes I drove; at other times, the ambulance had to be called. He was supposed to lose weight and to exercise. He did neither. He enjoyed eating a steak for dinner every night, which I gladly made for him, cooking something perhaps "healthier" but not tasting as good for myself.

Jack was such a workaholic that, even before his sickness, he often worked weekends, tucked away in his office in the basement. On those occasions I felt lonely, watching neighbors, especially the men, working in their gardens or being involved with their children. I used to think he missed out on watching them grow, and they, in turn, were deprived of his companionship. *They* didn't seem to feel that way. Only the other day, Debbie mentioned, "Daddy practically wrote a report for me, and do you remember when he posed as the governor of Alaska so I could 'interview' him on the tape recorder?"

Bradley, also, has not complained, and he is available and very attentive to his children—accompanying Ben on Boy Scouts weekends "like Daddy did with me, remember?" And he accepts Lindsay's invitation to join her for lunch at school.

When the children were little, Jack's interaction with them consisted mostly of either reading a bedtime story to them or making one up. The child had to contribute to move the story along and, possibly, make up the ending. He, and they, all loved it. By the time the kids reached school age, his influence was felt at the discussions during dinner—about school, something personal, or world affairs. His rules were obeyed. There was no television during the week, and Debbie, being the older, had to help Bradley with a homework problem if necessary.

BY 1979 DEBBIE HAD TO decide which university to attend. She had been offered a special schedule with small classes by the University of Pennsylvania, and a scholarship from Johns Hopkins University, both of which she turned down in favor of attending Cornell, which offered nothing. Jack was livid, saying, "There is no question where she should go."

Debbie, just as angry, ran upstairs and, before slamming her bedroom door, called down, "You can't make me go to Johns Hopkins. I won't go to college at all. I'll just get a job."

"This is pretty bad." I turned to Jack. "What do you think we should do?"

"You know what I think. It's up to you to decide. I won't be around."

Anger rose in my chest as I construed that remark as an easy way out, pushing all responsibility on me, but, instantly remembering the severity of his illness, I let it go. Instead, still feeling strong as long as he was around, I went upstairs after a few minutes and told Debbie, "I don't want money to come between us and make for a bad relationship. Money is in short supply, but you can go to Cornell if that's what you want—if you're willing to work in the summer and somehow make up the money you would get at Johns Hopkins."

I did not guess what her answer would be. Without a moment's hesitation, she turned to me, her face brightening as she said, "That's fine with me. I'll do that." We hugged, and I kissed her.

Debbie kept her word. She made up the money every year. That moment in her room was probably the beginning of a relationship between us that has lasted—strong, loving, and supportive of each other.

DURING JACK'S SIXTH AND LAST year of sickness, Bradley was in college—SUNY at Binghamton—and Debbie had graduated. Bradley had worked during vacations of his last high school year, loading trucks at night, to save money. He worked hard, which affected his social life, because he had to sleep during the day. Debbie took a year off, working before entering law school. Jack was worried that she would not continue her studies. I tried to reassure him, because I sincerely felt that she would follow her dream of becoming a lawyer.

Visits to doctors, and confinements in the hospital, became more frequent. The doctor provided a little machine in his office, which, with a mask over Jack's mouth and nose, allowed him to inhale oxygen and medicine, and restore his breathing. On one such occasion, I asked, "Is it possible for us to buy such a machine to have at home?"

"Yes, of course you can buy one," he answered.

I wondered why that suggestion had never crossed the doctor's lips.

Jack used the machine several times a day, including two or three times at night. He placed it on the desk in the bedroom, and of course turned the light on, which kept me awake. Every night I thought of sleeping in one of the other bedrooms, but it took me weeks to act, because I knew I could never move back again to sleep next to Jack.

Just after his sixty-fifth birthday, he entered the hospital for the last time. He spent almost six months in the intensive care unit, never well enough to be transferred to a room. In one way it was a relief, because he received the benefits of attentive nursing care. In the beginning, I visited during the three prescribed times every day, later cutting it to twice daily. He suffered much, largely due to the doctor's desire to keep him alive. Jack had always said to me, "There's no substitute for life." I did not tell this to the doctor, but there was nothing in writing, and I could not, in good conscience, stop the doctor even when, in answer to my question, "Will Jack come out of the hospital?" he answered, "Not unless you believe in miracles." So it was pitiful to watch him. There was nothing left to talk about that interested him. Stroking him, holding his hand, and just being there was comforting to him. For me, his brother Seymour's, and his wife Dotty's, visits every night were most helpful. Once or twice Seymour took the doctor to task on my behalf, and Dotty's support to me was outstanding. It continued after Jack's death.

AFTER JACK DIED—ON FEBRUARY 4, 1984—one of my friends remarked, "You must feel relieved that you don't have to run to the hospital every day."

"Not at all," I told her. "It's become a way of life and a routine, and now something is missing." We had both known he was going to die, and I'd tried to prepare myself, silently practicing making decisions before asking his opinion, but when I received that phone call from the doctor, I felt totally lost. Any self-confidence I had attained was gone. I moved through my daily schedule—fortunately I had my job—as if slightly tipsy. It took almost three years before I felt totally "sober" again.

40

ON MY OWN

LIVING ALONE FOR THE FIRST time in my life felt terrible. Whatever strength and self-confidence I had acquired disappeared after Jack died, and I was afraid of sinking into a depression. I felt I had hit bottom. A year after Jack died, almost to the day, the hospital tried to collect money from me in a very belligerent manner instead of from the insurance company, claiming his coverage had run out. It wasn't so. Also, Jack had borrowed on his life insurance policies, and I worried if there would be enough money for college tuitions and whether I would have to sell the house. That part was just too much to handle.

Months passed, and one day, while out on a walk, I decided, *I can't go on like this. I am going to change. I'm going to make the next years some of the best of my life.*

I looked for an additional job to supplement the two days I was working, and started to work full-time, which helped financially as well as psychologically. I volunteered at the Bergen County Parent Workshop, which involved leading a group of six or eight parents in problem solving regarding their children. If their teenage youngsters had committed a minor offense, the court ordered them to register at the Parent Workshop for a six-week course given one evening a week. Word spread, and parents flocked to participate. They brought problems they encountered with their children of any age, not only court ordered cases. The leaders and parents shared the same printed material as we guided them through the sessions, eliciting their thoughts and feelings, and involving them in little exercises. At one point the coordinators from the various groups decided to do the same for themselves. The six women I joined at a weekly meeting proved very therapeutic for me. I spoke freely and honestly, and received helpful feedback as well as support.

Ginny, our golden retriever, also showed her support by in-tuitively recognizing my moods and acting accordingly, laying her head on my lap when I was sad, joining me on a walk or drive, and becoming a true companion.

A year after Jack's death, during spring break in 1985, I par-ticipated in a seminar on family therapy in Killington, Vermont—a perfect choice for combining theory with skiing. The last day of the conference, a beautiful, sunny day, I decided to take one more run to finish a great week. Somebody brushed against me: I fell and broke my leg—the first accident in a lifetime of skiing. I was transported to Burlington, the nearest hospital, where I spent the next five weeks with my right leg, broken in three places, packed in plaster of Paris, hoisted on a bar.

After I shared the room with several different women, Betty Dorkin, a local, became my permanent roommate. She was a big woman, my senior by several years, her large brown eyes turned kindly towards me, ever considerate, and a delightful conversationalist. We shared our pleasure in art and music, and New York City in general, with which she was familiar from her prior Connecticut residence. Her minister visited her almost daily and, after a while, included me in their conversations. Between them they arranged for a rabbi to see me. He paid a short visit late one Friday afternoon, and I did not see him again. It was just as well—we didn't have much to talk about.

After Betty was discharged, the minister stopped by because, he explained, he was on the floor and thought he would say hello to me. I smiled coyly as I quickly pulled up the blanket to cover the magazine I had propped up on my good leg. One of my friends had sent me *Playgirl*, which had photographs of nude men.

The nurses made my lengthy stay most agreeable. They washed my hair; they powdered my body carefully, preventing sores as I lay on my back for weeks. In the mornings, while washing me, they moved to the other side of the bed so I could watch Phil Donahue's TV show; they brought the cafeteria menu to let me choose different food (I had neither asked for it nor complained); they took telephone messages for me when my line was busy. Most important, they followed my instructions carefully about what to do with my leg one weekend while my doctor was on a ski trip. He was furious when, on his return, he found the leg positioned at a wrong angle. He asked which nurse was responsible. Trying to protect her, I claimed ignorance. He was angry enough to call a meeting to make his displeasure known to all of them.

Bradley came to visit me during his college break. Always kind and thoughtful, he brought me chocolate and ran errands, some of which I invented so he wouldn't spend all his free time sitting in the hospital. One thing he brought with him was the student aid form, which I found more stressful to fill out than preparing income tax, because they asked for future earnings. I pinned a note to the form, explaining why the figures were from memory, and returned it to Emory Law School. They accepted it.

The day of my discharge finally approached. The bone had healed in two places but not in the third. With a new plaster of Paris cast, I practiced walking with crutches, ready for Debbie, who had taken off from law school, to come and take me home. Her big dog, my suitcase, the crutches, and I were arranged on the back seat. I don't know what was on top of what as she drove home, full speed ahead. I thought it best to close my eyes. Luckily, I fell asleep.

I hobbled around on crutches until later that summer, when the third break in the femur that had not healed required an operation.

The surgeon at Columbia Presbyterian Hospital in New York City asked for a fee of several thousand dollars, half to be paid in advance, and his first available date was three months hence. My good friends Rose and Manny, had a daughter—a physician—who recommended a doctor at Johns Hopkins Hospital specializing in that type of operation. I made an appointment for a second opinion, realizing by that time that no amount of "doing the right thing" or self-willed talk was going to heal that leg. It happened that he had a cancellation two days later, and since I liked his manner, his strong, steady handshake, his recommendation, and his fee—set at half the surgeon's in New York!—I stayed on at Rose and Manny's house in Baltimore, Manny not too pleased that Ginny, my dog, would be their house guest while I was in the hospital. By the time I left, Manny had learned to love her. He missed his walks with her and her company, he reported.

The operation went well, but what a difference in the two hospitals. There was neither privacy nor individuality. When I was ready to be taken to the operating room, my personal belongings were piled at the bottom of the stretcher because, after the operation, I would have to occupy a different room.

The following week, sitting in a wheelchair in a corridor waiting for physical therapy, I was placed next to a man who reminded me of Jack, partly in looks but mostly because he had tubes going in and out of every part of his body, which was how I had remembered Jack for a long time. I just fell apart. At that point, I lost my appetite, didn't eat, and forced myself to drink clear, overly salted soup until I couldn't even swallow that.

"If you won't eat or drink," a nurse somewhere in the room warned me harshly, "we'll just put a tube in you to force-feed you."

"I want to see my doctor," I answered. I was going to ask him to be discharged.

Fortunately, Bradley arrived. He had hardly stepped into the room when I half begged, half ordered him, "Just get me *out* of here. Whatever they want to do, don't sign anything, and don't let them do anything to me. I have to get *out*."

A day later, when the surgeon made his rounds, he said, "I think you're right. You'll be better off at home."

I still needed crutches, which I found very tiring even just going back and forth from the refrigerator to the stove. I called Meals on Wheels. The man delivering the food rang the bell, the dog barked, and he put the packages down by the door and ran away. He was afraid of dogs.

Ginny brought everything in for me, piece by piece. First, two slices of bread in a paper bag; secondly, a piece of fruit; then a small carton of milk on the next trip out; and, finally, the main dish wrapped in a foil container. She dropped each item in my lap as I sat by the door in a wheelchair, rewarding her with a dog biscuit. She had not been trained for that, yet she never touched any of the food. She also brought the newspaper in promptly, for which I had trained her, and picked up anything I dropped. In the past, she had ignored the paper many times, running off instead to investigate the neighbors' garbage. She seemed to understand something was different, and decided to become helpful and obedient.

THE FIRST COUPLE OF WEEKS after my return home, friends and neighbors visited frequently. My old friend Herbert from Vienna, who then lived near Philadelphia, stayed a couple of nights, as did one of my neighbors, and during the day I just left the door unlocked. Sometimes, one or the other would stay too long, which wore me out, but I never complained, knowing that the momentum would not keep up, and it was a comfort to feel their concern. They brought fruit, cooked dishes, ice cream, and they tidied up. I cried one day because I could not find the salt shaker in my own house. I did have help from various hired women a couple of hours in the morning. They assisted with taking a shower and dressing, but beyond that, I was glad when it was time for them to leave. One of them talked incessantly. She declared, "You are not *listening* to me." She was right. I had tuned her out. Another one, concerned that each of her curls was in place and checking her fingernails every few minutes, thumbed through one after another of her magazines. When I asked, "Would you mind vacuuming the foyer and living room?" she told me,

"That's not my job. I'm only supposed to take care of you and your room."

"You know," I lied, "I can't sit in the living room because the dog sheds, and I'm allergic to those hairs on the carpet."

Bradley was settled in Atlanta, attending Emory Law School. Debbie was at law school in New York. Neither of them was knowledgeable enough to be of help to me when it came to finances or other matters that needed to be taken care of, including me. Watching their father die and their mother acting needy was more than they were able to deal with. Just the same, Debbie drove home weekends and once during the week. I accumulated chores for her to do, all of which went unattended. Law school left no time for that. I adjusted, not easily at first, but concluded that my relationship with my daughter was more important than the dirty dishes in the sink or the clothes not hung up. On Friday nights we luxuriated on my bed as we watched *Dallas*.

A couple of months later, I had to fly to Baltimore for a checkup. That good-looking surgeon looked at my leg, smiled, and proudly announced, "Beautiful, just beautiful. A perfect straight line."

"Oh, really? Everything is all right?" I asked, wondering how he could consider the long, ugly, red line, under which a foot-long rod was lodged, to be beautiful. Of course, he was referring to his handiwork, but he was right. It healed well, the line is hardly visible, and I never suffered any complications.

"Are you sure the leg won't be shorter than the other one?" I asked. That was my big worry.

"You'll be fine if you do all the exercises." He assured me that I would be able to do everything unless I wanted to ski again or ride a motorcycle, in which case he would operate to take the long rod out. None of my friends skiied, and to take a chance that my children, maybe, would accompany me once a year did not seem worth undertaking another operation and hospital stay.

"Swimming would be good, too," he added in his kind manner. That made me join the Jewish Community Center to enable me to swim several times a week. I followed his instructions religiously, performing the boring, time consuming exercises for a whole year to make sure I would not end up with a limp. Actually, that leg became the stronger one, and no limp.

At the airport on the way back from Baltimore, half the passengers were in wheelchairs, looking much older than I. Must be a plane for handicapped people, I thought. Upon arrival at Newark, all the "handicapped" got out of their seats, marched out, and I was left sitting because the flight attendant had forgotten to hand me my crutches.

In addition to all the physical exercise, I went for psychotherapy for a while. As I adjusted slowly to being without Jack, I found that living alone had its perks. I could come and go as I pleased without having to rush home to make dinner, and I ate when and what I wished. I was, perhaps for the first time in my life (before or after my marriage), not responsible for anybody's well being, nor did I have to justify anything I wanted to do. Time helped in the healing process, but little things pushed me a step closer to independence and self-confidence.

One day, the clothes dryer stopped working. I investigated the cause in order to describe it to the repair man over the phone. While I was dabbling around, it got fixed. Voila!

With each problem that I could "fix" myself, coupled with making my own decisions, my independence grew. Making decisions was no longer as difficult as it had been. I had perennially had trouble deciding between what I wanted to do and what I should do, and how it would affect or be liked by my husband, or my mother (who lived with us for twelve years), or my children.

My financial situation was not great, but not as bad as I had feared. I made money working full time again, and I lived frugally.

After a while, I took a course locally—"Woman On Her Own." It was geared toward divorcees and widows, full of good advice of how to handle your money, and many other 'how to' sessions. Clued in, I carefully and gingerly invested in the stock market. I was lucky, did well, and between the loans the kids took out, plus help from me, they both made it through law school.

41

A NEW LIFE

I T TOOK TIME AND HARD work, emotionally and financially, to become independent. Gone were the days when I felt I needed a man to take care of me. Once I was ready to "date" again, I was fortunate in having the company of men, but I didn't want to get married to be a caretaker. I had done my share of caretaking of sick people, all of whom I loved—my father, my mother, my little boy, my husband. My poor father received the least nursing, my mother a good share; to little Richard, my son, during his fatal disease, I gladly gave all; and my husband, covering his six years of illness, had all my attention. I was fifty-eight when Jack died, healthy and, after a while, began to take pleasure in and valued a freedom I had never experienced before.

Also, many of the men of my generation were old fashioned enough to expect a male/female division of labor. It wasn't as much a question of work, as of the inequality of the sexes that still seemed to prevail, that bothered me.

I continued working—full time instead of just two days a

week, invested in the stock market, and traveled. My trips took me to New Zealand, China, and countries between in one direction, and to South America in another, always returning to Europe to savor my own culture. I also took advantage of New York's offerings—visiting museums, renewing my opera subscription, and adding the New York Philharmonic as well as Off-Broadway theaters. I learned to play bridge, joined a book club, signed up for lecture series, continued my support group sessions, made new friends, and kept my old ones.

I was out of the doldrums and in a position to cover my needs and satisfy my whims.

I discovered a secret: I was neither responsible for anyone, nor was it necessary to justify my decisions, my needs, my wants, my likes or dislikes. In the past, when my sister wanted to see me on a given day, my inability to do so was unacceptable to her. She would pry for the reason, usually a previous engagement, and typically suggest I change *that* appointment. Her insistence used to be so unpleasant that I resorted to little white lies, which made me uncomfortable. I determined that, with a sister or good friends, it should be acceptable to just say, "I don't feel like it," provided you made a counter offer.

I was fortunate then to meet a woman who personified the sister I missed and had always dreamt of having. Edith and I met at a temple gathering one evening, and we quickly became best friends. Her piercing brown eyes and thin nose made for an alert expression, and she was fast to surmise a new situation. The trust and understanding we soon developed led to mutual nurturing and support. No need to make excuses about not seeing each

other if one or the other was busy. On the contrary, we understood. We shared confidences and looked forward to spending
time together. Little jokes and laughs abounded in our relationship.

Both of us widowed, we were in touch daily, traveled to Europe (her male friend was unable to travel with her), and, although quite different, got along very well. She kept kosher (I
did not), which made it difficult for her in Prague the summer of
1991 to order dinner in a restaurant. We were there long after
the Russians had pulled out, but the menu still featured meat and
potatoes—no vegetables. The young waiter spoke neither German nor English, nor did he make any effort to understand that
she wanted hot tea. We had struggled for several minutes when,
suddenly, I blurted out, "*Horky*," meaning "hot." The word appeared out of nowhere. I hadn't thought of it in over fifty years,
since I'd heard it at the Austrian/Czech border, where the vendor
outside the train sold *horky parky*. We jokingly used the word
horky for a long time afterwards.

We ate many crepes too while in Prague—at her suggestion—
to make up for skimpy luncheons or dinners, often returning for
seconds to a street vendor we found near our hotel.

Edith left most of the planning of the trip to me, and since
she was always agreeable to my suggestions, I fell into becoming
her guide. We left Prague and drove to Austria, where she had
wanted to go, and at my suggestion stayed in the countryside,
near Gmunden. It's a beautiful area where lakes and mountains
abound. Her energy level, considerably lower than mine, made
her take a nap after lunch. I took that opportunity one day to

drive around, exploring nearby little towns. By three o'clock I was back and woke her up. "Edith," I cried excitedly, "you've got to come with me. I found a gorgeous spot overlooking the lake with a little restaurant where we can go for a *Jause*. We can have our afternoon tea in that village and watch the sailboats while we eat cake."

Rubbing her eyes, she got up, not angry, actually smiling, and said, "Sure. I know you can't resist a good piece of cake—so Viennese." We returned to that place again and again—and Edith, not being from Vienna, liked it as much as I did.

It was a very sad day when Edith died of cancer three years after we met. So many of us knew her that she became immortalized through us frequently quoting her. Her daughter, who lived in Cleveland, kept in touch with me for a couple of years, helping both of us to remember Edith.

WHEN I FELT I HAD hit bottom at one point after Jack's death, I resolved to spend the next years as some of the best of my life. Fortunately, that happened. Edith was part of it.

Another person was a young man I met in 1987, three years after Jack died. We fell in love and lived together happily for five years. Parting was painful for both of us—we tried several times—but we thought it best, because he was more than two decades my junior. We were so bonded that we have never parted in some ways.

SOME YEARS AFTER I HAD taken his "Woman on Her Own" course, I sought out Mr. Levy to see if he would act as my financial advisor. He had done that for several women who had been in his class. After a lengthy discussion during which I asked for explanations of some of his more dogmatic statements, he said, "I can't work with you. You're too independent." He relented before I left, but I decided to continue on my own—a wise decision. I did well.

I had resumed my life. I was able to help my children financially, and my social life was thriving. Almost to my own surprise, I found I was independent at last.

NOW, A WORD TO YOU, my grandchildren: What may seem insignificant, like living freely in the way you choose, I recognize as a treasure. As each of you reaches a certain age, I am reminded of my childhood under the Nazis and of my early teenage war years in England, where I kept my Jewish tradition in an all-Gentile environment. But it also triggers the insight that perseverance was not only life-saving during difficult periods, but played a significant role in pursuing education and a career as well. Determination to leave old stuff behind and move on has been instrumental in shaping the journey towards a wonderful, exciting, and rewarding life. I hope that you will aim high but stay humble, show tolerance, and enjoy loving relationships, and it will be enormously pleasing to see you grow up as honest and liberal, considerate of other people and animals, and happy in your chosen careers and hobbies. You're on your way, and I love each of you very much.

I felt that the appropriate ending of this book occurred at a moment in my life when I achieved what I've come to see as my independence, which happened before you, my grandchildren, were born, and is the reason you are not included in the story. Much has happened since then. I have had marvelous rewards, satisfactions, and love in my life. My greatest joy has been the satisfaction of knowing that you, Debbie and Bradley, are wonderful, decent human beings, married to caring spouses, Jon and Sandy, and to watch you, my five grandchildren—each different and each lovable—as you grow up. In order of age, you are: Jack, the oldest, born in 1996 and now eighteen; then Ben, a year younger at seventeen; Lindsay and Meera, both fourteen; and Reyna, age seven. Both boys are handsome, and the three girls are beautiful.

All of you are smart, all of you have inquisitive minds, and each of you gives me a reason to smile.

FAREWELLS AND FORTUNES

When I left Czechoslovakia in 1939 to join the Kindertransport in Vienna, bound for London, I had no way of knowing that I would never see any of the relatives I was in contact with again. The exception was Ernst, the husband of my aunt Yelli.

I visited him in 1998 in Sydney, Australia, some sixty years later. He was ninety-two, bald, a thin, small figure hobbling on a cane. He shared his lovely house with his second wife Elli, overlooking the bay, swimming pool in the back. A large painting of a woman in the living room had a remarkable likeness to my aunt Yelli. I remembered Aunt Rosl's comments that Ernst, who had worked in the bakery in the Terezin (Theresienstadt) camp, sneaked bread out for Elli but none for Yelli, his wife at the time, and I wondered silently if my favorite, wonderful aunt Yelli had had to suffer because of her. I never fully believed that rumor—partly I didn't want to—and also aunt Rosl was prone to exaggerate. I wanted desperately to ask him if, in fact, he'd only brought bread for Elli (not his wife then), but she did not leave the room.

When she finally did, to make coffee, I couldn't bring myself to talk about it. Ernst showed me photos of his little son, Stefan, killed in Auschwitz, mumbling, "*Nebich, nebich*" (Yiddish for "pity, what a shame") several times, sadly shaking his head. A thought flashed through my head: Whatever he had done, or hadn't done, he'd gone through hell. I adopted the same attitude towards Elli when she returned with the coffee—it wasn't up to me to judge. I never asked that burning question so vital to me a few moments earlier.

Ironically, Ernst referred to Yelli's nurturing nature and supportive manner that made her care for a little girl, a distant relative of his, at Auschwitz. That, too, triggered something: it became crystal clear why I always liked being in Misslitz/Miroslav so much. Irene's bullying had played a big role, but it had also been Yelli's caring manner, how she looked out for my interests, how important she made me feel, and how her physical love substituted for its absence in my mother that drew me there.

It was a bittersweet reunion with Ernst. We were both dissolved in tears when we kissed good-bye, knowing it would be the last time we'd see each other. Embracing me, his kisses covered my tear-washed cheeks, my neck, my hands, back to the face, to the point where I pulled away. It was just too much, too heart-wrenching, the glorious past and the foreseeable future all mixed up and tugging away at us.

All other close relatives perished in the Holocaust.

Benedikt and Therese Steiner, my paternal grandparents, who lived at 29 Moss Gasse, Vienna III, were forced to move to another address in Vienna before being arrested and transported to Terezin, Czechoslovakia, where they both perished.

Tante Hansi and uncle Karl (my father's brother) were killed in Auschwitz.

Willy, their son, died in New York City.

Ernst, my father's younger brother, was killed in a concentration camp in Poland.

Babi (Adele Deutsch), my maternal grandmother, and her sister, Tanta Hanni, died in Terezin.

Aunt Yelli and her son, my favorite little cousin, Stefan, aged five, were gassed in Auschwitz.

Aunt Gretl and her husband, Hans Wilheim, were murdered in Auschwitz.

Leo, my mother' brother, was shot on a death march in 1945, shortly before the war ended.

Gerti, Leo's wife, was killed in Auschwitz.

Trude Hauser, a cousin, was forced into prostitution, her fate and place of death unknown.

Those were the closest relatives. More than twenty others were murdered in the Holocaust as well.

Lorly and Edgar died in Pittsburgh—-she of cancer, he of Parkinson's disease.

My childhood friend Herbert lives near Philadelphia.

ABOUT THE AUTHOR

Lisl Malkin grew up in Vienna and England. A social worker in the United States, she specialized in counseling children and parents. Now retired, she lives in Northern New Jersey.

338

CPSIA information can be obtained at www.ICGtesting.com
Printed in the USA
LVOW12s1731170214

374035LV00003B/33/P